PATHS
BEYOND
EGO

For books written by the editor, see the last page of this book.

A NEW
CONSCIOUSNESS
READER

This *New Consciousness Reader* is part of a new series of original and classic writing by renowned experts on leading-edge concepts in personal development, psychology, spiritual growth, and healing. Other books in this series include:

The Awakened Warrior
EDITED BY RICK FIELDS

Dreamtime and Dreamwork
EDITED BY STANLEY KRIPPNER, PH.D.

The Erotic Impulse
EDITED BY DAVID STEINBERG

Fathers, Sons, and Daughters
EDITED BY CHARLES SCULL, PH.D.

Healers on Healing
EDITED BY RICHARD CARLSON, PH.D., AND BENJAMIN SHIELD

In the Company of Others
EDITED BY CLAUDE WHITMYER

Meeting the Shadow
EDITED BY CONNIE ZWEIG
AND JEREMIAH ABRAMS

Mirrors of the Self
EDITED BY CHRISTINE DOWNING

The New Paradigm in Business
EDITED BY MICHAEL RAY AND ALAN RINZLER
FOR THE WORLD BUSINESS ACADEMY

Paths Beyond Ego
EDITED BY ROGER WALSH, M.D., PH.D., AND FRANCES VAUGHAN, PH.D.

Reclaiming the Inner Child
EDITED BY JEREMIAH ABRAMS

Spiritual Emergency
EDITED BY STANISLAV GROF, M.D., AND CHRISTINA GROF

To Be a Man
EDITED BY KEITH THOMPSON

To Be a Woman
EDITED BY CONNIE ZWEIG

The Truth About the Truth
EDITED BY WALTER TRUETT ANDERSON

What Survives?
EDITED BY GARY DOORE, PH.D.

Who Am I?
EDITED BY ROBERT FRAGER

FOUNDING SERIES EDITOR: CONNIE ZWEIG, PH.D.

PATHS
BEYOND
EGO

The Transpersonal Vision

❏

Edited by

ROGER WALSH, M.D., Ph.D.

and

FRANCES VAUGHAN, Ph.D.

Jeremy P Tarcher / Penguin
a member of
Penguin Group (USA) Inc.
New York

Most Tarcher/Penguin books are available at special quantity
discounts for bulk purchases for sales promotions, premiums,
fund-raising, and educational needs. Special books or book excerpts
also can be created to fit specific needs.
For details, write Penguin
Special Markets, 375 Hudson Street
New York, NY 10014

This book is dedicated to
the awakening of transpersonal vision.

Jeremy P.Tarcher / Penguin
a member of
Penguin Group (USA) Inc.
375 Hudson Street
New York, NY 10014
www.penguin.com

Library of Congress Cataloging-in-Publication Data

Paths beyond ego : the transpersonal vision / edited by Roger Walsh
and Frances Vaughan.
p.   cm.
Includes bibliographical references.
ISBN 0-87477-678-3 (alk. paper)
1. Transpersonal psychology.   2. Altered states of consciousness.
I. Walsh, Roger N.   II. Vaughan, Frances E.
BF204.7.P38   1993   93-6705 CIP
150.19'8—dc20

Design by Irving Perkins Associates
Cover design by Susan Shankin

Printed in the United States of America

23 24 25 26 27

Contents

PART I

THE VARIETIES OF TRANSPERSONAL EXPERIENCE

SECTION ONE

THE RIDDLE OF CONSCIOUSNESS

SECTION TWO

MEDITATION: ROYAL ROAD TO THE TRANSPERSONAL

PART II

THE FARTHER REACHES OF DEVELOPMENT

Foreword

John E. Mack, M.D.

WE ARE witnessing a battle for the human soul between two opposing ontologies. In one view, the physical or material world is the ultimate, if not the only, reality, and the behaviors and experiences of living organisms, including ourselves, can be understood within the framework of potentially identifiable mechanisms. In this worldview consciousness is a function of the human brain, and its farthest reaches and greatest depths are, in theory, fathomable through the researches of neuroscience and psychodynamic formulations. In this view, life, in James Carse's words, is a finite game.

In the transpersonal view, the physical world and all its laws represent only one of an indeterminable number of possible realities whose qualities we can only begin to apprehend through the evolution of our consciousness. In this view, consciousness pervades all realities and is the primary source or creative principle of existence, including the energy-matter of the physical world. Until recently, Western philosophy and science, including psychology, have been dominated by the first view. The transpersonal vision is opening our minds, hearts, and spirits to the second. In this view, life is an infinite game.

Each worldview, the materialist and the transpersonal, has its accompanying epistemology (way of acquiring knowledge), and each has its consequences for human well-being and the fate of the earth. In the materialist universe we know the world at a distance, through our senses and the machines and instruments through which we can extend their reach, and by reasoned analysis of the observations that our empirical enterprises yield. We take pride in the objectivity that this way of knowing reflects, and we are suspicious of subjectivity and emotion, which are thought to distort the truth. In this framework, we rely on ordinary consciousness for information about ourselves and the surrounding environment and regard nonordinary states principally as exotic, pathological, or interesting for recreational purposes.

In the transpersonal universe or universes, we seek to know our worlds close up, relying on feeling and contemplation, as well as observation and reason, to gain information about a range of possible realities. In this universe we take subjectivity for granted and depend on direct experience, intuition, and imagination for discoveries about the inner and outer worlds. A transpersonal epistemology appreciates the necessity of ordinary states of consciousness for mapping the terrain of the physical universe, but nonordinary states are seen as powerful means of extending our knowledge beyond the four dimensions of the Newtonian/Einsteinian universe.

The consequences of the materialist worldview are all too familiar. By restricting the scope of reality and the domain of personal fulfillment to the physical world, while excluding from consciousness the power of spiritual realms, human beings are ravishing the earth and massacring one another with instruments of ever greater technological sophistication in the quest for power, dominance, and material satisfaction. The outcome of the continued enactment of this view will be the breakdown of the earth's living systems and the termination of human life as we know it. Psychology, in this paradigm, has limited its healing potential by following a therapeutic model in which one person treats the illness or problems of another, separate, individual, whose relevant world is confined to a few principle relationships.

The transpersonal vision offers the possibility of a different future for humankind and other living creatures. Through a deeper exploration of ourselves and the worlds in which we participate, transpersonal psychology enables human beings to discover their inseparability from all life and their appropriate place in the great chain of being. Central to this unfolding awareness is the rediscovery of the power of ancient methods of achieving altered states of consciousness, such as meditation, yoga, shamanic journeys, and the judicious use of psychedelic plants. New methods of self-exploration, such as the Grof holotropic breathwork method and modified forms of hypnosis, enable many people to experience realms of the unconscious and the mythic and spiritual universes from which we have cut ourselves off. Transpersonal psychology certainly has therapeutic applications. But its greater focus is upon healing, transformation, personal growth, and spiritual opening.

The poet Rilke once wrote that the senses by which we could grasp the spirit world have atrophied. The transpersonal vision, as set forth by its pioneers in this book, shows the way that these senses might be reawakened and opened to domains of being of which we have perhaps never before been conscious. If and when this occurs, we may again discover the sacred in ourselves and nature. It will then become unthinkable to foul the earth-nest of creation that has been mysteriously lent to each of us for such a brief time. For as we explore the multiple dimensions of universes of unlimited possibility, we may at the same time learn to participate in a harmonious relationship with our fellow human beings and other living species through a consciousness that is forever evolving.

Preface

WHEN IN the late 1970s we began preparing *Beyond Ego: Transpersonal Dimensions in Psychology*, our goal was to provide the first comprehensive overview of the exciting new field of transpersonal psychology. One of our challenges was to find enough review articles. Our challenge in editing a new overview for the nineties and the twenty-first century has been quite different: both easier and more difficult. It has been easier in the sense that the transpersonal field has expanded dramatically and good papers are abundant; it has been harder in that selecting among them is more challenging.

It rapidly became clear that transpersonal exploration has expanded far beyond its foundation discipline of psychology to encompass fields such as transpersonal psychiatry, anthropology, sociology, and ecology, thereby creating a multidisciplinary, transpersonal movement. It also became clear that in order to reflect this dramatic growth, more than a new edition of *Beyond Ego* was required; what was called for was a new book. The result is this book: *Paths Beyond Ego: The Transpersonal Vision*.

In preparing *Paths Beyond Ego* we had several aims. First, we wanted to provide an easily readable introduction. Transpersonal studies are of potential interest to an exceptionally wide range of people, from medical and mental health practitioners, researchers, and clinicians to social scientists, philosophers, theologians, and spiritual practitioners. We therefore wanted to provide a clear introduction to the field that required a minimum of specialized knowledge and would be accessible to readers from diverse backgrounds.

Within the available space we sought to provide as comprehensive an overview as possible. Therefore, we tried to include outstanding reviews of all the major transpersonal areas. In order to include as many areas and articles as possible, articles have been edited and condensed. Readers who want more detailed discussions of particular topics can consult the original articles as well as the recommended reading list.

We certainly hoped to convey a sense of the excitement of cutting-edge

work in this field. We therefore sought articles that build on the foundation of earlier work and also point to fascinating emerging possibilities.
One disappointment, however, was the small number of women authors.

In addition to an introduction and overview, we also wanted to provide
an integration of the field. We therefore chose articles of broad integrative
scope and attempted to write introductions that point to connections and
common themes wherever possible. Such an attempt seems particularly
important for a field that stands at the crossroads of an extraordinarily
wide range of disciplines and points to the interconnection and interdependence of all things.

Acknowledgments

The editors would like to express their appreciation to the many people who contributed to the publication of this book. They include all those who have created and explored the transpersonal vision; the authors whose writings appear herein; Connie Zweig, who provided excellent editorial assistance; our agent John White; and Bonnie L'Allier, whose administrative and secretarial support were invaluable. In addition we would like to thank the following people who served as consultants and reviewed sections of the book: Warwick Fox, Jayne Gackenbach, Charles Grob, John Levy, Robert McDermott, Phillip Novak, Leni Schwartz, Deane Shapiro, and especially Ken Wilber. Thanks also to all our friends and colleagues who have supported our work.

For further information on this and other books by Roger Walsh and Frances Vaughan, see the website essentialspirituality.com.

❑

Introduction

WE ARE astoundingly ingenious creatures. We have gone to the moon, split the atom, unraveled the genetic code, and probed the birth of the universe. Indeed, modern civilization stands as a monument to the boundless creativity of the human intellect.

Yet, while evidence of our intellectual and technological genius is all around us, there is growing concern that in other ways we have seriously underestimated ourselves. In part because of the blinding brilliance of our technological triumphs, we have distracted and dissociated ourselves from our inner world, sought outside for answers that can only be found within, denied the subjective and the sacred, overlooked latent capacities of mind, imperiled our planet, and lived in a collective trance—a contracted, distorted state of mind that goes unrecognized because we share it and take it to be "normality."

There exist within us, however, latent but unexplored creative capacities, depths of psyche, states of consciousness, and stages of development undreamed of by most people. Transpersonal disciplines have emerged to explore these possibilities, and they emerged first in psychology.

THE EVOLUTION OF PSYCHOLOGY

Western psychology was born from two distinct sources: the laboratory and experimental science on one hand, and hospitals and clinical concerns on the other. In its practitioners' efforts to establish it as a legitimate science, they modeled experimental psychology on physics, focused on observable, measurable behavior, and shied away from the unobservable world of inner experience. Experimental psychology became dominated by behaviorism.

Clinical psychology and psychiatry, on the other hand, were born of a concern for treating pathology. Since much suffering stems from unconscious forces, clinical work focused on the subjective and the unconscious. Clinical psychiatry and psychology became dominated by psychoanalysis. Psychoanalysis and behaviorism thus laid the foundations of clinical and experimental psychology, which they dominated for most of the first half of the twentieth century, becoming known as the first and second forces of Western psychology.

But by the sixties there was growing concern that along with the many contributions made by these schools of thought, there were also significant restrictions and distortions. Increasingly it appeared that they could not do justice to the full range of human experience. They focused on psychopathology or generalized from simple laboratory-controlled conditions to the complexities of daily life, and they ignored crucial dimensions of human experience, such as consciousness and exceptional psychological well-being.

In addition, they sometimes pathologized vital transpersonal experiences. For example, Freud interpreted such experiences as reflections of infantile helplessness, while other psychoanalysts dismissed them as "regressions to union with the breast," or "narcissistic neuroses." As the philosopher Jacob Needleman put it, "Freudianism institutionalized the underestimation of human possibility."[1]

Humanistic psychology emerged in response to these concerns. In the words of Abraham Maslow, a founding father of both humanistic and transpersonal psychology, "This point of view in no way denies the usual Freudian picture, but it does add to it and supplement it. To oversimplify the matter somewhat, it is as if Freud supplied to us the sick half of psychology, and we must now fill it out with the healthy half. Perhaps this health psychology will give us more possibility of controlling and improving our lives and for making ourselves better people."[2]

Humanistic psychologists wanted to study human experience and what was most central to life and well-being, rather than what was easily measured in the laboratory. One discovery in particular was to have an enormous impact and eventually give birth to transpersonal psychology. Exceptionally psychologically healthy people tend to have "peak experiences": brief but extremely intense, blissful, meaningful, and beneficial experiences of expanded identity and union with the universe. Similar experiences have been recognized across history and have been called mystical, spiritual, and unitive experiences, or in the East, samadhi and satori.

Eventually researchers recognized that various Eastern traditions describe whole families of peak experiences, and claim to have methods for inducing them at will. It soon became apparent that peak experiences have been highly valued throughout history, are the focus of several Asian disciplines, and yet seem to have been significantly underestimated—even pathologized—in the modern Western world. Transpersonal psychology arose in part to explore these experiences.

Of course, humanistic and transpersonal studies did not arise in a cultural vacuum. Rather, they both reflected and fed the dramatic changes occurring during the sixties within the culture at large. These included the birth of the human potential movement and the questioning of the materialistic dream, both of which led some people to look within for the enduring satisfaction that external success and acquisitions had seductively promised, but failed to provide.

Psychedelics also had a powerful impact and unleashed an unprecedented range and intensity of experiences on a society ill equipped to assimilate them. For the first time in history, a significant proportion of the culture experienced alternate states of consciousness. Some of these were clearly painful and problematic. Yet others were transcendent states that demonstrated to an unsuspecting world the plasticity of consciousness, the broad range of its potential states, the limitations and distortions of our usual state, and the possibility of more desirable ones.

At the same time, the introduction of Asian meditative disciplines offered ways of reaching similar states and insights through non-drug means. Suddenly, experiences that for centuries had appeared to many Westerners as nonsensical or pathological became valid and valued in the lives of a sizable minority. Western culture has never been the same since.

The many social effects included interest in Asian cultures and traditions and in spiritual practices as diverse as yoga, shamanism, and Christian contemplation. Dissatisfaction with conventional values led to alternate life-styles such as voluntary simplicity and ecological sensitivity, which flourished to express and support the new perspectives. Within universities new research fields explored topics such as meditation, biofeedback, psychedelics, and states of consciousness. Yesterday's cultural curiosity had become today's mainstream research. Transpersonal psychologists sought to integrate these novel findings into a new discipline, and they were soon joined by researchers in psychiatry, anthropology, sociology, and ecology.

DEFINITION AND DESCRIPTION

What, then, is the transpersonal?

Transpersonal experiences may be defined as experiences in which the sense of identity or self extends beyond (*trans*) the individual or personal to encompass wider aspects of humankind, life, *psyche*, and cosmos.

Transpersonal disciplines study transpersonal experiences and related phenomena. Practitioners seek to expand the scope of their disciplines to include the study of transpersonal phenomena and to bring their particular disciplinary expertise to this study.[3]

Transpersonal psychology is the psychological study of transpersonal experiences and their correlates. These correlates include the nature, varieties, causes, and effects of transpersonal experiences and development, as well as the psychologies, philosophies, disciplines, arts, cultures, life-styles, reactions, and religions that are inspired by them, or that seek to induce, express, apply, or understand them.

Transpersonal psychiatry is the area of psychiatry that focuses on the study of transpersonal experiences and phenomena. Its focus is similar to transpersonal psychology, with a particular interest in the clinical and biomedical aspects of transpersonal phenomena.

Transpersonal anthropology is the cross-cultural study of transpersonal phenomena and the relationship between consciousness and culture.

Transpersonal sociology studies the social dimensions, implications, and expressions of transpersonal phenomena.

Transpersonal ecology studies the ecological dimensions, implications, and applications of transpersonal phenomena.

The *transpersonal movement* is the interdisciplinary movement that in-cludes and integrates individual transpersonal disciplines.

These definitions describe the focus and purpose of transpersonal disci-plines. It is important to note what these definitions do not do, however. They do not exclude the personal, limit the type of expansion of identity, tie transpersonal disciplines to any particular philosophy or worldview, or limit research to a particular method.

Transpersonal disciplines do not exclude or invalidate the personal realm. Rather, they set personal concerns within a larger context that acknowledges the importance of both personal and transpersonal experi-ences. Indeed, one interpretation of the term *transpersonal* is that the transcendent is expressed through (*trans*) the personal.

Likewise the definitions do not specify limits on the direction or extent of expansion of the sense of identity. Some ecologists emphasize the importance of horizontal expansion of identity to encompass the earth and life, while simultaneously denying the value or validity of vertical tran-scendence. On the other hand, for some spiritual practitioners this vertical expansion of identity to encompass transcendent images and realms is central, while others value identification with both the vertical (tran-scendent) and the horizontal (immanent) realms.

These definitions do not commit the transpersonal disciplines or their practitioners to any specific interpretation of transpersonal experiences. In particular they do not tie the disciplines to any particular ontology, meta-physics, or worldview, nor to any specific doctrine, philosophy, or reli-gion. By focusing on experiences, the definitions allow for multiple interpretations of these experiences and the insights into human nature and the cosmos that they offer. Transpersonal experiences have long been interpreted in many different ways, and this will doubtless continue. A transpersonalist could be religious or nonreligious, theist or atheist. A definition of transpersonal disciplines that focuses on experience thus makes room for a range of diverse but valuable and complementary views.

Finally, these definitions do not place limits on the methods for studying or researching transpersonal experiences. Rather, any valid epistemology (way of acquiring knowledge) is welcome. In practice, transpersonal researchers have encouraged an eclectic, interdisciplinary, integrative approach that makes appropriate use of all the so-called "three eyes of knowledge": the sensory, introspective-rational, and contemplative. This is in contrast to many other schools, which effectively advocate or rely on a single epistemology. For example, behaviorism has centered on sensory data and science, introspective schools such as psychoanalysis have emphasized mental observation, while yogic approaches focus on contemplation. To date, the transpersonal disciplines stand alone in adopting an eclectic epistemology that seeks to include science, philosophy, introspection, and contemplation and to integrate them in a comprehensive investigation adequate to the many dimensions of human experience and human nature.

Transpersonal disciplines, therefore, tend to be exceptionally wide-ranging, interdisciplinary, and integrative. Their investigations include higher developmental possibilities and what Maslow called "the farther reaches of human nature." This investigation builds on and integrates knowledge from fields such as neuroscience, cognitive science, anthropology, philosophy, and comparative religion and incorporates Eastern as well as Western perspectives. Topics of particular interest include consciousness and altered states, mythology, meditation, yoga, mysticism, lucid dreaming, psychedelics, values, ethics, relationships, exceptional capacities and psychological well-being, transconventional development, transpersonal emotions such as love and compassion, motives such as altruism and service, and transpersonal pathologies and therapies.

RELATIONSHIP TO RELIGION

Several of these topics overlap with areas of religious studies. This raises the question of the relationship of transpersonal disciplines to religion. Of course much depends on definitions. As Ken Wilber points out, "One of the great difficulties in discussing religion . . . is that it is not an 'it.' In my opinion, 'it' has at least a dozen different, major, largely exclusive meanings, and unfortunately these are not always, not even usually, distinguished in the literature."[4]

One simple definition of religion is that which is concerned with, or related to, the sacred. Since some, but not all, transpersonal experiences are experiences of the sacred, and since some, but not all, religious experiences are transpersonal, there is clearly some overlap between transpersonal experiences and religious experiences. Transpersonal disciplines, however, are also interested in transpersonal experiences that are not religious, and in research, interpretations, psychologies, and philosophies devoid of religious overtones. Transpersonal disciplines espouse no creed or dogma, demand no particular religious convictions, espouse an open-minded scientific, philosophical, and experiential testing of all claims, and usually assume that transpersonal experiences can be interpreted either religiously or nonreligiously according to individual preference. Transpersonal disciplines and religion should therefore be regarded as distinct fields with partially overlapping areas of interest and also significant differences. Likewise, although they share some areas of interest, transpersonal psychology and transpersonal anthropology are clearly distinct from the psychology and anthropology of religion.

MULTISTATE DISCIPLINES

It is vitally important to note that transpersonal disciplines are multistate disciplines. Like Western culture, mainstream disciplines such as psychology and anthropology are predominantly unistate. That is, they are centered in, and focus on, a single state of consciousness—namely our usual waking state—and accord significantly less attention and importance to alternate states.

By contrast, multistate cultures accord more attention and value to states such as dreams and contemplation and therefore derive significant parts of their worldviews from multiple states. Examples of such multistate enterprises include shamanic tribal cultures, Buddhist psychology, and Taoist philosophy.

Traditional transpersonal disciplines, such as yoga and contemplation and their associated psychologies and philosophies, are designed to induce and illuminate multiple states. They are therefore clearly multistate disciplines. Contemporary transpersonal disciplines are attempts to forge modern multistate disciplines to bring the understanding, expression, and induction of transpersonal experiences and phenomena to the modern world and to combine the best of ancient and cross-cultural wisdom with contemporary disciplines.

Because they are multistate systems, transpersonal disciplines may be inherently broader than conventional disciplines, encompassing and valuing a wider range of human experiences and possibilities. This breadth extends to encompassing the contributions of multiple schools of thought. Having seen the ways in which any school or theory provides a selective perspective that highlights some aspects of behavior and neglects or obscures others, transpersonalists are especially interested in the contributions and integration of diverse schools.

For example, rather than advocating the exclusive dominance of one perspective, transpersonal psychology suggests that apparently conflicting schools may address different perspectives, dimensions, and stages of human experience and may therefore be partly complementary. Thus, Freudian psychology is concerned with important issues of early development, while existential psychology speaks to universal issues confronting mature adults. Behavior therapy demonstrates the importance of environmental reinforcers in controlling behavior, while cognitive therapies illuminate the power of unrecognized thoughts and beliefs. Jungian psychology reminds us of the archetypal depths and power of the collective unconscious and the therapeutic potency of images and symbols. Asian systems such as Buddhist, yogic, and Vedantic psychologies complement Western approaches by describing stages of transpersonal development and providing techniques for realizing them.

Although transpersonal psychology includes areas beyond the usual scope of mainstream Western schools, it values the many contributions of these schools. It does not seek to replace them but rather to integrate them within a larger vision of human possibility. This is the transpersonal vision.

Of course, the transpersonal vision presented here is not complete or final. It, too, will doubtless yield in its turn to a still more comprehensive viewpoint.

And yet if we only knew how each loss of one's viewpoint is a progress and how life changes when one passes from the stage of the closed truth to the stage of the open truth—a truth like life itself, too great to be trapped by points of view, because it embraces every point of view . . . a truth great enough to deny itself and pass endlessly into a higher truth.[5]

THE IMPORTANCE OF THE TRANSPERSONAL VISION

Across centuries and cultures transpersonal experiences have been regarded as vitally or even supremely important. In our own time the transpersonal vision and transpersonal disciplines are crucially important for many reasons. They draw attention to a neglected, misunderstood family of experiences; provide new understandings of ancient ideas, religious traditions, and contemplative practices; offer more generous views of human nature; and point to unsuspected human possibilities.

Transpersonal disciplines seek to research and rehabilitate transpersonal experiences that for too long have been dismissed as irrational or patho-logical. As the chapters of this book amply demonstrate, these experi-ences are regarded more accurately as healthy progressions than as pathological regressions. As Ken Wilber clearly argues, such experiences are not "regression in the service of the ego, but evolution and tran-scendence of the ego."[6]

The rehabilitation and appreciation of transpersonal experiences has enormous cross-cultural significance. It allows us to better appreciate many other cultures as well as their philosophies, religions, and art, and to integrate much historical and cross-cultural data.

In the first half of the twentieth century many Western anthropologists adopted the psychoanalytic perspective and therefore devalued transper-sonal experiences. Since these experiences have been so widespread and valued in other cultures, the natural tendency was to reinforce Western biases that devalued other cultures. Eminent scholars could then un-blinkingly reach conclusions such as: "The obvious similarities between schizophrenic regressions and the practices of Yoga and Zen merely indicate that the general trend in Oriental cultures is to withdraw into the self from an overbearingly difficult physical and social reality."[7]

Now that transpersonal experiences and processes are better under-stood, we can evaluate other cultures better and learn from their transper-sonal wisdom accumulated over thousands of years. We can, in effect, reclaim what has been called "the Great Tradition": the sum total of humankind's cross-cultural religious-philosophical wisdom.

Just why transpersonal experiences have been valued throughout his-tory is becoming clearer as we research them more closely. They offer significant psychological and social benefits. Transpersonal experiences can often, though certainly not invariably, produce dramatic, enduring, beneficial psychological changes. They can provide a sense of meaning and purpose, resolve existential quandaries, and inspire compassionate concern for humankind and the earth. Indeed, a single transpersonal experience can sometimes change a person's life forever. Moreover, grow-ing evidence, discussed at various places throughout this book, suggests that a lack of such experiences may underlie a significant amount of the individual, social, and global pathology that surrounds and threatens us.

Transpersonal experiences also point to a cornucopia of human possi-bilities. They suggest that certain emotions, motives, cognitive capacities, and states of consciousness can be cultivated and refined to degrees well beyond the norm.

For example, contemplative traditions suggest that beneficent emo-tions such as love and compassion can be expanded to encompass not only all people but all life. Likewise they claim—and initial research supports their claim—that attention can be stabilized, perceptions sensitized, and motives such as altruism and self-transcendence strengthened. The possibility of heightening capacities such as these suggests that psychological development may proceed far beyond what we formerly regarded as the ceiling for human possibilities.

Transpersonal experiences occur in altered states of consciousness, and the study of both has made clear just how dramatically we have underestimated the plasticity of human consciousness and its range of potential states. Until the second half of the twentieth century, Western psychology recognized only a handful of states of consciousness; other than normal waking and sleeping states, most of these—such as intoxication, delirium, and psychosis—were pathological. Now, however, research has demonstrated numerous alternate states, and the number and variety of recognized states continue to grow.

The range of techniques for inducing these states is vast and includes both ancient and modern methods. Some time-honored methods are physiological strategies such as fasting, sleep deprivation, and exposure to heat and cold; others are psychological methods such as solitude, chanting, drumming, dance, meditation, and yoga. Modern additions range from isolation tanks to biofeedback.

While many alternate states may confer no particular advantage or may even be disadvantageous, others are associated with heightened capacities such as those discussed earlier. Two key implications follow: higher states of consciousness—states in which people have capacities above and beyond the usual—may be available to us all. And our usual state of consciousness, which we usually assume to be the best, is actually suboptimal.

One finding has far-reaching implications: states of consciousness may exhibit what is called state specificity or state-specific limitations. This means that what is learned or understood in one state of consciousness may be less easily comprehended in another. Thus even profound understandings gained in an alternate state may be incomprehensible to someone who has never accessed the state.

This implies that the ability to appreciate and understand transpersonal experiences, as well as their associated disciplines and life-styles, may depend on the extent of one's experience of these alternate states. State specificity suggests one important reason why transpersonal experiences and traditions have been underestimated and why undertaking practices to cultivate these experiences may be necessary for understanding them.

Transpersonal disciplines offer radical reinterpretations and illuminations of certain aspects of religions and contemplative practices. From this perspective the contemplative and mystical core of the world's great religions can be seen as multistate traditions for inducing specific transpersonal states of consciousness, especially those states that offer what has been called enlightenment, liberation, or salvation. The philosophies and psychologies that accompany these traditions can be seen as expressing the knowledge gained from these states. The contemplative practices by which these liberating states are induced can be regarded in part as transpersonal technologies or technologies of transcendence. This perspective offers a new and illuminating understanding of disciplines that have often seemed mysterious.

Almost invariably, people who have deep transpersonal experiences begin to entertain a larger view of human nature and the cosmos. They discover an inner universe as vast and mysterious as the outer, and realms of experience inaccessible to physical instruments. These are realms of mind and consciousness. People who discover them may conclude that we exist in these realms as much as or more than in the realm of the senses and physical world.

As with human nature, so too with the cosmos. Transpersonal experiences often suggest that there are nonphysical realms of existence of enormous scope. From this viewpoint existence is seen as multilayered, and the physical universe, so often assumed to be the totality of existence, now appears as only one of multiple realms.

Whatever understanding of humankind and the cosmos they may eventually unveil, to date transpersonal disciplines stand alone in the scope of their search. They advocate an eclectic, integrative quest that includes personal and transpersonal, ancient and modern, East and West, knowledge and wisdom, art and philosophy, science and religion, introspection and contemplation. Only by such a comprehensive approach can we hope for a vision that reflects the extraordinary possibilities of humankind and the cosmos: a transpersonal vision.

PART I

❏

The Varieties of Transpersonal Experience

SECTION ONE

◻

THE RIDDLE OF CONSCIOUSNESS

In the history of the collective as in the history of the individual, everything depends on the development of consciousness.

CARL JUNG[1]

THE STUDY of consciousness and altered states of consciousness is central to transpersonal psychology. Yet there is remarkably little discussion of what consciousness is. This dearth of discussion mirrors psychology in general, which under the sway of behaviorism and the quest for objectivity long dismissed consciousness as a topic unfit for polite conversation. Although it regained partial respectability in the eighties, confusion continues regarding the nature, importance, and even existence of consciousness, let alone the best means to study it.[2]

This confusion in psychology reflects centuries of confusion in philosophy. Indeed, the nature of consciousness is one of the most fundamental and difficult of all philosophical questions. At one extreme consciousness has been dismissed as fictitious, "the name of a nonentity," according to William James. At the other extreme it has been lauded as the fundamental substrate of reality (a philosophical position known as absolute idealism). It also has been regarded as a mere epiphenomenon of matter (materialism) or as one aspect of a more basic reality that is fundamentally neither mental nor physical but can exhibit qualities of both (dual aspect theory, or neutral monism). Consciousness has been looked down on as a disease

13

of life (Nietzsche) and looked up to as infinite being-bliss: the *Sat-chit-ananda* (being-consciousness-bliss) of Vedanta. Small wonder, then, that "so far there is no good theory of consciousness. There is not even agreement about what a theory of consciousness would be like."[3]

For most of psychology and science, consciousness is an epiphenomenon not readily amenable to scientific research, while for much of Western philosophy consciousness is a classical conundrum that does not yield to conceptual analysis. Somehow consciousness seems to slip through scientific research and conceptual analysis like water through a net.

Yet from the perspective of several Eastern and some Western philosophical and religious traditions, this is to be expected. While most of Western psychology assumes that consciousness is a property or product of the personal mind and brain, these traditions assume that consciousness is an aspect of the Absolute, Atman-Brahman, God, Void, or Mind.

According to these traditions, our usual state of mind is said to be clouded, deluded, dreamlike, or entranced. In this state we assume that the individual psyche is the source of consciousness rather than a creation or component of it. Here are the words of Patanjali, who compiled the classic text of yoga:

> *The mind does not shine by its own light.*
> *It too is an object, illumined by the Self. . . .*
> *But the Self is boundless.*
> *It is the pure Consciousness that illumines the*
> *   contents of the mind. . . .*
> *Egoism, the limiting sense of "I," results from the*
> *   individual intellect's attributing the power of*
> *   consciousness to itself.*[4]

In this view, consciousness is not personal but transpersonal, not mental but transmental. In fact, as an aspect of the Absolute, it is said to be beyond space, time, qualities, concepts, categories, and limits of any kind. Hence, the ultimate nature of consciousness is said to be intangible and inconceivable. Even to attempt to describe this reality results in a paradox whereby, as Kant discovered, the opposite of any apparently valid statement is also valid. Almost fifteen hundred years before Kant, Nagarjuna—the founder of Madhyamaka Buddhism—reached virtually the same conclusion, "a conclusion echoed and amplified in succeeding generations by every major school of Eastern philosophy and psychology: Reason cannot grasp the essence of absolute reality, and when it tries, it generates only dualistic incompatibilities."[5]

From this perspective, then, it is not surprising that most schools of

Western philosophy, psychology, and science have failed to grasp the nature of consciousness. For in the words of the Third Zen Patriarch:

> To seek Mind with the (discriminating) mind
>   is the greatest of all mistakes. . . .
> The more you talk about it
> The further astray you wander from the truth.[6]

It is a mistake because, to use contemporary language, it is a "category error." That is, it is an attempt to use what St. Bonaventure called the eye of flesh (sensory perception) or the eye of mind (logic and philosophy), and their combination (science) to see what can only be seen with the eye of contemplation.[5]

The Asian traditions agree with St. Bonaventure. Consciousness cannot be perceived or adequately conceived; it can only be known through direct intuition. This direct intuition of consciousness and the transmental domain is said to develop wisdom (prajna) that allows one to escape from our distorted view of consciousness, self, and world.

The way out of this distortion is obviously to change our state of mind. Indeed, it is intriguing that although humans might not know what consciousness is, they have poured enormous effort into altering their experience of it. A cross-cultural survey found that fully 90 percent of several hundred societies had institutionalized one or more altered states.[7] People in traditional societies almost always view these states as sacred. Andrew Weil concluded that the "desire to alter consciousness periodically is an innate normal drive analogous to hunger or the sexual drive."[8]

From a perspective that regards consciousness as unchangeable and unqualifiable, the idea of changing states of consciousness makes no sense. What is really being changed is states of mind. Most Western psychologists, however, operate from the implicit assumption that consciousness is a function of the individual psyche and consequently speak of "states of consciousness." Because this term is so common in the literature we use it here as necessary.

One of the early assumptions about altered states of consciousness (ASCs) induced by practices such as meditation or yoga was that they were more or less equivalent. This reflected our ignorance of the broad range of possible ASCs. For example, the varieties of ASC that have been identified in Indian meditative and yogic practices alone include highly concentrated states such as the yogic samadhis or Buddhist jhanas; witness-consciousness states in which equanimity is so strong that stimuli have little or no effect on the observer; and states in which extremely refined inner stimuli become the objects of attention, such as the faint inner sounds of shabd yoga. Some practices lead to unitive states in which the sense of separation between self and world dissolves, as in some Zen satoris. In other states all objects or phenomena disappear, as in the Buddhist nirvana or Vedantic nirvikalpa samadhi; and in still others all phenomena are perceived as expressions or modifications of consciousness, such as sahaj samadhi.[9,10]

Until recently many of these states were regarded as pathological. There are several reasons for this. In the West we have traditionally recognized only a limited number of states of consciousness—waking, sleeping, and intoxication, for example—and have tended to deny or pathologize others. Witness the nineteenth-century surgeons who observed a leg amputation performed painlessly under hypnosis and concluded that the patient was a hardened rogue, bribed to pretend he felt no pain. As psychologist Charles Tart concluded, "they must have had very hard rogues in those days."[11] This dovetails with the tendency in clinical psychiatry and anthropology to pathologize unusual experiences, especially those of people from other cultures, and to assume that our own usual state is optimal.

Most researchers have had little direct experience of the ASCs they investigate. Yet classical descriptions, psychological and philosophical arguments, and personal reports by trained Western researchers [11,12] suggest that it may be difficult to fully appreciate and comprehend altered states without direct experience of them. Indeed, such experiences can radically alter one's worldview, and those who have them are particularly likely to regard consciousness as the primary constituent of reality.[2]

So Western academic evaluations of the altered states of consciousness induced by meditative-yogic disciplines have undergone a dramatic shift. Many initial evaluations assumed that such states were pathological, whereas several hundred studies now attest to their potential benefits. Historically, their goal of mystical union was regarded as the *summum bonum*, the greatest good and highest aspiration of human existence.

The existence of a wide range of states raises four key questions: (1) Which states are beneficial and transformative and which are dangerous and destructive? (2) How can we strengthen healthy states and transform destructive ones? These two questions are discussed in other sections of this book. (3) How can we identify, characterize, map, and compare individual states? (4) How can we develop an overarching framework or theory that lays out the whole spectrum of consciousness and the place of individual states within it? These two questions are the subject of the following essays.

In "Psychology, Reality, and Consciousness," Daniel Goleman points out that Western psychology is only one of many psychologies, some of them thousands of years old. Each psychology, indeed each culture, constructs a worldview and codifies experience in specific ways. Goleman suggests that Western psychology and culture have been largely unistate, focusing on our usual waking state. This has left us relatively unsophisticated about, and suspicious of, altered states and the means to induce them.

By comparison, many Eastern psychologies and cultures are multistate. They value altered states and have developed sophisticated techniques for inducing them and maps for describing them. Goleman concludes that integrating different psychologies may enrich both East and West.

In "Psychologia Perennis," Ken Wilber points out that throughout history a perennial philosophy and psychology have described many states of consciousness ranged along a spectrum. Different psychologies and therapies address different levels of this spectrum and can therefore be seen as complementary rather than oppositional. Each level is associated with specific experiences and a specific sense of identity, ranging from the drastically narrowed identity associated with egocentricity to that known as the Supreme Identity or cosmic consciousness, which has been considered both the source and goal of the great religions.

Charles Tart offers a valuable means for understanding altered states via "A Systems Approach to Consciousness." He points out that a state of consciousness is a highly complex system constructed of components such as attention, awareness, identity, and physiology. Different dynamic patterns of these components result in different states, and techniques for altering consciousness change patterns by modifying one or more components.

In "Mapping and Comparing States," Roger Walsh responds to two questions that have puzzled Western researchers ever since they realized that contemplative practices elicit ASCs: (1) Are the states induced by different practices identical or different? (2) Are they pathological and regressive or healthy and transcendent? The debate has persisted because until now there has been no way to precisely describe and compare states of consciousness. Walsh compares the states occurring in shamanism, Buddhism, yoga, and acute schizophrenia and shows that they differ significantly on several key dimensions of experience.

❑

I

Psychology, Reality, and Consciousness

Daniel Goleman

Attempts to forge a systematic and inclusive understanding of human behavior by no means originated with contemporary Western psychology. Our formal psychology as such is less than a hundred years old, and so represents a recent version of an endeavor probably as old as human history. It is also the product of European and American culture, society, and intellectual history, and as such is only one of innumerable "psychologies" (though for us by far the most familiar and comfortable) which have been articulated as an implicit or explicit part of the fabric of reality in every culture, present and past. If we are to arrive at the fullest possible understanding of human psychology, it behooves us to turn to these other systems of psychology, not as curiosities to be studied from our own vantage point, but as alternative lenses through which we may be allowed visions and insights which our own psychological viewpoints might obscure. While we may subsequently find some alternative viewpoints irrelevant to our own situation, we may also find much of value.

Individuals in each culture, observes Dorothy Lee (1950), codify experience in terms of the categories of their own linguistic system, grasping reality only as it is presented in code. Each culture punctuates and categorizes experience differently. The anthropologist recognizes that the study of a code different from our own can lead us to concepts and aspects of reality from which our own way of looking at the world excludes us.

Openness on the part of contemporary psychology may be a requisite to gaining what wisdom and insights regarding consciousness are contained in traditional psychologies. Each culture has a specialized vocabulary in those areas of existence which are most salient to its own mode of experiencing the world. In this light it is intriguing that our own culture has as its major technical vocabulary for describing inner experience a highly specialized nosology of psycho-pathology, while Asian cultures such as India have equally intricate vocabularies for altered states of consciousness and stages in spiritual development.

LaBarre (1947) points out that the outward expression of emotion is susceptible to great cross-cultural variation, even those expressions such as laughing and crying which are generally considered biologically determined. So with the experience and communication of states of awareness: culture molds awareness to conform to certain norms, limits the types of experience or categories for experience available to the individual, and determines the appropriateness or acceptability of a given state of awareness or its communication in the social situation.

Our normative cultural reality is state-specific. Insofar as "reality" is a consensually validated, but arbitrary, convention, an altered state of consciousness can represent an anti-social, unruly mode of being. This fear of the unpredictable may have been a major motivating force behind the repression in our culture of means for inducing altered states—e.g., psychedelics—or for a more general suspicion of techniques such as meditation.

While the cultural value system which has led to the preeminence of the waking state and the preclusion of altered states (except for alcohol intoxication) from the cultural norm has proved functional in terms of, say, economic growth, it has also rendered us as a culture relatively unsophisticated in terms of altered states of consciousness (ASC). Other "primitive' and traditional cultures, while less materially productive than our own, are far more knowledgeable than we in the intricacies of consciousness. Some cultures explicitly educate some or all members in altering consciousness, and many have developed "technologies" for this purpose— e.g., the Bushmen are trained to enter a trance via dancing, and to use the trance state for healing (Katz, 1973).

The religious teachings of the East contain psychological theories, just as our own psychologies reflect cosmologies. Within the context of their own respective cosmologies these traditional psychologies of the East are equal to our own in terms of an "empirical" adequacy determined not by the procedural canons of empirical science, but rather as interpretive schemes applicable to everyday life. Berger and Luckmann (1967, p. 178) observe:

> Insofar as psychological theories are elements of the social definition of reality, their reality-generating capacity is a characteristic they share with other legitimate theories. . . . If a psychology becomes socially established (that is, becomes generally recognized as an adequate interpretation of objective reality), it tends to realize itself forcefully in the phenomena it purports to interpret. . . . Psychologies produce a reality, which in turn serves as the basis for their verification.

The domain of many traditional psychologies encompasses the familiar territory of normal waking awareness, but extends also into states of consciousness of which the West has only recently become cognizant (and the existence of which may yet remain a mystery for most Western psychologists and laymen who have not themselves heard of or experienced them). The models of contemporary psychology, for example, foreclose the acknowledgment or investigation of a mode of being which is the central premise and *summum bonum* of virtually every Eastern psycho-spiritual system. Called variously "enlightenment," "Buddhahood," "liberation," the "awakened state," and so on, there is simply no fully equivalent category in contemporary psychology.[1] The paradigms of traditional Asian psychologies, however, are capable of encompassing the major categories of contemporary psychology as well as this other mode of consciousness.

Freud saw no way out of suffering but to bear it; the Buddhist psychologist offers an alternative: alter the processes of ordinary consciousness and thereby end suffering. The state of consciousness which transcends all the ordinary realms of being is the "Buddha realm." Buddhahood is attained by transforming ordinary consciousness, principally through meditation, and once attained is characterized by the extinction of all those states—e.g., anxiety, needfulness, pride—which mark the ordinary realms of existence. Buddhahood is a higher-order integration than any suggested by the developmental schema of contemporary psychology.

What is particularly intriguing about the Buddhist developmental schema is that it not only expands the constructs of contemporary psychology's view of what is possible, but also gives details of the means whereby such a change can occur, namely, that via meditation—an attentional manipulation—one can enter an altered state, and that through systematic retraining of attentional habits one can alter consciousness as a trait of being. Such an enduring alteration of the structure and process of consciousness is no longer an ASC, but represents an altered *trait* of consciousness, or ATC, where attributes of an ASC are assimilated in ordinary states of consciousness.

Though traditional and contemporary psychologies may partially overlap—e.g., in a common interest in attentional processes, or in an understanding of the inescapable nature of human suffering—each also thoroughly explores territory and techniques the other ignores or barely touches on. Psychoanalytic thought, for example, has charted aspects of what would be called "karma" in the East in far greater detail and complexity than any Eastern school of psychology. Eastern schools have developed an array of techniques for voluntarily altering consciousness and stabilizing in an ATC, and so establish a technology for dealing with realities beyond the mind as it is conceptualized in contemporary psychology or experienced in our usual state of consciousness.

To the extent that biography is the progenitor of psychology, these paradigmatic differences between traditional Eastern and contemporary Western psychology reflect differing experiences of being-in-the-world. Psychoanalytic thought, for example, gives a prominent place to the concept of reality-testing, which from the viewpoint of the relativity of states of consciousness is a state-bound test of "reality." The Western pathology of view is to equate "reality" with the world as perceived in waking state awareness, so denying access or credibility to reality as perceived in other states of consciousness. The complementary Eastern pathology is to see reality as wholly other than that of waking awareness, and so dismisses the physical world as illusory.

As in the evolution of science generally, in resolving any seeming conflicts in vision, paradigm, or worldview between Eastern and Western psychologies, an integratory effort may generate resolutions which would be higher-order formulations offering an understanding of states of consciousness and state-dependent realities at once more complex and more solidly grounded than any at present. The key for a progressive transfer to wider modes of apprehension for psychology as a whole as for the individual is the recognition, as William James said, that there is "always more . . ."

❑

2

Psychologia Perennis: The Spectrum of Consciousness

Ken Wilber

In the past few decades the West has witnessed an explosion of interest among psychologists, theologians, scientists, and philosophers alike in what Huxley (1970) has called *philosophia perennis* the 'perennial philosophy', a universal doctrine as to the nature of humankind and reality lying at the very heart of every major metaphysical tradition. What is frequently overlooked, however, is that corresponding to the perennial philosophy there exists what I would like to call a psychologia perennis, a 'perennial psychology'—a universal view as to the nature of human consciousness, which expresses the very same insights as the perennial philosophy but in more decidedly psychological language. The purpose of this paper—besides describing the fundamentals of the perennial psychology—is to outline a model of consciousness which remains faithful to the spirit of this universal doctrine yet at the same time gives ample consideration to the insights of such typically Western disciplines as ego-psychology, psychoanalysis, humanistic psychology, Jungian analysis, interpersonal psychology, and the like.

At the heart of this model, the "Spectrum of Consciousness", lies the insight that human personality is a multi-leveled manifestation or expression of a single Consciousness, just as in physics the electro-magnetic spectrum is viewed as a multi-banded expression of a single, characteristic electro-magnetic wave. More specifically, the Spectrum of Consciousness is a pluridimensional approach to human identity; that is to say, each level of the Spectrum is marked by a different and easily recognized sense of individual identity, which ranges from the Supreme Identity of cosmic consciousness through several gradations or bands to the drastically narrowed sense of identity associated with egoic consciousness. Out of these numerous levels or bands of consciousness, I have selected five major levels to discuss in connection with the *psychologia perennis* (*see* Fig. 1).

LEVELS OF THE SPECTRUM

The Level of Mind

The core insight of the *psychologia perennis* is that our 'innermost' consciousness is identical to the absolute and ultimate reality of the universe, known variously as Brahman, Tao, Dharmakaya, Allah, the Godhead—to name but a few—and which, for the sake of convenience, I will simply call 'Mind' (with a capital "M" to distinguish it from the apparent plurality of 'minds'). According to this universal tradition, Mind is what there is and all there is, spaceless and therefore infinite, timeless and therefore eternal, outside of which nothing exists.

On this level, we are identified with the universe, the All—or rather, we are the All. According to the *psychologia perennis*, this level is not an abnormal state of consciousness, nor even an altered state of consciousness, but rather the *only real* state of consciousness, all others being essentially illusions. In short, our innermost consciousness—known variously as the Atman, the Christ, Tathagatagarbha—is identical to the ultimate reality of the universe. This, then, is the Level of Mind, of cosmic consciousness, of humankind's Supreme Identity.

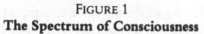

FIGURE 1
The Spectrum of Consciousness

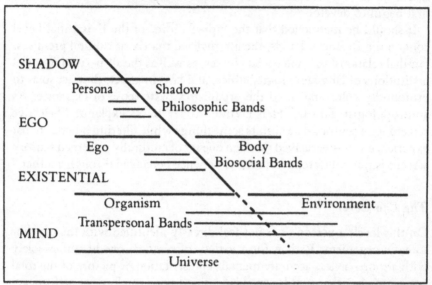

Some Prominent Nodes in the Spectrum of Consciousness. The major levels of identity are indicated by broad lines, while I have arbitrarily chosen three-line groupings to represent the auxiliary bands. The diagonal slash line is representative of the self/not-self boundary, so that, for example, to an individual identified with his persona, the shadow, the body, and the environment all appear as outside of self, as foreign, external, alien, and hence potentially threatening. The self/not-self boundary breaks at the Transpersonal Bands and vanishes at the Level of Mind.

The Transpersonal Bands

These bands represent the area of the Spectrum that is supra-individual, where one is not conscious of one's identity with the All and yet neither is identity confined to the boundaries of the individual organism. It is on these bands that the archetypes occur. In Mahayana Buddhism (Suzuki, 1968) these bands are known collectively as the 'supra-individual reposi-tory consciousness'; while in Hinduism (Deutsch, 1969) they are referred to as the *karana-sairia* or 'causal body'.

The Existential Level

Here humans are identified solely with the total psychophysical organism as it exists in space and time, for this is the first level where the line between self and other, organism and environment, is firmly drawn. This is also the level where rational thought processes, as well as personal will, first begin to develop.

It should be mentioned that the 'upper limits' of the Existential Level contain the Biosocial Bands, the internalized matrix of cultural premises, familial relationships, and social glosses, as well as the all-pervading social institutions of language, logic, ethics, and law. In effect, they act so as to profoundly color and mold the organism's basic sense of existence. As anthropologist Edward Hall (White, 1972, p. x) explains, "Selective screening of sensory data admits some things while filtering others, so that experience as it is perceived through one set of culturally patterned sensory screens is quite different from the experience perceived through another."

The Ego Level

On this level, a person does not feel directly identified with the psycho-somatic organism. Rather, for a variety of reasons, one identifies solely with a more-or-less accurate mental representation or picture of the total organism. In other words, one is identified with the Ego, or self-image. The total organism is thus split into a disembodied 'psyche', the ghost in the machine, and a 'soma', 'poor brother ass', with the person identified squarely with the psyche, the mind, the ego—a fact which one betrays by saying not "I *am* a body," but "I *have* a body." One feels that one exists *in* the body and not *as* the body. This level is identified almost exclusively with a mental picture of the total psychophysical organism, and therefore intellectual and symbolical processes predominate. Hence the Buddhists call this level the 'intellect', while the Hindus refer to it as the level of the ego split from and therefore trapped in the gross body.

The Shadow Level

Under certain circumstances, one can alienate various aspects of one's own psyche, dis-identify with them, and thus narrow the sphere of identity to only *parts* of the ego, which we may refer to as the persona. This level is that of the Shadow: identification with an impoverished and inaccurate self-image (i.e., the persona), while the rest of the psychic tendencies, those deemed too painful, 'evil', or undesirable, are alienated as the contents of the Shadow.

The above model is an extremely abbreviated description of the Spec-trum. As such, it does not fully represent the flow and interaction between the various bands. Nevertheless, it should be obvious that each level of the Spectrum represents an increasingly narrowed sphere of identity, from the universe to a facet of the universe called organism, from the organism to a facet of the organism called psyche, and from the psyche to a facet of the psyche called persona. (Each major level of the Spectrum is also marked by a different mode of knowing, a different dualism or set of dualisms, a different class of unconscious processes, and so on. For this paper, I have chosen to concentrate on the pluridimensionality of identity.)

EVOLUTION OF THE SPECTRUM

If it is true that the Level of Mind is the only reality, we might wonder just how it is that the other levels seem to exist at all. The answer is supplied by the *psychologia perennis* in the form of the doctrine of *maya*. *Maya* is any experience constituted by or stemming from dualism (specifically, the primary dualism of subject vs. object). According to Deutsch (1969, p. 28), "*Maya* is all experience that is constituted by, and follows from, the distinction between subject and object, between self and non-self." The perennial psychology declares all dualism to be not so much unreal as *illusory*. Cutting of the world into seer and seen, only *apparently* and not actually divides the world, for the world always remains indistinct from itself. Dualism, in other words, is illusory: it appears to exist but remains devoid of reality. In the same vein, the *psychologia perennis* declares that since the various levels of consciousness (except that of Mind itself) are the products of *maya* or dualism—as we will shortly explain—then they must exist only in an illusory fashion, with the *reality* of each level remaining always as Mind.

The *original* dualism or act of severance is mythologically referred to by the perennial philosophy as the separation of Heaven and Earth, Male and Female, Sun and Moon; epistemologically, it is the separation of subject and object, knower and known, observer and observed; ontologically, it is the separation of self and other, organism and environment. For our purposes, the most convenient labels for the two halves of this original dualism are subject and object, self and other, or simply organism and environment, for with its occurrence, human identity apparently (not actually) shifts from the nondual All to the organism. Our Supreme Identity becomes not lost but obscured, and thus is created "out of the Oneness of Mind" the next major level of the Spectrum: the Existential Level—the individual identified with the organism as against the environment. We might also mention that since this primary dualism separates the seer from the seen, the subject from the object, it simultaneously creates *space*.

As soon as one identifies exclusively with the organism, the problem of being vs. nullity—the problem of life vs. death—is created. The creation of the dualism of life vs. death is simultaneously the creation of *time*—for in the timelessness of the eternal Mind there is neither birth nor death, beginning nor end, past nor future. In other words, birth and death, past and future are one in the eternal Now, so that in separating birth from death humans necessarily separate past from future, and so consequently are thrown out of the timeless Now and into historical time. And that is the Existential Level: the person identified exclusively with the organism as it exists in *space* and *time*.

But the disruption of the unity of life and death—the creation of time itself—has yet another consequence. At the Existential Level, humans are now in panicked flight from death, and this very flight from death results in the creation of an idealized image of self called 'ego', for the ego, being essentially composed of fixed and stable symbols, *seems* to promise something that mere flesh will not: the everlasting escape from death embodied in static images. "The truth of the matter, according to Freud's later theory, is that the peculiar structure of the human ego results from its incapacity to accept reality, specifically the supreme reality of death" (Brown, 1959, p. 159). Man, in fleeing death, flees the mutable body and identifies with the seemingly undying idea of self. Hence identity shifts from the *total* psychophysical organism to the mental representation of that organism which thus creates the next major level of the Spectrum: the Ego Level, the person identified with a symbolic picture of self as against mortal body.

Finally, in the ultimate act of dualism, the person severs the unity of egoic tendencies and identifies with only a fraction of the psychic processes. One disowns, alienates, casts off the unwanted aspects of ego (which, through the process of egoic repression, nevertheless remains). In an attempt to make the self-image acceptable, one renders it inaccurate, thus creating the final level of the spectrum: the Shadow Level, the person identified with an inaccurate and greatly impoverished image of self called the persona, with the unwanted aspects of self projected as the Shadow.

Thus through successive dualisms (e.g., organism vs. environment, life vs. death, mind vs. body, persona vs. shadow) the various levels of the Spectrum of Consciousness evolve. Further, the 'level' of Mind is not actually one level among many but one without a second, and so we speak of the 'Level of Mind' only as a convenience. The levels of the Spectrum of Consciousness are thus not at all discrete but, like any spectrum, infinitely shade into one another. According to the *psychologia perennis*, these levels of the Spectrum exist, but only in an illusory fashion, much as the images seen on a television screen are unreal as actual events but exist as mere pictures. Thus the reality of each level is always nothing but Mind, and the actual levels themselves appear independently real only to those who are too enchanted to see through the illusion, who are unable to realize that the world always remains indistinct from itself despite the appearance of dualisms.

THERAPIES ADDRESSING THE VARIOUS LEVELS

Such, then, is an extremely brief description of the *psychologia perennis* and its interpretation according to the Spectrum of Consciousness. In a general fashion, the major fields of Western psychotherapy are each concerned with a different level of the Spectrum. These schools need not overly concern themselves as to which is the 'correct' approach to human consciousness because each is more-or-less correct when addressing its own level. A truly integrated and encompassing psychology can and should make use of the complementary insights offered by each school of psychology.

Ego-Level Therapies

Common to this group of therapies is the belief that pathology results from some sort of breakdown in communication between the conscious and the unconscious processes of the psyche, from a split between the persona and the shadow, however the latter may be conceived. Pathology results when a person's *self-image is distorted* and rendered inaccurate, and 'cure' consists in the establishment of an accurate and therefore acceptable self-image.

If one alienates certain facets of oneself, one will render the self-image fraudulent. The alienated facets (i.e., the now 'unconscious' shadow) will nevertheless remain but will be projected so as to appear to exist 'outside', in the environment or in others. Therapy consists in contacting the shadow and eventually re-owning it, so that one's sense of identity expands, so to speak, to include all of the aspects of oneself which were once alienated. In this fashion, the split between the persona and shadow is healed, and the individual consequently evolves an accurate and acceptable self-image, a more-or-less correct mental representation of the total psychophysical organism. And that is precisely the aim of Ego-level therapies.

Existential-Level Therapies

Since the Existential Level is the level of the total organism not marked by the dualism of psyche vs. soma, these therapies deal primarily with actualizing the concrete, full human being, not cut asunder into an ego vs. a body. Their aim is not so much to develop an accurate image of the total organism as to *be* that total organism. Just as the Ego-Level therapies aim at 'expanding identity' to all facets of the psyche, Existential-Level therapies aim at extending identity to *all facets of the total organism*. This is clearly stated by Perls et al. (1951): "The aim is to extend the boundary of what you accept as yourself to include *all organic activities*." Or, as Perls later put it, "Lose your mind and come to your senses!" That is, come to the total organism.

But remember that the Existential Level is also the home of the two root dualisms, namely, that of subject vs. object (or self vs. other) and life vs. death (or being vs. nullity). Consequently, these are a major concern of many Existential-Level therapies. "Sickness unto death," "being and nothingness," "hell is others," "being-in-the-world," the "dialectic of crisis"—all are common themes for some forms of existential therapy, and accurately reflect the phenomenology of the level to which they address themselves.

Overall then, the Existential-Level therapies are concerned with the total psychophysical organism and the crises it may face as well as the incredible potentials it may display. This group of therapies would include the more noetic approaches—such as existential psychology, Gestalt therapy, logotherapy, humanistic psychology in general, and bioenergetics, as well as the more somatic approaches such as hatha yoga, structural integration, polarity therapy, and sensory awareness. Despite their many real differences, they all seek to authenticate the full and concrete human organism.

Biosocial-Band Therapies

Recall that we named the upper limits of the Existential Level 'the Biosocial Bands'. These bands represent the massive mappings of cultural patterns onto the organism itself, and they thus exert a profound and pervasive influence upon the entire organism's orientation and behavior. Among other things, they mold the structure of an individual's ego (Mead, 1964) and the pattern of thought processes (Whorf, 1956). More important, as far as pathology is concerned, these bands act as a screen or filter of reality. In the words of Erich Fromm (1970, p. 98–99, 104):

> The effect of society is not only to funnel fictions into our consciousness, but also to prevent awareness of reality. . . . Every society by its own practice of living and by the mode of relatedness, of feeling and perceiving, develops a system of categories which determines the forms of awareness. This system works, as it were, like a *socially conditioned filter*. . . . Experiences which cannot be filtered through remain outside of awareness; that is, they remain unconscious. . . .

The Biosocial-Band therapies are thus concerned with the very fundamental ways in which such social patterns as language and logic alter and distort awareness, and are obviously working on a 'deeper' level than that of purely individual distortions, repressions, and so on. Hence the social context of pathology most concerns these therapies.

Transpersonal-Band Therapies

The Transpersonal Bands represent those aspects or levels of consciousness that by their very nature are supra-individual. At this level the 'individual' is not yet completely identified with the All, and yet neither is identity confined to the conventional boundaries of the organism. Among other things, the Transpersonal Bands are the home of the 'primordial images' of the 'collective unconscious'.

Now these archetypes exert a profound effect upon every level of the Spectrum existing 'above' the Transpersonal Bands. It is entirely possible that this is a general phenomenon seen throughout the Spectrum; the vicissitudes of *any* level can dramatically affect all of the levels above it. But the point to be emphasized here is that the Transpersonal Bands can themselves be *directly* experienced. Carl Jung (1968, p. 110) himself realized this, for he stated that "Mystics are people who have a particularly vivid experience of the processes of the collective unconscious. Mystical experience is *experience of archetypes*."

A general characteristic of the Transpersonal Bands is a suspension of all dualisms (except some form of the primary dualism). This necessarily includes the dualisms of persona vs. shadow as well as ego vs. body. In undercutting these dualisms, one simultaneously undercuts the support of individual neuroses, both egoic and existential.

To say the same thing in a slightly different fashion, in recognizing a depth of one's identity that goes beyond one's individual and separate being, a person can more easily go beyond individual and separate neuroses. For one is no longer *exclusively* identified with just the separate-self sense and hence is no longer exclusively tied to purely personal problems. In a sense one can start to let go of fears and anxieties, depressions and obsessions, and begin to view them with impartiality. The Transpersonal Band therapy discloses—probably for the first time—a transposition from which one can comprehensively *look at* individual emotional and ideational complexes. But the fact that one can comprehensively *look at* them means that one has ceased using them as something *with which to look at*, and thus distort, reality. Further, the fact that one can look at them means that one is no longer exclusively identified with them. One's identity begins to touch that within which is beyond.

As such, the Transpersonal Bands are sometimes experienced as the supra-individual Witness: that which is capable of observing the flow of what is—without manipulating it. The Witness simply observes the stream of events both inside and outside the mind-body in a creatively detached fashion, since, in fact, the Witness is not exclusively identified with either. In other words, *when the individual realizes that mind and body can be perceived objectively, he spontaneously realizes that they cannot constitute a real subjective self.* This position of the Witness, or we might say, this state of Witnessing, is the foundation of all beginning Buddhist practice ('mindfulness') [and] of Psychosynthesis ('disidentification and the transpersonal Self').

Further, it seems to resemble very closely what Maslow called plateau experiences, which "represent a witnessing of the world. The plateau experience is a witnessing of reality. It involves seeing the symbolic, or the mythic, the poetic, the transcendent, the miraculous. . . . It's the transcending of time and space which becomes quite normal, so to speak." It is expressly through these types of experiences that one is fully initiated into the world of metamotivations, B-values, transcendent values, mythological and supra-individual awareness—in short, the spiritual dimension of Transpersonal Bands.

Level-of-Mind Therapies

This distinction between what I am calling—for lack of better terms—'lesser' and 'true' mysticism is again the distinction between the transpersonal Witness and Mind. The transpersonal Witness is a 'position' of Witnessing reality. But notice that this state of the transpersonal Witness still contains a subtle form of the primary dualism, namely, the witness vs. what is witnessed. It is when this last trace of dualism is finally and completely shattered that one awakens to Mind, for at that moment (which is *this* moment) the witness and the witnessed are one and the same.

This is not at all to denigrate the position of the transpersonal self or Witness, for it can not only be highly therapeutic in itself, but it can frequently act as a type of springboard to Mind. Nevertheless it is not to be confused with Mind itself.

Such, then, is the major difference between the lesser mystical states of the transpersonal self, and the true mystical state which is Mind. In one, a person may witness reality; in the other he or she is reality. While one invariably retains some subtle form of the primary dualism, the other does not. The individual goes right to the very bottom of his or her being to find who or what is doing the seeing, and *ultimately* finds—instead of a transpersonal self—nothing other than what is seen, which Blyth called "the experience by the universe of the universe."

Therapies aimed at this level—like those of any level—are trying to heal a particular dualism, in this case, the primary dualism of subject vs. object. And the collapse of the dualism between subject and object is simultaneously the collapse of the dualism between past and future, life and death, so that one awakens, as if from a dream, to the spaceless and timeless world of cosmic consciousness. Therapies—and at this level we use the term 'therapies' only as a concession to language—addressing this level include Mahayana Buddhism, Taoism, Vedanta, Hinduism, Sufism, and certain forms of Christian mysticism.

CONCLUDING REMARKS

Having thus finished the above very abstract outline, a few points must at least be touched upon. First, the levels of the Spectrum of Consciousness, like any spectrum, infinitely shade and grade into one another, and in no way can they be finally separated from one another. We have merely picked out a few prominent 'nodes' in the Spectrum for discussion, so it immediately follows that the assignment of different schools of psychotherapy to one level or band is only a rough approximation. Second, when we assign a particular school to one major level of the Spectrum, this is done on the basis of a somewhat arbitrary 'deepest' level which that school recognizes. Generally speaking, the therapies of any one level recognize and even utilize the psychotherapeutic disciplines of the levels 'above' it. Thus, to place Jungian psychology on the Transpersonal Bands is not to imply that Jung had nothing to say about the Shadow Level, or the Biosocial Bands. Indeed he did have much to offer regarding those levels. Third, it *is*, however, generally the case that the therapies of any one level tend to view experience of *any* level 'beneath' theirs as being pathological, and are hence quick to explain away all lower levels with a diagnostic fury, as witness the stance of orthodox psychoanalysis on mysticism. Fourth, since the descent of the Spectrum of Consciousness is, in one sense or another, an expanding of identity from the persona to the ego or the organism to the cosmos, we could just as well speak of a progressive disidentification or a progressive *detachment* from all *exclusive* identifications. When it comes to the Level of Mind, it does not matter whether we say the individual is identified with *everything* or whether the individual is identified with *nothing*—both are logically meaningless anyway. To elucidate the former only makes the complex story of the Spectrum of Consciousness a little easier to tell. Fifth, since each level of the Spectrum is marked by a different sense of identity, each level will have more-or-less characteristic features associated with it. For instance, the different levels seem to produce different dreams, different needs, and different symptoms—to mention a few. For example, transpersonal anxiety, existential anxiety, and shadow anxiety are different beasts indeed, and simply must not be treated the same. The indiscriminate use of a single therapeutic technique for all symptoms may have the most unfortunate effects.

In this regard, the question might arise as to what effect, if any, therapeutic procedures on the upper levels (Shadow, Ego, Existential) have or might have on a person's development on or towards the lower levels (Transpersonal, Mind). Although an extended discussion of this topic is quite beyond the scope of this paper, the following may be said. The descent of the Spectrum of Consciousness can be described as a process of surrendering exclusive, narrowed, and partial identifications so as to discover broader and more encompassing ones down the Spectrum. To the extent an individual can let go of exclusive attachments on the upper bands of the Spectrum—and this, in essence, is the aim of upper level therapies—descent is thereby facilitated.

Theoretically, in totally healing the major dualism characteristic of any given level, the individual would be expected to necessarily, and quite spontaneously, descend to the next level. For example, in healing and wholing the split between persona and shadow, the individual—almost by definition—has descended to the Ego Level. In fully healing and wholing the split between ego and body, the individual has spontaneously descended to the Existential Level, and so on. Once on the new level, the individual will likely become more sensitive to that level's characteristics—its dreams, its dualisms, its class of 'dys-eases', its potentials for growth, its needs. This phenomenon of spontaneous descent, which is *potentially* inherent in everyone, is an almost exact analogue of Maslow's (1968) hierarchical needs—that is, neurotic needs (Shadow Level), basic needs (Ego and Existential Levels) and meta-needs (Transpersonal Bands: Mind has no needs for there is nothing outside it). As soon as an individual clears up one set of needs, the next set spontaneously emerges, and failure to satisfy these emergent needs will result in a different set of problems.

Thus, on the Shadow Level, the basic needs are not satisfied. Through repression, alienation, or some other projective mechanism, individuals fail to recognize the nature of their basic needs. And since, as is well known, one cannot get enough of what one does not really need, a whole battery of insatiable neurotic needs develop. If, on the other hand, these neurotic needs can be understood and displaced, so that the underlying basic needs can emerge (hierarchically), the individual can begin to act on them so as to find thereby the way to a larger fulfillment. One also finds— again, almost by definition—one's way to a lower level of the Spectrum. And by the time the individual reaches the Existential Level, an entirely new set of needs, the meta-needs, begin to emerge, carrying with them a call, sometimes a demand, to transcendence. Acting upon these meta-needs initiates one into the world of the Transpersonal Bands; shunning them throws one into the grips of a meta-pathology.

In light of the above, it would not be reckless to conclude that therapeutic measures on the upper levels of the Spectrum may indeed facilitate the descent to the lower levels. This does not mean that a descent to the Transpersonal Bands or the Level of Mind always *requires* upper-level therapy, even in the cases where it is indicated. It might certainly help, but may not be mandatory since lower-level therapies may in a real sense reduce the work to be done on the upper levels. If this were not the case, meditation practices would probably never be useful to a neurotic unless he had undergone something akin to complete psychoanalysis.

I have only extended the *psychologia perennis* by suggesting that not only do these levels apparently exist, as maintained by the perennial psychology, but also that pathology can occur on any of these levels (except, of course, on the Level of Mind), and thus the great contribution of Western psychologies lies precisely in addressing themselves to *these* pathologies.

Thus it is possible to see the grand complementarity of Eastern and Western approaches to consciousness and 'psychotherapy'. On the one hand, the overriding concern of the Eastern explorers of consciousness (and by 'Eastern' we really mean the *psychologia perennis* in general, geographically East or West being irrelevant) has always been with the Level of Mind, and thus they gave little, if any, attention to the pathologies that could develop on the other levels. This is understandable, for the perennial psychology maintains that *all* pathology stems from ignorance of Mind. Thus, although they were perfectly aware of the various levels of the Spectrum, and although they mapped them in detail, they felt that 'curing' a pathology on any of these levels was not much more than a waste of time, for the root ignorance of the subject-object dualism would still remain. The West, on the other hand, has been—at least since the seventeenth century—almost completely bereft of even the least conception of the perennial philosophy, and hence, when the study of psychopathology began to develop in this metaphysical vacuum, Western scientists had no choice but to seek out the roots of neuroses and psychoses in one or more of the 'upper' levels of the Spectrum (such as the Ego or Biosocial Levels). It is suggested that on their own levels they are *all* correct, and taken together they form a complementary approach to consciousness that spans the entire Spectrum.

❑

3

The Systems Approach to Consciousness

Charles Tart

Our ordinary state of consciousness is not something natural or given, but a highly complex construction, a specialized tool for coping with our environment and the people in it, a tool that is useful for doing some things but not very useful, and even dangerous, for doing other things. As we look at consciousness closely, we see that it can be analyzed into many parts. Yet these parts function together in a pattern: they form a system. While the components of consciousness can be studied in isolation, they exist as parts of a complex system, consciousness, and can be fully understood only when we see this function in the overall system. Similarly, understanding the complexity of consciousness requires seeing it as a system and understanding the parts. For this reason, I refer to my approach to states of consciousness as a systems approach.

To understand the constructed system we call a state of consciousness, we begin with some theoretical postulates based on human experience. The first postulate is the existence of a basic awareness. Because some volitional control of the focus of awareness is possible, we generally refer to it as *attention/awareness*. We must also recognize the existence of *self-awareness*, the awareness of being aware.

Further basic postulates deal with *structures*, those relatively permanent structures/functions/subsystems of the mind/brain that act on information to transform it in various ways. Arithmetical skills, for example, constitute a (set of related) structure(s). The structures of particular interest to us are those that require some amount of attention/awareness to activate them. Attention/awareness acts as *psychological energy* in this sense. Most techniques for controlling the mind are ways of deploying attention/awareness energy and other kinds of energies so as to activate desired structures (traits, skills, attitudes) and deactivate undesired structures.

Psychological structures have individual characteristics that limit and shape the ways in which they can interact with one another. Thus the possibilities of any system built of psychological structures are shaped and limited both by the deployment of attention/awareness and other energies and by the characteristics of the structures comprising the system. The human biocomputer, in other words, has a large but limited number of possible modes of functioning.

Because we are creatures with a certain kind of body and nervous system, a large number of human potentials are in principle available to us. But each of us is born into a particular culture that selects and develops a small number of these potentials, rejects others, and is ignorant of many. The small number of experiential potentials selected by our culture, plus some random factors, constitute the structural elements from which our ordinary state of consciousness is constructed. We are at once the beneficiaries and the victims of our culture's particular selection. The possibility of tapping and developing latent potentials, which lie outside the cultural norm, by entering an altered state of consciousness, by temporarily *restructuring* consciousness, is the basis of the great interest in such states.

The terms *state of consciousness* and *altered state of consciousness* have come to be used too loosely, to mean whatever is on one's mind at the moment. The new term *discrete state of consciousness* (d-SoC) is proposed for greater precision. A d-SoC is a unique, dynamic pattern or configuration of psychological structures, an active system of psychological subsystems. Although the component structures/subsystems show some variation within a d-SoC, the overall pattern, the overall system properties remain recognizably the same. If, as you sit reading, you think, "I am dreaming," instead of "I am awake," you have changed a small cognitive element in your consciousness but not affected at all the basic pattern we call your waking state. In spite of subsystem variation and environmental variation, a d-SoC is stabilized by a number of processes so that it retains its identity and function. By analogy, an automobile remains an automobile whether on a road or in a garage (environmental change), whether you change the brand of spark plugs or the color of the seat covers (internal variation).

Examples of d-SoCs are the ordinary waking state, nondreaming sleep, dreaming sleep, hypnosis, alcohol intoxication, marijuana intoxication, and meditative states.

A *discrete altered state of consciousness* (d-ASC) refers to a d-SoC that is different from some *baseline state of consciousness* (b-SoC). Usually the ordinary state is taken as the baseline state. A d-ASC is a new system with unique properties of its own, a restructuring of consciousness. *Altered* is intended as a purely descriptive term, carrying no values.

Our current knowledge of human consciousness and d-SoC is highly fragmented and chaotic. The main purpose of the systems approach presented here is organizational: it allows us to relate what formerly disparate bits of data and supplies numerous methodological consequences for guiding future research. It makes the general prediction that the number of d-SoCs available to human beings is definitely limited, although we do not yet know those limits. It further provides a paradigm for making more specific predictions to sharpen our knowledge of the structures and subsystems that make up human consciousness.

There are enormously important individual differences in the structure of d-SoCs. If we map the experiential space in which two people function, one person may show two discrete, separated clusters of experiential functioning (two d-SoCs); while the other, the second, makes no special effort and does not experience the contrast of pattern and structure differences associated with the two regions (the two d-SoCs). Thus what is a special *state* of consciousness for one person may be an everyday experience for another. Great confusion results if we do not watch for these differences: unfortunately, many widely used experimental procedures are not sensitive to these individual differences.

Induction of a d-ASC involves two basic operations that, if successful, lead to the d-ASC from the b-SoC. First we apply *disruptive forces* to the b-SoC—psychological and/or physiological actions that disrupt the stabilization processes discussed above either by interfering with them or by withdrawing attention/awareness energy or other kinds of energies from them. Because a b-SoC is a complex system, with multiple stabilization processes operating simultaneously, induction may not work. A psychedelic drug, for example, may not produce a d-ASC because psychological stabilization processes hold the b-SoC stable in spite of the disrupting action of the drug on a physiological level.

If induction is proceeding successfully, the disrupting forces push various structures/subsystems to their limits of stable functioning and then beyond, destroying the integrity of the system and disrupting the stability of the b-SoC as a system. Then, in the second part of the induction process, we apply *patterning forces* during this transitional, disorganized period—psychological and/or physiological actions that pattern structures/subsystems into a new system, the desired d-ASC. The new system, the d-ASC, must develop its own stabilization process if it is to last.

Deinduction, return to the b-SoC, is the same process as induction. The d-ASC is disrupted, a transitional period occurs, and the b-SoC is reconstructed by patterning forces. The subject transits back to his or her customary region of experiential space.

Psychedelic drugs like marijuana or LSD do not have invariant psychological effects, even though much misguided research assumes they do. In the present approach such drugs are disrupting and patterning forces whose effects occur in combination with other psychological factors, all mediated by the operating d-SoC. Consider the so-called reverse tolerance effect of marijuana that allows new users to consume very large quantities of the drug with no feeling of being stoned (in a d-ASC) but later to use much smaller quantities of marijuana to achieve the d-ASC. This is not paradoxical in the systems approach, even though it is paradoxical in the standard pharmacological approach. The physiological action of the marijuana is not sufficient to disrupt the ordinary d-SoC until additional psychological factors disrupt enough of the stabilization processes of the b-SoC to allow transition to the d-ASC. These additional psychological forces are usually "a little help from my friends," the instructions for deployment of attention/awareness energy given by experienced users who know what functioning in the d-ASC of marijuana intoxication is like. These instructions also serve as patterning forces to shape the d-ASC, to teach the new user how to employ the physiological effects of the drug to form a new system of consciousness.

The systems approach can also be applied within the ordinary d-SoC to deal with *identity states*, those rapid shifts in the central core of a person's identity and concerns that are overlooked for many reasons, and emotional states. Similarly the systems approach indicates that latent human potential can be developed and used in various d-ASCs, so that learning to shift into the d-ASC appropriate for dealing with a particular problem is part of psychological growth. At the opposite extreme, certain kinds of psychopathology, such as multiple personality, can be treated as d-ASCs.

One of the most important consequences of the systems approach is the deduction that we need to develop *state-specific sciences*. Insofar as a "normal" d-SoC is a semi-arbitrary way of structuring consciousness, a way that loses some human potentials while developing others, the sciences we have developed are one-state sciences. They are limited in important ways. Our ordinary sciences have been very successful in dealing with the physical world, but not very successful in dealing with particularly human psychological problems. If we apply scientific method to developing sciences within various d-ASCs, we can evolve sciences based on radically different perceptions, logics, and communications, and so gain new views complementary to our current ones.

❑
4

Mapping and Comparing States

Roger Walsh

The number of recognized states of consciousness has increased dramatically, but there is considerable confusion over how best to describe and compare such states. This paper aims (1) to introduce a method for describing, mapping, and comparing altered states of consciousness (ASCs), by identifying key dimensions of experience; (2) to locate specific states on these dimensions; and then (3) to compare them.

Here we will compare shamanic, yogic, Buddhist, and schizophrenic states since these are important, powerful, and common and are sometimes described as identical. Witness, for example, the claim that "shamans, yogis and Buddhists alike are accessing the same state of consciousness,"[1] and that the shaman "experiences existential unity—the samadhi of the Hindus or what Western spiritualists and mystics call enlightenment, illumination, *unio mystica*".[2]

To begin with shamanic states, it is important to recognize that shamans employ a wide variety of techniques, and each may induce its own unique state. Here we will focus on states occurring during the shamanic journey. In it, shamans first enter an altered state of consciousness (ASC), perhaps with the aid of fasting, drumming, dancing, or drugs. They then usually experience leaving the body and journeying as a disembodied soul or free spirit to other realms to meet with spirits in order to gain from them information and power with which to help their fellow tribespeople.[3,4]

How, then, do we describe and map shamanic journey states? We can begin with a careful description of the raw experiences. The dimensions of experience that seem particularly helpful for such mapping include (1) degree of control, especially the ability to enter and leave the ASC at will and to control experiences while in the ASC; (2) degree of awareness of the environment; (3) ability to communicate; (4) concentration; (5) energy or arousal; (6) calm; (7) emotional state; (8) sense of identity; (9) whether out-of-body experiences (OOBE) occur; and (10) type of inner experience.[3]

MAPPING SHAMANIC JOURNEY STATES

We can now map shamanic journey states on these dimensions as follows. *Control:* One of the defining characteristics of shamans is their ability to control their states of consciousness. Master shamans can enter and leave the journey state at will with aids such as drumming and rituals. They can also partly control the type of images and experiences that occur.

Awareness of the environment and ability to communicate: During journeys, awareness of the environment is significantly reduced. Yet in spite of shamans' other-world adventures they may be able to communicate with their audiences and treat them to a blow-by-blow account of the worlds, spirits, and battles they encounter.

Concentration: Shamans are known for their good concentration.[5] During a journey they must focus for long periods without distraction, but their attention is not fixed immovably on a single object as is the yogi's. Rather their attention is fluid, moving freely and choicefully from one thing to another as their journeys unfold.

Energy/arousal, calm, and emotions: Since they are roaming between worlds, battling spirits and interceding with gods, it is small wonder that shamans may feel energetically aroused and their emotions may range from dread and despair to pleasure and excitement. Calm is not a word applied to many shamanic journeys.

Sense of identity and out-of-body experience: One of the defining characteristics of the shamanic journey is an out-of-body experience, a sense of being a free spirit unshackled from the body and physical constraints, and hence the journey state is sometimes described as ecstatic.

Content of the journey experience: The shaman's experiences are remarkably rich and highly organized.[4] Unlike the chaotic images of schizophrenic disturbances they are coherent and purposeful, reflecting both the journey's purpose and the shamanic cosmology.

These then are the experiences that make up the shamanic journey, and they are summarized in the accompanying table. Let us now use this map to compare this state with those of schizophrenia on the one hand and yoga and Buddhist meditation on the other.

Shamanic and Schizophrenic States

Until recently the majority view among Western researchers was that shamans are psychologically disturbed, and schizophrenia was a common diagnosis. Yet there are many reasons why such a diagnosis seems inaccurate.[3] One of them is that phenomenological mapping reveals major differences between shamanic and schizophrenic states of consciousness.

Comparison of the States of Consciousness Occurring in Shamanic Journeys, Advanced Yogic and Buddhist Meditation, and Schizophrenia

Dimension	Shamanism	Buddhist (Vipassana) Insight Meditation	Patanjali's Yoga	Schizophrenia
Control				
ability to enter and leave ASC at will	Yes	Yes	Yes	↓↓ Dramatic reduction of control
ability to control the content of experience	↑ Partial	↑ Partial	↑↑ Extreme control in some samadhis	↓↓
Awareness of Environment	↓	↓	↓↓ Reduced sensory and body awareness	↓ Often decreased and distorted
Ability to Communicate	Sometimes	Usually	None	↓ Communication is usually distorted
Concentration	↑ Fluid	↑ Fluid	↑↑ Fixed	↓↓ Fixed
Arousal	↑	↓ Usually	↑↓	↑↑ Agitation may be extreme

Calm	→	↑ Usually	↑↑ Extreme peace	
Affect	+ (positive feelings) or − (negative feelings)	+ or − + Tends to increase as practice deepens	++ Ineffable bliss	Usually very negative though rarely positive, often distorted and inappropriate
Self sense	Separate self sense, may be a non physical "soul"	Self sense is deconstructed into a changing flux: "no self"	Unchanging transcendent Self or purusha	Disintegrated, loss of ego boundaries. Unable to distinguish self and others
OOBE	Yes, controlled ecstasy ("ecstasis")	No	No. Loss of body awareness ("enstasis")	Rarely, uncontrolled
Content	Organized coherent imagery determined by shamanic cosmology and purpose of journey	Deconstruction of complex experiences into their constituent stimuli. Stimuli are further deconstructed into a continuous flux	Single object ("samadhi with support") or pure consciousness ("samadhi without support")	Often disorganized and fragmented

Another reason is that many people who claim that shamanic and schizophrenic states are equivalent seem to assume that there is only one shamanic altered state and one schizophrenic state. Yet this is certainly false.

To simplify things we will focus on the state that occurs in an acute schizophrenic episode. This can be one of the most devastating experiences any human being can undergo. Psychological disorganization is extreme and disrupts emotions, thought, perception, and identity. Victims can be completely overwhelmed, plunged into a nightmare of terror and confusion, haunted by hallucinations, swept from their usual sense of reality and identity, and lost in a private autistic world. We can map the acute schizophrenic episode and compare it to the shamanic state as follows:

Control is almost entirely lost. Awareness of the environment may be reduced when the person is preoccupied with hallucinations, and thinking may be so fragmented that the person can hardly communicate. Concentration is drastically reduced, and the patient is usually highly aroused and agitated. Emotional responses are often distorted, bizarre, and extremely painful.

So destructive is the process that the schizophrenic's experience is usually highly disorganized, identity fragments, and the schizophrenic may consequently feel that he or she is disintegrating, dissolving, or dying. This may occasionally result in a sense of being outside the body, but the experience is brief and uncontrolled. The whole experience is an incoherent fragmented nightmare. This schizophrenic experience is obviously very different from the shamanic journey, and the differences are summarized in the table.

To these experiential differences are added differences in social functioning. Shamans may display considerable intellectual, artistic, and leadership skills, yet such skills and contributions are very rare amongst schizophrenics.[4,5]

Clearly then, acute schizophrenic episodes and shamanic journeys are very different, and schizophrenics and shamans function very differently in society. Although early researchers sometimes regarded shamans as schizophrenic, this assessment is certainly not appropriate.

Comparisons Among Practices

Recently there has been a growing tendency to equate shamans with masters of various spiritual traditions, especially Buddhism and yoga. When shamanic, Buddhist, and yogic states are compared carefully, however, significant differences leap into view.

As we have already seen there are probably multiple shamanic states. In Buddhism and yoga the situation is even more complex. Buddhism, for example, has literally dozens of meditation practices, and the states they induce can differ dramatically. Moreover, each meditation practice may evolve through several distinct stages and states. The result is that a practitioner in a tradition such as Buddhism may access not one but literally dozens of altered states in the course of training.[6]

It seems, therefore, that comparing the states accessed in shamanism and other traditions is a complex business. Those who wish to claim that shamans and masters of other traditions are equivalent and that they access identical states of consciousness will need to make multiple comparisons between multiple states on multiple dimensions. This has simply not been done. In fact, when we actually make direct comparisons we find not identity, but rather major differences. Let us briefly outline some yogic and Buddhist meditation practices and then compare some of the advanced states that occur in them with the shamanic journey state.

Classical yoga is a concentration practice in which the mind is stilled until it can be fixed with unwavering attention on inner experience such as the breath, an image, or a mantra. To do this the yogi withdraws attention from the body and outer world to focus inward "like a tortoise withdrawing his limbs into his shell." Finally all objects drop away and the yogi experiences samadhi or ecstatic mystical union with the Self.[7,8]

Whereas classical yoga is a concentration practice, the central Buddhist practice, called insight or Vipassana meditation, is an awareness practice. Whereas yoga emphasizes the development of unwavering attention on inner objects, insight meditation emphasizes fluid attention to all objects, both inner and outer. Here all stimuli are examined as precisely and minutely as awareness will allow. The aim is to examine and understand the workings of senses, body, and mind as fully as possible and thereby to cut through the distortions and misunderstandings that usually cloud awareness.[6]

These three practices produce experiences and states with some experiential and functional similarities, e.g., heightened concentration, but also with significant differences. In contrast to schizophrenia, in which control is drastically reduced, all three disciplines enhance self-control. Practitioners are able to enter and leave their respective states at will, although shamans may require external assistance such as drugs or drumming. Both shamans and insight meditators exert partial control over their experiences in the ASC, while yogis in samadhi have almost complete ability to halt thought and some other mental processes. Indeed, the second line of Patanjali's classic yoga text states that: "Yoga is the control of thought-waves in the mind."

Perceptual sensitivity to the environment shows dramatic differences between the three states. Both ancient and modern descriptions as well as recent psychological tests suggest that Buddhist insight meditators may show dramatic increases in perceptual sensitivity to the environment.[9] In the shamanic journey, by contrast, awareness of the environment is usually somewhat reduced, while in advanced yogic states it is drastically reduced, even to the point of nonawareness. Indeed, Eliade defined samadhi as "an invulnerable state in which perception of the external world is absent."[7]

These differences in environmental awareness are reflected in differences in communication. Shamans may communicate with spectators during their journeys, and Buddhist meditators can do so if necessary. However, even attempting to speak may be sufficient to break a yogi's fierce, one-pointed concentration.

Concentration training appears to be widespread among authentic spiritual practices, including shamanism, Buddhism, and yoga, but the type and depth of concentration can differ dramatically. In both shamanism and Buddhist insight meditation, attention moves fluidly from one object to another. This is in marked contrast to advanced yogic practice, where attention is fixed unshakably on a single object.

There are also significant differences in arousal or energy levels. Shamans are usually aroused during their journey and may even dance or become highly agitated. Buddhist insight meditators gradually develop greater calm, while in yogic samadhi calm may become so profound that many mental processes cease temporarily.

The sense of identity differs drastically among the three practices. The shaman usually retains a sense of being a separate individual, though now perhaps identified as a soul or spirit rather than as a body. This is not the case with the Buddhist meditator, whose microscopic awareness becomes so sensitive that it is able to dissect the sense of self into its component stimuli. Thus, the meditator perceives not a solid unchanging ego or self sense, but rather a ceaseless flux of thoughts and images of which that ego is composed. This is the experience of "no self" in which the sense of a permanent egoic self is recognized as an illusory product of imprecise awareness that arises in much the same way as an apparently continuous movie arises from a series of still frames. Precise awareness penetrates this egoic illusion and hence frees the meditator from egocentric ways of thinking and acting.

The yogi's experience shows both similarities with and differences from that of the shaman and Buddhist. It is different in that in the higher reaches of meditation, attention fixes immovably on consciousness and consequently this is what the yogi now experiences him- or herself to be—pure consciousness. This is similar to the Buddhist experience inasmuch as the egoic self sense is recognized as illusory and is transcended.

The yogi's experience of pure consciousness contrasts dramatically with the complex images of the journey that fill the shaman's awareness. The Buddhist meditator has yet a third type of experience. Here awareness becomes so sensitive that all experiences are eventually broken down or deconstructed into their components, and the meditator perceives a ceaseless flux of microscopic images that arise and pass away with extreme rapidity.[6]

One of the defining characteristics of shamanism is soul flight, which is a form of out-of-body experience (OOBE), ecstasy or "ecstasis." Neither the yogi nor Buddhist meditator experiences this. In fact, the yogi may become so inwardly concentrated as to lose all awareness of the body and become absorbed in the inner bliss of samadhi, a condition sometimes called "enstasis." Eliade, whose theoretical knowledge of both shamanism and yoga was probably as extensive as anyone's, was very clear on the difference between the two. In his classic book on yoga, he stated emphatically:

Yoga cannot possibly be confused with shamanism or classed among the techniques of ecstasy. The goal of classic yoga remains perfect *autonomy*, enstasis, while shamanism is characterized by . . . ecstatic flight.[10]

IS THERE A CORE MYSTICAL EXPERIENCE?

One of the major questions that has dominated discussion of mysticism since the publication of William James's classic work, *The Varieties of Religious Experience*, is whether or not there is any core mystical experience that is common across cultures and traditions. Some philosophers say yes, but "constructionists," who argue that all experience, including mystical experience, is constructed from and filtered through a variety of inescapable personal and cultural experiences, say no. Since the comparisons made above clearly indicate significant differences between shamanic, yogic, and Buddhist experiences, they would seem to favor the constructionists and argue against the existence of a common core mystical experience.

Yet this may be only part of the story, for while the meditative experiences described above are indeed advanced, they are not the most advanced. At the very highest reaches of meditation, transcendent experiences of a wholly different kind, radically discontinuous from all that have gone before, are said to occur. These are the samadhi of yoga and the nirvana of Buddhism.

Here descriptions and comparisons fail! For these experiences are said to be ineffable, indescribable, beyond space, time, and limits of any kind.

In the words of the Third Zen Patriarch:

> To this ultimate finality
> no law or description applies. . . .
> The more you talk and think about it
> the further astray you wander from the truth.[11]

Are the yogic samadhi and Buddhist nirvana the same? The question does not apply. The answer, at least for yoga and Buddhism, to the question of whether there exists a common core mystical experience may be neither yes nor no. To quote Wittgenstein, "Whereof one cannot speak, thereof one must be silent."

And what of shamanism? Do its practitioners access similar states? Most authorities think not.[12] Yet there is some indirect evidence that although such states are not the focus or goal of shamanism, experiences of mystical union may occasionally occur.[3]

SECTION TWO

❑

MEDITATION: ROYAL ROAD TO THE TRANSPERSONAL

We must close our eyes
and invoke a new manner of seeing. . .
a wakefulness that is the birthright of us all,
though few put it to use.

—PLOTINUS[1]

cultural definition of normality

WHEN HISTORIANS look back on the twentieth century, they may find that two of the most important breakthroughs in Western psychology were not discoveries of new knowledge but recognitions of old wisdom.

First, psychological maturation can continue far beyond our arbitrary, culture-bound definitions of normality. There exist further developmental possibilities latent within us all. As William James pointed out, "Most people live, whether physically, intellectually or morally, in a very restricted circle of their potential being. They make use of a very small portion of their possible consciousness. . . . We all have reservoirs of life to draw upon, of which we do not dream."

Wm James

Second, techniques exist for realizing transpersonal potentials. These techniques are part of an art or technology that has been refined over thousands of years in hundreds of cultures, and constitutes the contemplative core of the world's great religious traditions. This is the art or technology of transcendence, designed to catalyze transpersonal development. As such, it is based on two fundamental assumptions about the nature and potentials of the mind.

The first assumption is that our usual state of mind is suboptimal. In fact, the mind has been described as clouded, distorted, dreamlike, entranced and largely out of control. This has been recognized by psychologists and mystics of both East and West. Freud's culture-shaking recognition that "man is not even master in his own house . . . his own mind,"[2] echoed the Bhagavad Gita's despairing cry two thousand years earlier:

> Restless man's mind is,
> So strongly shaken
> In the grip of the senses:
> Gross and grown hard
> With stubborn desire. . . .
> Truly, I think
> The wind is no wilder.[3]

In the words of Ram Dass, "We are all prisoners of our own mind. This realization is the first step on the journey to freedom."[4] Pir Vilayat Khan put it even more succinctly, "The bind is in the mind."

The second assumption is that although the untrained mind is clouded and out of control, it can be trained and clarified and this training catalyzes transpersonal potentials. The sages of both East and West, past and present, agree on this. Socrates said: "In order that the mind should see light instead of darkness, so the entire soul must be turned away from this changing world, until its eye can bear to contemplate reality and that supreme splendor which we call the Good. Hence there may well be an art whose aim would be to effect this very thing."[5] Likewise, according to Ramana Maharshi, "All scriptures without any exception proclaim that for salvation mind should be subdued."[6]

Although practices and techniques vary widely, there seem to be six common elements that constitute the heart of the art of transcendence: ethical training; development of concentration; emotional transformation; a redirection of motivation from egocentric, deficiency-based needs to higher motives, such as self-transcendence, refinement of awareness, and the cultivation of wisdom.

Ethics is widely regarded as an essential foundation of transpersonal development. Contemplative traditions, however, view ethics not in terms of conventional morality but rather as an essential discipline for training the mind. Contemplative introspection renders it painfully apparent that unethical behavior both stems from and reinforces destructive mental factors such as greed and anger. Conversely, ethical behavior undermines these and cultivates mental factors such as kindness, compassion, and calm. Ultimately, after transpersonal maturation occurs, ethical

Meditation a path to train the mind.

behavior is said to flow spontaneously as a natural expression of identification with all people and all life. For a person at this stage, which corresponds to Lawrence Kohlberg's highest stage of moral development, "whatever is . . . thought to be necessary for sentient beings happens all the time of its own accord."[7]

Attentional training and the cultivation of concentration are regarded as essential for overcoming the fickle wanderlust of the untrained mind. As E. F. Schumacher observed of attention, "No topic occupies a more central place in all traditional teaching; and no subject suffers more neglect, misunderstanding, and distortion in the thinking of the modern world."[8]

Attentional training is certainly misunderstood by Western psychology, which has unquestioningly accepted William James's century-old conclusion that: "Attention cannot be continuously sustained."[9] Yet James went further: "The faculty of voluntarily bringing back a wandering attention over and over again is the very root of judgment, character and will. No one is *compos sui* if he have it not. An education which would improve this faculty would be the education par excellence. . . . It is easier to define this ideal than to give practical direction for bringing it about."[10] Here, then, we have a stark contrast between traditional Western psychology, which says attention *cannot* be sustained, and the art of transcendence, which says that attention can and *must* be sustained if we are to mature beyond conventional developmental limits.

Being able to direct attention at will is so important because the mind tends to take on qualities of the objects to which it attends. For example, if we think of an angry person, we tend to feel angry; if of a loving person, we tend to feel loving. The person who can control attention can, therefore, control and cultivate specific emotions and motives. Ultimately, said the Indian sage Ramakrishna, the mind of such a person "is under his control; he is not under the control of his mind."[11]

Ethical behavior and attentional stability facilitate the third element of the art of transcendence: emotional transformation. There are three components to emotional transformation.

The first is the reduction of inappropriate destructive emotions such as fear and anger, a process which is well known in Western therapy. Of course, what is implied here is not repression or suppression but rather clear awareness of such emotions and consciously relinquishing them where appropriate.

The second component is the cultivation of positive emotions such as love, joy, and compassion. Whereas conventional Western therapies have excellent techniques for reducing negative emotions, they have virtually none for enhancing positive emotions such as these. In contrast, the art of transcendence contains a wealth of practices for cultivating these emotions to an intensity and extent undreamed of in Western psychology. Thus, for example, the Buddhist's compassion, the Bhakti's love, and the Christian's agape are said to reach their full flowering only when they unconditionally and unwaveringly encompass all creatures, without exception and without reserve.

This mindboggling intensity and scope of positive emotion is facilitated by a third component of emotional transformation: the cultivation of equanimity, an emotional imperturbability which allows love and compassion to remain unconditional and unwavering even under duress. This capacity is the Stoic's *apatheia*, the Christian Father's *divine apatheia*, the Buddhist's equanimity, the Taoist principle of "the equality of things," which leads beyond "the trouble of preferring one thing to another," and the contemporary philosopher Franklin Merrell-Wolff's "high indifference."

Ethical behavior, attentional stability, and emotional transformation all work together, along with practices such as meditation, to redirect motivation along healthier, more transpersonal directions. The net effect is a reduction in the intensity and compulsivity of motivation and a change in its direction, variety, and focus. Most important, the compulsive power of both addiction and aversion is reduced.

As motivation becomes less scattered and more focused, the things desired become more subtle, more internal; there is less emphasis on getting and more on giving. Desires gradually become less self-centered and more self-transcendent.

Traditionally this motivational shift was seen as "purification" or as "giving up attachment to the world." In contemporary terms it is movement up Maslow's hierarchy of needs, Arnold Toynbee's process of "etherealization," and the means for reaching the philosopher Kierkegaard's goal in which "purity of heart is to will one thing."

The reduction of compulsive craving is said to result in a corresponding reduction in intrapsychic conflict and suffering, a claim now supported by studies of advanced meditators. [12] In the words of the Athenian philosopher Epicurus, "If you want to make a man happy, add not to his riches but take away from his desires." This is not to imply that redirecting motives and relinquishing craving is necessarily easy. In Aristotle's estimation, "I count him braver who overcomes his desires than him who conquers his enemies; for the hardest victory is the victory over self." [13]

The great wisdom traditions agree that in our usual untrained state of mind, awareness and perception are insensitive and impaired: fragmented by attentional instability, colored by clouding emotions, and distorted by scattered desires. Accordingly we are said to mistake shadows for reality (Plato) because we see "through a glass darkly" (St. Paul), a "reducing valve" (Aldous Huxley), or "narrow chinks" (Blake). William Blake put it poetically:

> If the doors of perception were cleansed
> everything would appear to man as it is, infinite.
> For man has closed himself up,
> 'til he sees all things thro' narrow chinks of his cavern.[14]

The fifth element of the art of transcendence, therefore, aims to refine perception and awareness and render them more sensitive, more accurate, and more appreciative of the freshness and novelty of each moment of experience. One of the primary tools for this is meditation.

Meditators notice that both internal and external perception become more sensitive, colors seem brighter, and the inner world becomes more available through a process known as "introspective sensitization." The validity of these subjective experiences has recently found experimental support from research that indicates that meditators' perceptual processing becomes more sensitive and rapid and empathy more accurate.

As the psychiatric historian Henri Ellenberger observed, "The natural tendency of the mind is to roam through the past and the future; it requires a certain effort to keep one's attention in the present."[15] Meditation is training in precisely that effort. The result is a present-centered freshness of perception variously described as mindfulness (Buddhism), anuragga (Hinduism), the "sacrament of the present moment" (Christianity), the "draught of forgetfulness," in which one forgets the past and comes anew into each present moment (Steiner); and as a characteristic of self-actualizers (Maslow).

When we see things clearly, accurately, sensitively, and freshly we can respond empathically and appropriately. Thus both ancient wisdom traditions and modern psychotherapies agree with Fritz Perls, the founder of Gestalt therapy, that "awareness per se—by and of itself—can be curative."[16]

The sixth quality cultivated by the technology of transcendence is wisdom, which is something significantly more than knowledge. Whereas knowledge is something we have, wisdom is something we become. Developing it requires self-transformation. This transformation is fostered by opening defenselessly to the reality of "things as they are," including the enormous extent of suffering in the world. In the words of the psalms, this is the recognition that we are "as dust . . . our lives are but toil and trouble, they are soon gone, they come to an end like a sigh" (Psalm 90); "what man can live and never see death?" (Psalm 89).

In our own time, existentialism has emphasized this recognition most forcefully. With its graphic description of the inevitable existential challenges of meaninglessness, freedom, and death it has rediscovered aspects of the Buddha's first noble truth, which holds that unsatisfactoriness is an inherent part of existence. Both existentialism and the wisdom traditions agree that, in the words of Thomas Hardy, "if a way to the Better there be, it exacts a full look at the Worst."[17]

Whereas existentialism leaves us marooned in a no-exit situation of heightened awareness of existential limits and suffering, the art or technology of transcendence offers a way out. For existentialism, wisdom consists of recognizing these painful facts of life and accepting them with authenticity, resoluteness (Heidegger), and courage (Tillich). For contemplative traditions this existential attitude is a preliminary rather than a final wisdom and is used to redirect motivation away from trivial, egocentric pursuits toward the contemplative practices that lead to deeper wisdom. This deeper wisdom recognizes that the sense of being marooned in a no-exit situation of limits and suffering can be transcended through transforming the self that seems to suffer. Such wisdom springs from the development of direct intuitive insight into the nature of mind, self, consciousness, and cosmos. This insight matures into the direct intuitive wisdom—beyond words, thoughts, concepts, or even images of any kind—which transforms and liberates. And with this liberation the goal of the art of transcendence is realized.

These, then, seem to be six essential, common elements, qualities or processes that constitute the heart of the art of transcendence. Of course different practices and traditions focus more on some processes than on others. For example, Indian philosophy divides practices into various yogas. All of them acknowledge ethics as an essential foundation. Raja yoga emphasizes meditation and the training of attention and awareness; Bhakti yoga is more emotional and focuses on the cultivation of love; Karma yoga uses work in the world to refine motivation; and Jnana yoga hones the intellect and wisdom. It seems, however, that to the extent a tradition is authentic—that is, capable of fostering transpersonal development and transcendence[18]—it will incorporate all the elements of the technology of transcendence.

Almost all paths include some form of meditation. Meditation is central because it works directly on so many processes essential to transpersonal development. At its best it stabilizes attention, transforms emotions and motivation, cultivates awareness, heightens sensitivity to unethical behavior, and fosters wisdom. If dreams are the royal road to the unconscious, meditation is the royal road to the transpersonal.

What then is meditation? The term refers to a family of practices that train attention in order to bring mental processes under greater voluntary control and to cultivate specific mental qualities such as awareness, insight, concentration, equanimity, and love. It aims for development of optimal states of consciousness and psychological well-being.

The term "yoga" refers to a family of practices with the same aims as meditation, but in addition to meditation, yogas encompass ethics, lifestyle, body posture, breathing, and intellectual study. The origins of meditation and yoga are lost in antiquity, but they are at least four thousand years old and perhaps considerably older, and specific practices have evolved over centuries.

There are many varieties of meditation and meditative experiences. The best known involve sitting quietly, but other practices include walking, dancing, and bringing conscious awareness to everyday activities. Meditation can focus on an almost infinite variety of objects, ranging from dead corpses to the breath to sublime mind states. Needless to say, these many practices result in a wide range of experiences. Even within a single tradition such as Sufism, different meditative practices have overlapping but also distinct effects.

These different practices are often divided into two major types: concentration and awareness practices. Concentration meditations attempt to focus attention unwaveringly on a single object such as the breath. Awareness practices, on the other hand, open awareness in a choiceless, nonjudgmental manner to whatever experiences arise.

The history of meditation in the West has had many distinct phases. At various times in their long histories, Judaism, Christianity, and Islam offered various meditative techniques, but they never attained the popularity and centrality that such techniques enjoy in Asian traditions such as Hinduism and Buddhism.

In the twentieth century, initial reports of the results of Asian meditation met with skepticism from Western psychologists and psychiatrists. This skepticism was especially strong in the psychoanalytic community, which for the most part dismissed meditation, along with practices such as shamanism and yoga, as primitive or regressive and diagnosed their practitioners as pathological. The eminent psychoanalyst Franz Alexander, for example, titled one of his papers "Buddhist Training as an Artificial Catatonia."[19] Yet as Ken Wilber has pointed out, the "facile equation of the mystic with the psychotic can be done only by demonstrating one's ignorance of the subtleties involved."[20] Alexander's proclamation now stands as a classic example of the "pre/trans fallacy" and mistaking the transpersonal for the prepersonal.

Since the 1960's meditation has become widely accepted and there has been a veritable explosion of popular, professional, and research interest. It has been estimated that by 1980 over six million people in the United States alone had learned some form of meditation.

Indeed, meditation is still spreading and influencing Western culture. The historian Arnold Toynbee predicted that one of the major events of the twentieth century would be the introduction of Buddhism to the West, but the introduction of meditative techniques from diverse Asian traditions may have a combined, cumulative effect significantly greater than that of Buddhism alone. The introduction—or, better, the reintroduction—of meditation to the West may prove to be one of the most significant events of the twentieth century.

The varieties of impact are many. Literally millions of people meditate for personal growth or the relief of psychological or psychosomatic disturbances.

Others use it as part of a spiritual practice. Some who practice Asian meditations are drawn deeply into the corresponding Asian philosophies and religions. Other practitioners report a more paradoxical effect of developing greater appreciation of their own Judeo-Christian heritage, especially its more contemplative dimensions.

Not surprisingly, Judaism and Christianity also have been affected. On one hand, the influx of Asian meditation has prompted a renewed interest in Western forms of meditation; on the other hand, some fundamentalists have denounced meditation as the work of the devil and proclaimed that the resultant quietness of mind makes Satan's entry all the easier. The traditional response to both questions and criticisms of meditation is the advice to test it for yourself.

While meditation has had an effect on Western culture, Western culture is also affecting meditation. Traditionally, meditation has been practiced in cultural-religious contexts of strong faith and unquestioning acceptance by people with little background in psychology, science, and research. Now meditation is also practiced in secular settings and subjected to appropriately skeptical scrutiny by clinicians and researchers. Consequently, new questions are emerging. For example, scientists are asking how meditation can best be researched, precisely what effects it has, how it works, and which practices work best for different people.

Clinicians are trying to determine which psychological and psychosomatic disorders meditation can help, as well as the complications and risks of practice. Historically, the issue of complications rarely has been addressed, yet it is now clear that meditation, like any powerful therapy, can be stressful for some people. Western clinicians are therefore breaking new ground in identifying the complications of meditation practice and the ways to use psychotherapy to treat them.

Since meditation is a central technique for transpersonal development, it is of both theoretical and practical interest to transpersonalists. Informal surveys suggest that most of them have tried it and a majority practice regularly.

On the practical side, meditation offers many benefits for psychological and somatic well-being. Psychotherapists report that the practice of meditation—by the therapist, client, or both—can complement and catalyze therapy. In addition to cultivating healthy qualities such as calm and equanimity, it can enhance empathy and provide insight into mental processes and the origins of pathology. On the theoretical side, meditation practice and research offer insights into the nature of mind, maturation, and transpersonal experiences.

Theory and practice are also linked. Without direct experience, transpersonal concepts and systems remain what Immanuel Kant called "empty," or devoid of experiential grounding. Meditation practice is, therefore, vital for a deep understanding of meditation experiences. As the philosopher Philip Novak pointed out, the "deepest insights are *available* to the intellect, and powerfully so, but it is only when those insights are discovered and absorbed by a psyche made especially keen and receptive by long coursing in meditative discipline, that they begin to find their fullest realization and effectiveness."[21]

To recommend meditation practice is easy; to do it can be difficult. Just sitting still for half an hour can be arduous at first. Most people who have tried to train the mind agree that it is one of the most challenging and rewarding tasks a person can undertake and has rightly been called "the art of arts and science of sciences."

The papers in this section describe the experiences, stages, benefits and difficulties of meditation. Jack Kornfield describes "The Seven Factors of Enlightenment"—mindfulness, energy, investigation, rapture, concentration, calm, and equanimity—that are key mental qualities said by Buddhist psychology to characterize the enlightened mind and to be cultivated by meditation. Different meditations and therapies are compared by assessing the extent to which they foster and balance these factors.

In "Meditation Research: The State of the Art," Roger Walsh summarizes the results of the hundreds of research studies that have now been done.

Meditation can clearly produce profound experiences and healings, but no single psychological or contemplative technique is effective for all issues. One of the intriguing research questions of our time is therefore which psychological dimensions and problems are effectively healed or transformed by specific meditations and which are left relatively untouched. In an historically novel event, a number of advanced meditators and teachers have begun to seek psychotherapy to heal difficulties unresolved by meditation. Jack Kornfield, who is both a meditation teacher and psychologist, suggests that "even the best meditators have old wounds to heal" (in his article of the same name) and that a skillful combination of meditation and psychotherapy may be superior to either alone.

5

The Seven Factors of Enlightenment

Jack Kornfield

There are several major categories of meditation. The two most fundamental distinctions in meditation are concentration and insight. Concentration meditation is an entire range or class of meditations in which the
emphasis is to train the mind by focusing it fixedly on a particular object.
Concentration means to focus on the breath, a mantra, a candle flame,
and so forth in such a way that it excludes other distractions, other
thoughts and inputs. The mind, being energy, can be concentrated in the
same way a laser can concentrate light energy. The power of concentration can serve to transcend, or to attain a whole range of states of mind
that are altered, or of different perceptions from normal ones. They are
often quite blissful in that they are undisturbed, or peaceful or tranquil.
In addition to providing access to many altered states, the power of
concentration can also be applied to the dissection of ourselves, our
experiences, and to the understanding of what makes up our world of
consciousness and experience.

Awareness-training, the other major class of meditation, doesn't attempt to take the mind away from ongoing experience to focus it on a
single object to create different states. Rather it works with present experience, cultivating awareness and attention to the moment-to-moment flow
of what make up our life—sight, sound, taste, smell, thought, and feelings.
It uses them as the meditation object, as a way to see who we are. In the
process of awareness-training meditators also begin to answer the questions about how negative states arise and how to work with them in our
own minds and experience. Later, when awareness becomes well-
developed they can gain access to other levels of experience that transcend
our normal daily consciousness.

Meditation which involves devotion or surrender can also be assigned
to this second class, because to pay attention carefully is itself a devotional
practice. It is a surrender to what is actually happening in each moment

without trying to alter or change or put a conceptual framework around it. In that attentive meditation, the second class, one works with a realm of experiencing that lies between the suppression of feelings, impulses, and ideas—not pushing them aside at all—and the other extreme of necessarily acting on them. This cultivates a state of mind which allows us to be open, to observe and experience fully the entire range of mental and physical reality without either suppressing it or acting it out. Through the procedure of paying attention, greater awareness, concentration and new understanding can gradually develop.

I'd like to present a model which comes from Buddhist psychology. It is called the Factors of Enlightenment and may be helpful in understanding the way meditation works. The Factors of Enlightenment are seven qualities of mind described in the traditional literature which are the definition of a healthy or enlightened mind. They are cultivated to become present in such a way that they determine one's relationship to each moment of experience.

Mindfulness, central to the seven qualities, is followed by two groups of factors which must be in balance. The first group includes energy, investigation and rapture; the second set of factors is concentration, tranquillity and equanimity. The first three comprise a very active quality of mind. Here energy means the effort to stay conscious or aware; investigation means looking very deeply at experience, exploring the process of ourselves, while rapture means joy and interest in the mind. These three must be balanced with concentration, tranquillity and equanimity. Concentration is one-pointedness, stillness, the ability to focus the mind in a powerful way; tranquillity is an inner kind of silence, a silent investigation rather than thought-filled; equanimity is calm balance in relation to the changing circumstances of experience. Mindful-

FIGURE 1
The Factors of Enlightenment

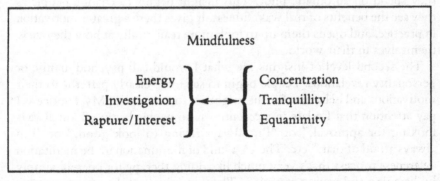

Mindfulness

Energy   Concentration
Investigation } ←→ { Tranquillity
Rapture/Interest   Equanimity

ness when cultivated becomes the cause for the arising of all these seven qualities. It's the key meditation factor that develops the others and brings them into balance.

In Western psychology there is much emphasis on the active factors, which include investigation and energy devoted to understanding of one's self. But the West has unfortunately lacked an understanding of the importance of the complementary factors of concentration and tranquillity. Without cultivating concentration and tranquillity, the mind's power is limited and the range of understanding that is available is rather small in scope.

Conversely there is often difficulty in Eastern traditions because of too much emphasis on concentration and tranquillity. They may lead to wonderful experiences of rapture, silence of mind, and trance or Jhana states. But without the balance of investigation and energetic observation of how things really are, such practice will not lead to a deeper understanding of self and the freedom of enlightenment.

To understand ourselves in practice is to employ the tools of focusing and concentrating the mind and then to apply them with awareness and investigation. What's interesting about this model is that it doesn't take a specific form—Sufi, Buddhist, Hindu, or psychotherapeutic. As it said in *The Lazy Man's Guide to Enlightenment*, "enlightenment doesn't care how you get there." Any method that will cultivate these qualities of mind and bring them into balance is good. Whatever techniques can bring you to a place of stillness, clarity, and openness will lead to a direct understanding of the basic spiritual truths. The true nature of ourself is always here to view if we cultivate our ability to see. When we understand spiritual practice as simply the cultivation of certain mental qualities, we can understand a wide range of seemingly diverse traditions.

There seem to be several levels of development that people go through and many ways to describe these levels. At the first level people simply realize how asleep they are, which is one of the most important insights of all. In trying to pay attention to themselves and be present as much as possible all day long, people become astonished by how much of the time they spend on automatic pilot. This insight begins to change people as they see the benefits of real wakefulness. It gives them a greater motivation in practice, and opens them up to look more realistically at how they view themselves in their world.

The second level of insights are what I would call psychodynamic or personality revelations. People begin to see more clearly patterns to their motivations and behavior. So one might see for example, "My, I notice as I pay attention that I relate in a certain way to people because I am always looking for approval," or "I'm always trying to look good," or "I'm always afraid of that," etc. There's a kind of illumination in the meditation awareness process that's very much like doing therapy for oneself, simply by listening and paying attention. These insights and the acceptance that comes with a nonjudgmental awareness of our patterns promotes mental balance and understanding, so it can lessen our neurotic identification and suffering.

Beyond psychological insight in practice there are levels which are often talked about in the Eastern classical literature. Some of these are levels of the different trance or Jhana states, very high levels of absorption or concentration. These concentration states have the drawback of leading primarily to altered state changes but not necessarily to fundamental long-term trait changes.

A second array of experiences beyond the psychodynamic and awareness of personality level is a progression of insights. This level of awareness brings an illumination of how the mind is constructed. One begins to see how the whole process of desire and motivation works in the mind, quite apart from the content of any particular desire. Further insights into the process of mind lead to seeing more deeply that everything we are is in constant change. There can arise a clear vision of the dissolution of self from moment to moment, and this often leads to a realm of fear and terror, and a kind of inner death. Later there arises from this awareness a spontaneous process of letting go of personal motivation, and with this grows an awareness of loving or 'Bodhisattva' consciousness. As the solidity of the self breaks down, there is a vision of the true connection between all of us. From this arises a spontaneous kind of warmth and compassion. Greater understanding leads to all kinds of altruistic states and eventually the highest kinds of enlightenment, in which we can see our existence as a play in the energy field that is the whole world.

In order to understand this wide range of meditation experience our meditation research must examine the various traditions and techniques from the point of view of how they are simply means to effect changes in arrays of our mental factors. Each technique alters the way that we relate to our experiences and if we look, very different practices and traditions often work to cultivate inwardly the same qualities, such as concentration, tranquillity, or greater awareness and balance. In particular, the seven factors of enlightenment can then also be seen as simply another model or description of mind coming into balance so that it can see more clearly the nature of our experience.

❑

6

Meditation Research: The State of the Art

Roger Walsh

There are enough research projects here to keep squadrons of
scientists busy for the next century.
—ABRAHAM MASLOW,
The Farther Reaches of Human Nature

Meditation research is a young but vigorous field. Over fifteen hundred publications have appeared and have demonstrated psychological, physiological, and chemical effects. Different types of meditation appear to elicit overlapping but also distinct effects. The most frequently studied practice has been Transcendental Meditation (TM).

Transpersonal psychologists have researched meditation hoping to forge a mutually beneficial link between the practices of the consciousness disciplines and the experimental techniques of science. However, in the past the variables examined, e.g., heart and respiration rate, have often been relatively gross and tangential to the subtle transpersonal shifts in awareness, emotions, and values that constitute the traditional goals of meditation.

EFFECTS OF MEDITATION

Psychological

The range of experiences that can emerge during meditation is enormous. Experiences may be pleasant or painful, and intense emotions such as love or anger can alternate with periods of calm and equanimity. Although the idea of meditation as simply a relaxation response is a vast oversimplification, the general trend as meditation practice continues is toward greater calm, positive emotions, and perceptual and introspective sensitivity. Advanced experiences include profound peace, concentration and joy, intense positive emotions of love and compassion, penetrating insights into the nature of mind, and a variety of transcendent states that can run the gamut of classical mystical experiences. [1,2]

Enhanced perceptual ability allows insight into psychological processes and habits. One of the first insights is how extraordinarily out of control, unaware, fantasy-filled, and dreamlike our usual state of mind is. Classical claims that the untrained mind is like a "wild drunken monkey" and that taming it is "the art of arts and science of sciences" soon make sense to the beginning meditator. To date most knowledge of meditative experiences has come from personal accounts, and there has been little systematic phenomenological research.

However, there have been a large number of experimental studies of meditation's effects on personality, performance, and perception. Intriguing findings include evidence for enhanced creativity, perceptual sensitivity, empathy, lucid dreaming, self-actualization, a positive sense of self control, and marital satisfaction. [2,3,4] Studies of TM suggest that it may foster maturation as measured by scales of ego, moral and cognitive development, intelligence, academic achievement, self-actualization and states of consciousness. [1,5]

A fascinating study of perception examined the Rorschach test responses of Buddhist meditators ranging from beginners to enlightened masters. [2,6] Beginners showed normal response patterns, whereas subjects with greater concentration saw not the usual images, such as animals and people, but simply the patterns of light and dark on the Rorschach cards. That is, their minds showed little tendency to elaborate these patterns into organized images, a finding consistent with the claim that concentration focuses the mind and reduces the number of associations.

Further striking findings characterized subjects who had had an initial experience of nirvana and thereby reached the first of the four classic stages of Buddhist enlightenment. At first glance their Rorschach tests were not obviously different from those of nonmeditators. There was, however, a difference in their accounts of the test: these subjects viewed the images they saw as creations of their own minds and were aware of the moment-by-moment process by which their stream of consciousness became organized into images.

Interestingly, the initially enlightened subjects displayed evidence of normal conflicts around issues such as dependency, sexuality, and aggression. However, they showed remarkably little defensiveness and reactivity to these conflicts. In other words, they accepted and were unperturbed by their neuroses.

Those few meditators at the third stage of enlightenment gave reports that were unique in four ways. First, these meditation masters saw not only the images but the ink blot itself as a projection of mind. Second, they showed no evidence of drive conflicts and appeared free of psychological conflicts usually considered an inescapable part of human existence. This finding is consistent with classic claims that psychological suffering can be dramatically reduced in advanced stages of meditation.

The third and fourth unique features were that these masters systematically linked their responses to all ten cards into an integrated response on a single theme. The result was a systematic teaching about the nature of human suffering and its alleviation. In other words, the meditation masters transformed the Rorschach testing into a teaching for the testers.

Physiological Variables

Physiological research began with sporadic investigations of spectacular yogic feats such as altering body temperature and heart rate. When some of these claims proved valid, more systematic investigation was begun. The introduction of better controls led to the recognition that many physiological effects initially assumed to be unique to meditation could actually be induced by other self-control strategies such as relaxation, biofeedback, or self-hypnosis.[7] This led some researchers to assume prematurely that there is little that is unique to meditation or its effects.

For example, initial studies of metabolic effects reported marked reductions in metabolic rate—as shown by reduced oxygen consumption, carbon dioxide production, and blood lactate levels—and suggested that transcendental meditation led to a unique hypometabolic state. Subsequent studies confirmed a reduced metabolic rate, but better controls suggested that the effects were not unique to meditation.[2]

The cardiovascular system is clearly affected.[2,4] During meditation the heart rate drops, and with regular practice blood pressure also falls. Meditation can therefore be a useful treatment for mild high blood pressure, but the benefits dissipate if practice is discontinued. Certain practitioners can increase blood flow to the body periphery, thereby raising the temperature of fingers and toes. Tibetan Tumo masters who specialize in this are reported to demonstrate their mastery by meditating seminaked in the snows of the Tibetan winter.

Blood chemistry may also shift.[2,4] Hormone levels may be modified, lactate levels—sometimes regarded as a measure of relaxation—may fall, and cholesterol may be reduced.

In summary, it is clear that meditation elicits significant physiological effects. While a few studies of TM have reported distinct patterns of blood flows and hormone levels, overall it is not yet clear to what extent the physiological effects are unique to meditation.

Electroencephalograph (EEG)

The most common measure of brain activity during meditation has been the EEG. This provides a measure of cerebral electrical activity that is valuable but gross, comparable to measuring activity in Chicago by placing a dozen microphones around it. While it remains unclear whether there are patterns unique to meditation, intriguing findings have emerged.

With most meditative practices the EEG slows, and alpha waves (eight to thirteen cycles per second) increase in amount and amplitude. In more advanced practitioners even greater slowing may occur, and theta (four to seven cycles) patterns may appear. These findings are consistent with deep relaxation.

Not only do the brain waves slow but they may also show increasing synchronization or coherence between different cortical areas. Some TM researchers suggest that this provides a basis for enhanced creativity and psychological growth. [1]

However, it is always difficult in EEG research to extrapolate from brain waves to specific states of mind, and it is usefully humbling to realize that increased coherence can also occur in epilepsy and schizophrenia.

Some skeptics have attempted to explain (away) meditation as merely the effect of drowsiness or even sleep, but this explanation fails for several reasons. While meditators, especially novices, may become drowsy, this is recognized by contemplative traditions as a specific trap: the "defilement of sloth and torpor," as Buddhists picturesquely describe it. Second, the experience of nondrowsy meditation is very different from sleep. Finally, the EEG pattern of meditation is quite distinct from that of sleep. [4,8]

It is increasingly recognized that the left and right cerebral hemispheres have distinct, though overlapping, functions. Because meditation may reduce left-hemisphere functions such as verbal analysis, meditation might involve either a reduction of left-hemisphere activity and/or an activation of the right hemisphere. There is preliminary evidence of some enhanced right-hemisphere skills in meditators such as the ability to remember and discriminate musical tones. However, EEG studies suggest that while there may be relative left-hemisphere deactivation during the initial few minutes of a sitting, thereafter both hemispheres seem to be affected equally.[8,9]

Yogis and Zen practitioners may respond differently to sensory stimulation, in ways consistent with their respective methods and goals of practice. Yogis, whose practice involves internal focus and withdrawal of attention from the senses, showed little EEG response to repeated noises. Zen monks, however, whose practice involves open receptivity to all stimuli, showed continued EEG responsiveness to a repeated sound, rather than habituating to it as nonmeditators would.[4] Although other studies have found less clearcut differences,[8] these findings remain intriguing because the electrophysiological data are consistent with both the different goals and experiences of yogic and Zen practitioners.

Moreover, the lack of EEG habituation in the Zen monks is consistent with other reports. Continuous freshness of perception is characteristic of both Maslow's self-actualizers and contemplatives who practice, for example, the Buddhist's "mindfulness" or the Christian's "sacrament of the present moment."

Therapeutic Effects

Many effects of meditation seem beneficial, and research suggests that it can be therapeutic for various psychological and psychosomatic disorders. Responsive psychological disorders include anxiety, phobias, post-traumatic stress, muscle tension, insomnia, and mild depression. Regular long-term meditation seems to reduce both legal and illegal drug use and to help prisoners by reducing anxiety, aggression, and recidivism.

Psychosomatic benefits may include reduction of blood pressure, cholesterol, and the severity of asthma, migraine and chronic pain.[2,3,10]

These therapeutic effects may reflect enhanced general psychological and physical health. In fact, TM meditators use less than normal amounts of psychiatric and medical care, and meditators in their mid fifties measured twelve years younger on scales of physical aging than members of control groups.[11] Of course, how much of this superior general health is actually due to meditation and how much to associated factors such as prior good health and a healthy life-style is unclear.

One well-controlled study clearly demonstrated dramatic effects on the aged. A group of nursing-home residents whose average age was eighty-one and who learned TM performed better on multiple measures of learning and mental health than did residents who were taught relaxation, given other mental training, or left untreated. Most striking, however, was that after three years all the meditators were alive, whereas only 63 percent of the untreated residents were still alive.[1] For thousands of years yogis have claimed that contemplative practices increase longevity, a claim that can no longer be ignored.

The most startling research claim is that meditators can exert "action-at-a-distance." TM researchers see fundamental reality as a field of consciousness. They therefore argue that minds are interconnected and that meditation groups of sufficient size can influence nonmeditating individuals and society at large. Several studies report that TM groups have beneficially influenced social problems. These benefits include re-duced rates of crime, violent death, traffic accidents, terrorism, and, when a group meditated in the Middle East, the intensity of conflict in Lebanon.[12]

These findings are certainly dramatic. However, most of this and other research on TM has been conducted by members of the TM organization. Unconscious biases can easily affect research findings, so studies by researchers independent of the TM organization are essential. If the find-ings of "action-at-a-distance" are independently and reliably confirmed, then the implications—for everything from philosophy and physics to peace and politics—will be remarkable.

In summary, meditation may produce a large number of effects and therapeutic benefits. However, some experimental designs and control groups have been less than ideal, most meditation subjects have been mere beginners by traditional standards, and it is often unclear whether med-itation is necessarily more effective for clinical disorders than other self-regulation strategies such as relaxation training, biofeedback, and self-hypnosis. On the other hand, meditators often report that the practice is more meaningful, enjoyable, and easier to continue than other ap-proaches and fosters an interest in self-exploration.[2,10]

Complications

A general principle in psychiatry states that any therapy powerful enough to be helpful is also powerful enough to be harmful. This seems to hold true for meditation, though serious casualties are rare. While meditators may experience psychological difficulties at any stage, problems are more frequent in beginners, those doing intense practice without adequate supervision, and in people with preexisting psychopathology. Some diffi-cult experiences may ultimately prove to be cathartic and beneficial, a process TM calls "unstressing."

The range of difficulties is wide. It may include emotional lability with episodes of anxiety, agitation, depression, and euphoria. Psychological conflicts may surface and somatic symptoms such as muscle or gastroin-testinal spasms may appear. Meditators may ruminate obsessively or be confronted by painful existential questions. On rare occasions, defenses may be overwhelmed, resulting in a psychotic break, especially in those with a history of previous psychosis.[13] Advanced practitioners may also experience difficulties, although they are more likely to be subtler and to involve existential or spiritual concerns.[14] Development at any level involves challenges.

Given that meditation can produce both benefits and difficulties, can we predict which people will be affected? Studies of TM suggest that those who persist successfully share certain traits. They are more interested in internal experiences, more open to unusual ones, and feel high self-control. They may be less emotionally labile and possess high concentration and alpha-wave activity. They seem less psychologically disturbed and more open to recognizing and acknowledging unfavorable personal characteristics. Future research may identify those people who will respond optimally and those at risk for negative effects, as well as means of enhancing favorable responses.

Exactly how meditation produces its many effects remains unclear. Many mechanisms have been suggested. Possible physiological processes include lowered arousal and increased hemispheric synchronization. Possible psychological mechanisms include relaxation, desensitization, dehypnosis, and development of self-control skills, insight and self-understanding.[2] Perhaps the most encompassing explanation is the classic one: namely that meditation fosters psychological development.[6]

CONCLUSION

While much has been learned experimentally about meditation, research is still in its early stages. As yet relatively little can be said about the relationships between the traditional goals of meditation and experimental measures. More attention has been given to heart rate than heart opening. Future research will need to pay more attention to advanced practitioners and their transpersonal goals such as enhanced concentration, ethics, love, compassion, generosity, wisdom and service.[15] The vision of a mutually enriching bridge between meditation and science remains only partly realized, but it also remains worth seeking.

❑
7

Even the Best Meditators Have Old Wounds to Heal: Combining Meditation and Psychotherapy

Jack Kornfield

For most people, meditation practice doesn't "do it all." At best, it's one important piece of a complex path of opening and awakening. I used to believe that meditation led to the higher, more universal truths, and that psychology, personality, and our own "little dramas" were a separate, lower realm. I wish it worked that way, but experience and the nondual nature of reality don't bear it out. If we are to end suffering and find freedom, we can't keep these two levels of our lives separate.

The various compartments of our minds and bodies are only semi-permeable to awareness. Awareness of certain aspects does not automatically carry over to the other aspects, especially when our fear and woundedness are deep. Thus, we frequently find meditators who are deeply aware of breath or body but are almost totally unaware of feelings, and others who understand the mind but have no wise relation to the body.

Mindfulness works only when we are willing to direct attention to every area of our suffering. This doesn't mean getting caught in our personal histories, as many people fear, but learning how to address them so that we can actually free ourselves from the big and painful "blocks" of our past. Such healing work is often best done in a therapeutic relationship with another person.

Meditation and spiritual practice can easily be used to suppress and avoid feeling or to escape from difficult areas of our lives. Our sorrows are hard to touch. Many people resist the personal and psychological roots of their suffering; there is so much pain in truly experiencing our bodies, our personal histories, our limitations. It can even be harder than facing the universal suffering that surfaces in sitting. We fear the personal and its sorrow because we have not learned how it can serve as our practice and open our hearts.

We need to look at our whole life and ask ourselves, "Where am I awake, and what am I avoiding? Do I use my practice to hide? In what areas am I conscious, and where am I fearful, caught, or unfree?"

There are many areas of growth (grief and other unfinished business, communication and maturing of relationships, sexuality and intimacy, career and work issues, certain fears and phobias, early wounds, and more) where good Western therapy is on the whole much quicker and more successful than meditation. These crucial aspects of our being can't just be written off as "personality stuff." Freud said he wanted to help people to love and work. If we can't love well and give meaningful work to the Earth, then what is our spiritual practice for? Meditation can help in these areas. But if, after sitting for a while, you discover that you still have work to do, find a good therapist or some other way to effectively address these issues.

Of course, there are many mediocre therapists and many limited kinds of therapy. Just as in meditation, you should look for the best. Many new therapies have been developed with a strong spiritual basis, such as psychosynthesis, Reichian breath work, sand play, and a whole array of transpersonal psychologies. The best therapy, like the best meditation practice, uses awareness to heal the heart, and is concerned not so much with our stories, as with fear and attachment and their release, and with bringing mindfulness to areas of delusion, grasping, and unnecessary suffering. One can, at times, find the deepest realizations of selflessness and non-attachment through some of the methods of transpersonal psychology.

Does this mean we should trade meditation for psychotherapy? Not at all. Therapy isn't the solution either. Consciousness is! And consciousness grows in spirals. If you seek freedom, the most important thing I can tell you is that spiritual practice always develops in cycles. There are inner times when silence is necessary, followed by outer times for living and integrating the silent realizations, as well as times to get help from a deep and therapeutic relationship with another person. These are equally important phases of practice. It is not a question of first developing a self and then letting go of it. Both go on all the time. Any period of practice may include samadhi and stillness, followed by new levels of experiencing wounds and family history, followed by great letting go, followed by experiences of the void, followed by more personal problems. It is possible to work with all of these levels in the context of a spiritual practice. What is required is the courage to face the totality of what arises. Only then can we find the deep healing we seek—for ourselves and for our planet.

In short, we have to expand our notion of practice to include all of life. Like the Zen ox-herding pictures, the spiritual journey takes us deep into the forest and leads us back to the marketplace again and again, until we are able to find compassion and the sure heart's release in every realm.

SECTION THREE

◻

LUCID DREAMING

We are such stuff
As dreams are made on, and our little life
Is rounded with a sleep.
            —SHAKESPEARE, *The Tempest*

FROM ANCIENT times, dreams have been regarded as a source of inspiration, mystery, and messages. For shamans, dreams served notice of their sacred vocation, while for the prophets of Israel dreams were messages from God. Recall, for example, this passage from the Bible: "Hear my words: If there be a prophet among you, I the Lord make myself known to him in a vision, I speak with him in a dream."[1] In ancient Mediterranean cultures, dreams were regarded as a source of healing, and people flocked to the temple of the god Asklepios to incubate healing dreams. Recently, dreams have been regarded psychologically as "the royal road to the unconscious" (Freud) and as messages of healing and intuitive wisdom from the unconscious (Jung). Hence, dreams hold considerable transpersonal interest.

However they are interpreted, dreams are a nightly miracle in which a whole universe arises populated with people, places, and creatures that seem solid, independent and "real." Moreover, in our dreams we appear to possess an equally solid, "real" body that seems to be the source and support of our lives, our pleasures, and our pains, whose eyes and ears provide sensory input, and whose death means our death. In short, this dream world and body seem to create and control us. Yet this seemingly objective universe is a creation of our own minds, a subjective, illusory, transient production that we create and control.

71

When we awaken, we say, "It was only a dream," implying that it was unreal. In the technical terms of Indian philosophy we "subrate" it. That is, we accord it less validity or ontological status in light of our waking consciousness. Yet in spite of each awakening, night after night, time after time, we take our dreams to be "real" and therefore flee and fight, laugh and cry, curse and rejoice within the dream.

However, most of us have had at least one experience of suddenly realizing that "it's only a dream" while in the midst of some apparently dramatic adventure or terrifying threat. At that moment we become "lucid"; we are dreaming yet we know that we are dreaming. That moment can result in a sense of relief, delight, wonder, and freedom. Then we are free to confront our monsters, fulfill our desires, or seek our highest goals, knowing that we are creators, not victims, of our experience. For as the philosopher Nietzsche exclaimed, "Perhaps many a one will, like myself, recollect having sometimes called out cheeringly and not without success amid the dangers and terrors of dreamlife: 'it is a dream! I will dream on!' "[2]

For most of us such lucid dreams are rare and beyond our ability to induce. Is there any way of cultivating our ability to awaken in our dreams at will? The answer from a variety of contemplative traditions and dream explorers is yes. As long ago as the fourth century, the classical yoga sutras of Patanjali recommended "witnessing the process of dreaming or dreamless sleep."[3] Four centuries later, Tibetan Buddhists devised a sophisticated dream yoga. In the twelfth century the sufi mystic Ibn El-Arabi, a religious and philosophical genius known in the Arab world as "the greatest master," claimed that "a person must control his thoughts in a dream. The training of this alertness . . . will produce great benefits for the individual. Everyone should apply himself to the attainment of this ability of such great value."[4] More recently a number of explorers and spiritual masters such as Sri Aurobindo and Rudolf Steiner also have reported success with lucid dreaming.

For decades Western researchers dismissed such reports as impossible. Then, in the 1970's, in one of the greatest breakthroughs in the history of dream research, two investigators provided experimental proof of lucid dreaming. Working independently and quite unknown to each other, Alan Worsley in Britain and Stephen LaBerge in California both learned to dream lucidly. Then, while being monitored electrophysiologically in a sleep laboratory, they signaled by means of eye movements that they were dreaming, *and knew it*. Their EEG's (electroencephalograms) showed the characteristic patterns of REM (rapid eye movement) sleep, during which dreaming typically occurs, thereby validating their reports. For the first time in history someone had brought back a message from the world of dreams while still dreaming. Dream research and our understanding of dreaming have never been the same since. Interestingly, for some time LaBerge was unable to get his reports published because reviewers simply refused to believe that lucid dreaming was possible. [2]

Since then, with the aid of eye movement signaling and electrophysiological measures, researchers have been able to study such things as the frequency and duration of lucid dreams, their physiological effects on the brain and the body, the psychological characteristics of those who have them, the means for inducing them more reliably, and their potential for healing and transpersonal exploration. Lucid dreaming also has inspired thought on the philosophical, practical, and transpersonal implications of both dreams and lucidity.

One of the striking philosophical implications concerns the nature of our waking world. After all, if night after night we mistake our dream world and bodies for objective, "real" things that exist quite independently of our minds and that seem to control us, perhaps we do the same with our waking world and bodies. How do we know that the waking state is not also a dream? For as Tibetan Buddhists point out, "there is no characteristic of waking experience that clearly distinguishes it from dreaming." [5]

A variety of philosophers and mystical traditions have agreed. The philosopher Schopenhauer suggested that the universe is "a vast dream, dreamed by a single being, in such a way that all the dream characters dream too." [6] The great Zen scholar D. T. Suzuki argued, "As long as we are in the dream we do not realize that we are all dreaming." [7] Likewise, a contemporary Christian teaching points out:

> Dreams show you that you have the power to make a world as you would have it be, and that because you want it you see it. And while you see it you do not doubt that it is real. Yet here is a world, clearly within your mind, that seems to be outside. . . . You seem to waken, and the dream is gone. Yet what you fail to recognize is that what caused the dream has not gone with it. Your wish to make another world that is not real remains with you. And what you seem to waken to is but another form of this same world you see in dreams. All your time is spent in dreaming. Your sleeping and your waking dreams have different forms, and that is all. [8]

This perspective is, of course, a form of philosophical idealism, the metaphysical view that what we take to be external reality is a creation of mind. Though not widely popular in these materialistic times, this position has been held by some of the world's greatest philosophers of both East and West. Hegel, for example, claimed, "Spirit is alone Reality. It is the inner being of the world." [9] The fact that no philosopher has ever been able to demonstrate the existence of an outside world is no surprise to idealists. [10]

Lucid dreamers have a powerful realization of how convincingly objective and material a dream world can seem, and how dramatic a personal awakening can be. The lucid dreamer experiences with startling clarity that what seemed an unquestionably external, objective, material, and independent world is in fact an internal, subjective, immaterial, and dependent creation of mind. Some begin to question their previous worldviews, to wonder whether the waking world could also be a dream, and to agree with Nietzsche that "we invent the largest part of the thing experienced. We are much greater artists than we know."[11]

This suggests important philosophical and practical implications for our usual waking state. While dreaming, we usually assume that our state of consciousness is clear and accurate and that we are seeing things "as they really are." Only when we awaken or become lucid do we subrate our previous dream consciousness and recognize its distortions. Two questions follow: Could our usual waking state of consciousness be similarly distorted? If this is so, is there a way to "wake up" and become lucid in daily life?

For centuries the great religious traditions have answered yes, our usual state is distorted. And yes, we can awaken. Indeed, contemplative disciplines urge us to recognize the limitations of our usual state of consciousness and offer practices for awakening from it to the undistorted state known as enlightenment.

This raises two additional questions about lucidity. The first: Is it possible to further refine lucidity so as to extend it into dreamless sleep, waking states, or both? The second: Is it possible to cultivate higher states of consciousness within dreams, and thereby develop what Charles Tart calls "high dreams"?

Both personal reports and recent research suggest that the answer to both questions is yes. Sages such as Aurobindo and Steiner, as well as Western meditation students in retreat, have described being able to maintain continuous lucidity throughout much of the night in both dreams and dreamless sleep. Advanced TM practitioners also report this experience, and some even describe being able to "witness" their dreams. By this they mean that in dreams, or even in dreamless sleep, they remain identified with pure consciousness and therefore simply observe the figures and dramas in their dreams without being perturbed by them. Moreover, this equanimous witnessing can extend to daytime waking life. According to the TM Vedic tradition, the first stage of enlightenment is reached when witnessing becomes imperturbable and unbroken.

Evidently yoga and meditation can induce lucid dreaming, and lucid dreaming can itself be used as a meditation. Indeed, lucidity seems to spontaneously motivate dreamers to do just that. Experienced practitioners report that even the thrill of repetitive wish fulfillment in dreams eventually fades, leaving dreamers longing for something more meaningful and profound than playing out another sensual fantasy. These people rediscover the ancient idea that sensory pleasures alone can never be enduringly satisfying.

At this point dreamers may begin to seek transpersonal experiences and to use lucid dreaming as a transpersonal technique. To do this they employ three strategies. First, they actively seek within the dream for a spiritual experience, be it a symbol, a teacher, or a deity. Second, they may adopt a more passive approach, turning control of the dream over to a "higher power," whether that power is conceived to be an inner guide, Self, or God.

In the third strategy they begin a meditative-yogic practice *while still in the dream.* By far the most sophisticated such practice is the twelve-hundred-year-old Tibetan Buddhist "dream yoga." According to the Dalai Lama, Tibetan yogis are taught to develop lucidity, first in their dreams, and then in their nondream sleep, seeking to remain continuously aware twenty-four hours a day.[12] Meanwhile, during daylight hours they cultivate the awareness that their waking experience is also a dream. The ideal result is unbroken awareness, the sense that all experience is a dream, and ultimately "the Great Realization."

> The final step leads to the Great Realization, that nothing within the *Samsara* (existence) is or can be other than unreal like dreams. The Universal Creation, with its many mansions of existence from the lowest to the highest Buddha paradise, and every phenomenal thing therein, organic and inorganic, matter or form, in its innumerable physical aspects, as gases, solids, heat, cold, radiations, colours, energies, electronic elements, are but the content of the Supreme Dream. With the dawning of this Divine Wisdom, the microcosmic aspect of the Macrocosm becomes fully awakened; the dewdrop slips back into the Shining Sea, in *Nirvanic* Blissfulness and At-one-ment, possessed of All Possessions, Knower of the All-Knowledge, Creator of All Creations—the One Mind, Reality Itself.[13]

The papers in this chapter describe the benefits of lucid dreaming, ways to cultivate it, and the farther reaches of lucidity. Psychologist Judith Malamud outlines the benefits of lucidity and the possibility of becoming lucid during waking life. Stephen LaBerge, the pioneer who proved the existence of lucid dreams experimentally, describes how to induce them. Jayne Gackenbach and Jane Bosveld explore the farther reaches of lucidity, including witnessing in both dreaming and dreamless sleep. Sri Aurobindo, one of this century's greatest intellectual and religious geniuses, provides a personal account of developing continuous awareness throughout the night. Finally, Stephen LaBerge summarizes Tibetan dream yoga and the remarkable evolution it describes from lucidity to enlightenment.

> *Dreams are real while they last.*
> *Can we say more of life?*
> HAVELOCK ELLIS

8

Benefits of Lucid Dreaming

Judith Malamud

Once dreamers become aware of the implications of the fact that they are dreaming, they may be able to create less anxious, more gratifying dreams and even to experience inner growth while dreaming. Several researchers have reported success in alleviating unpleasant dreams and recurrent night-mares by inducing lucidity. Pleasure experiences can be programmed and wishes that would be impossible or illegal to gratify in waking life can be freely indulged.

At higher levels of lucidity, the lucid dream state consists of a self-reflective cognitive set and awareness of freedom, safety, and insulation from waking life consequences, combined with vivid perceptual experi-ence, access to "autonomous processes," and the potential for powerful emotional impact. Hence, the lucid dream state may be ideal for fostering personality change via "corrective emotional experiences." Lucid dream-ing may be suitable for desensitization of phobias and rehearsal of more appropriate behavior. Garfield reported that students in a "Creative Dreaming" course learned to apply the principle "confront and conquer danger" in their dreams. These students reportedly experienced waking carryover effects of greater self-confidence and more assertive behavior. Because lucidity fosters awareness of the self-reflecting aspects of the dream environment, lucid dreams may be conducive to dialogue with one's own projections, in the form of other dream characters, during the dream itself. Rogo suggested that patients could train themselves to meet a "dream-helper" in lucid dreams. Whether lucidity training can actually produce constructive personality change remains to be verified by re-search, which, considering recent advance in lucidity induction tech-niques, should now be feasible.

Lucidity permits consciously directed access to the creativity that abounds in dreams. In lucid dreams, one can perform experiments to test one's powers of imagination, seek out dream adventures, or study interest-ing images for later reproduction as literary or artistic work.

Preliminary research suggests that the brain, and to a lesser extent, the body, are affected by certain kinds of dreamed activities in much the same way as they would be affected by the corresponding waking activities. Further research may point to medical applications. I wonder, for example, whether inducing lucid dreams of healing could be combined with waking visualization techniques for combating disease.

Waking experience can be enhanced by awareness of the implication of *dreaming*, namely, that one is cocreator of a self-mirroring world of experience that, because of its subjectivity, is but one of many alternate realities. Awareness of oneself as a creative source involves an increased sense of responsibility for one's past and current experience, as well as awareness of one's power to create future experience. Even if this sense of responsibility is merely acknowledged intellectually, it may inspire deliberate attempts to "take charge" of one's life and may encourage an inquiring attitude toward one's own unconscious motives and life-shaping behaviors.

❏

9

Learning Lucid Dreaming

Stephen LaBerge

For the most part, those who want to remember their dreams can do so, and those who do not want to do not. For many people, simply having the intention to remember, reminding themselves of this intention just before bed, is enough. One effective way to strengthen this resolve is to keep a dream journal beside your bed and record whatever you can remember of your dreams every time you wake up. As you record more dreams, you will remember more dreams. Reading over your dream journal can provide an added benefit: the more familiar you become with what your dreams are like, the easier it will be for you to recognize one while it is still happening.

An infallible method for developing your ability to remember dreams is to get in the habit of asking yourself, every time you wake up, "What was I dreaming?" This must be your first thought upon awakening. You must not give up too quickly if nothing is recalled at first, but persist patiently in the effort to remember, without moving or thinking of anything else.

In developing dream recall, as with any other skill, progress is sometimes slow. It is important not to be discouraged if you do not succeed at first. Virtually everyone who stays with it improves through practice.

Paul Tholey, a German psychologist, has recently described various techniques for inducing lucid dreams. According to Tholey, the most effective method for achieving lucidity is to develop "a critical-reflective attitude" toward your state of consciousness, by asking yourself whether or not you are dreaming while you are awake. He stresses the importance of asking the critical question ("Am I dreaming or not?") as frequently as possible, at least five to ten times a day, and in every situation that seems dreamlike. Asking the question at bedtime and while falling asleep is also favorable. Following this technique, most people will have their first lucid dream within a month, Tholey reports, and some will succeed on the very first night.

I developed a simple technique for maintaining conscious awareness during the transition from waking to sleep. The method is to count to yourself ("one, I'm dreaming; two, I'm dreaming," and so on) while drifting off to sleep, maintaining a certain level of vigilance as you do so. The result is that at some point—say, "forty-eight, I'm dreaming"—you will find that you *are* dreaming!

An important factor influencing the kind of results you are likely to obtain with the foregoing technique is *timing*. Rather than attempting to enter the lucid dream state at the beginning of your sleep cycle, you would do much better to try later in the night, toward morning, especially after already awakening from a dream.

There is another, and for most people far easier, way to become lucid in a dream: become very familiar with your dreams, get to know what is dreamlike about them, and simply *intend* to recognize that they are dreams while they are happening. Evidently, simply intending to recognize that one is dreaming is enough to increase the frequency of occurrence of lucid dreams.

Merely telling oneself to have a lucid dream can provide a starting point, at least, for deliberately inducing lucid dreams.

During the first year and a half of my research, I used self-suggestion for lucid-dream induction. Gradually, more self-observation led to the realization that a second psychological factor was involved: the intention to *remember* to be lucid during the next dream. This clarification of intention was accompanied by an immediate increase in my lucid dreams. Once I discovered that memory was the key to lucid dreaming, further practice and methodological refinements allowed me to arrive at my goal: a method by which I could reliably induce lucid dreams.

MNEMONIC INDUCTION OF LUCID DREAMS (MILD)

"Mnemonic induction of lucid dreams," or MILD, is based on nothing more complex or esoteric than our ability to remember that there are actions we wish to perform in the future.

The verbalization that I use to organize my intended effort is: "Next time I'm dreaming, I want to remember to recognize I'm dreaming." The "when" and "what" of the intended action must be clearly specified.

I generate this intention either immediately after awakening from an earlier REM period, or following a period of full wakefulness, as detailed below. An important point is that in order to produce the desired effect, it is necessary to do more than just mindlessly recite the phrase. You must really *intend* to have a lucid dream. Here is the recommended procedure spelled out step by step:

1. During the early morning, when you awaken spontaneously from a dream, go over the dream several times until you have memorized it.
2. Then, while lying in bed and returning to sleep, say to yourself, "Next time I'm dreaming, I want to remember to recognize I'm dreaming."
3. Visualize yourself as being back in the dream just rehearsed; only this time, see yourself realizing that you are, in fact, dreaming.
4. Repeat steps two and three until you feel your intention is clearly fixed or you fall asleep.

If all goes well, in a short time you will find yourself lucid in another dream.

The reason for the "early morning" specified in step one is that such dreams occur almost exclusively during the morning hours. Once I myself learned how to use MILD, I experienced as many as four lucid dreams in a single night, and indeed seemed able to attain lucidity on any night that I tried it. MILD also seems to work well for others, especially those who meet the requirements of high motivation and excellent dream recall.

❏

10

Beyond Lucidity: Moving Toward Pure Consciousness

Jayne Gackenbach and Jane Bosveld

If the theory that lucid dreaming is only one step along a continuum of human consciousness is correct, at least two important questions follow: What comes after lucid dreaming, and why should we care?

The evolution of self-reflective consciousness does not end with lucidity. One can move further along the continuum to a quieter, uninvolved state of awareness that is experienced as having no boundaries. This stage is known as witnessing.

In order to explore this continuum from lucidity to witnessing, Gackenbach, along with Robert Cranson and Charles Alexander of MIU, collected sleep experiences from five groups of TM meditators and four groups of controls. They were looking for distinctive characteristics of lucid dreams versus both witnessing dreams and witnessing during nondreaming sleep. The researchers described each state in the following way:

- A lucid dream is a dream in which you are actively thinking about the fact that you are dreaming.
- A witnessing dream is a dream in which you experience a quiet, peaceful, inner awareness or wakefulness completely separate from the dream.
- Witnessing in deep sleep is a dreamless sleep in which you experience a quiet, peaceful, inner state of awareness or wakefulness.

Here are examples from the TM meditators of the three states of awareness:

Lucid dreaming: "During a dream I will become aware of the dream as separate, then aware that I am dreaming. Then I begin to manipulate the story and the characters to create whatever situation I desire."

Witnessing dreaming: "Sometimes, whatever the content of the dream is, I feel an inner tranquillity of awareness that is removed from the dream. Sometimes I may even be caught up in the dream, but the inner awareness of peace remains."

Witnessing deep sleep: "It is a feeling of infinite expansion and bliss and nothing else. Then I become aware that I exist but there is no individual personality. Gradually I become aware that I am an individual, but there are no details of who, where, what, when, etc. Eventually, these details fill in and I might awaken."

The researchers found that the meditators reported experiencing all three phenomena more frequently than did the nonmeditating controls. But both meditators and nonmeditators reported more lucid dreams than witnessing dreams or witnessing in deep sleep, a finding that supports the theory that lucid dreams are easier to access no matter what one's training or personal skills and may therefore be a precursor to the other experiences.

In order to examine the differences among these three forms of sleeping consciousness, Gackenbach, Cranson, and Alexander turned to a group of highly advanced meditators and found a number of important differences among these states of sleeping consciousness. For one thing, feelings of separateness were much more common in witnessing dreams than in lucid ones: The subjects felt more separate or outside of the dream when they were witnessing. As one meditator put it, "There is me *and* the dream, two different realities."

Another difference involved positive emotions. Although lucid dreams were reported as being positive, witnessing in dreams and in dreamless sleep were felt to be even more so. The feeling in the latter two states is reminiscent of the idea of "bliss" in the Eastern religions, and, in fact, the term "bliss" was most often used to describe the witnessing state but virtually never used to describe lucidity. On the other hand, dream control was much more frequent during lucid dreaming than during witnessing dreams. In lucidity, the "will," or volitional capacity of the individual ego, can act on thoughts and desires, while in pure consciousness one is content and feels no desire to enter into the dream.

Gackenbach, along with Alexander (and other researchers), devised an experiment to see if there were any distinct physiological differences between the lucid dreams of LaBerge's subjects and a subject who was believed to be witnessing his dreams. They contacted an advanced TM practitioner who claimed that he witnessed at all times, including during sleep.

As expected, the man was capable of signaling that he was dreaming, and as with other lucid dreamers, his heart and respiration rates increased *with the eye movement signals.* But unlike other lucid dreamers, these signs of physical arousal dropped off dramatically once the eye signal had been made. The researchers reported that "the restfully alert state of Transcendental Consciousness was only momentarily disrupted during the signaling task and then quickly returned to the low arousal, silent, wakeful condition." Again, this was a study that evaluated only one subject and should be replicated with other advanced meditators.

These findings support the idea that there is indeed a developmental continuum in night consciousness, with lucidity emerging first, followed by witnessing in dreams, and finally witnessing in dreamless sleep. This continuum fits in nicely with the Vedic belief that pure consciousness provides the foundation for the development of stable higher states of consciousness or enlightenment. "According to the Maharishi," Alexander explains, "the first stable higher stage of consciousness, termed 'cosmic consciousness,' is defined as the maintenance of pure consciousness throughout the twenty-four-hour cycle of waking, dreaming, and deep sleep."

❏

II

Continuous Consciousness

Sri Aurobindo

What happens in sleep is that our consciousness withdraws from the field of its waking experiences; it is supposed to be resting, suspended or in abeyance, but that is a superficial view of the matter. What is in abeyance is the waking activities, what is at rest is the surface mind and the normal conscious action of the bodily part of us; but the inner consciousness is not suspended, it enters into new inner activities, only a part of which, a part happening or recorded in something of us that is near to the surface, we remember.

In fact, in what we call dreamless sleep, we have gone into a profounder and denser layer of the subconscient, a state too involved, too immersed or too obscure, dull and heavy to bring to the surface its structures, and we are dreaming there but unable to grasp or retain in the recording layer of subconscience these more obscure dream-figures.

If we develop our inner being, live more inwardly than most men do, then the balance is changed and a larger dream-consciousness opens before us; our dreams can take on a subliminal and no longer a subconscious character and can assume a reality and significance.

It is even possible to become wholly conscious in sleep and follow throughout from beginning to end or over large stretches the stages of our dream-experience; it is found that then we are aware of ourselves passing from state after state of consciousness to a brief period of luminous and peaceful dreamless rest, which is the true restorer of the energies of the waking nature, and then returning by the same way to the waking consciousness. It is normal, as we thus pass from state to state, to let the previous experiences slip away from us; in the return only the more vivid or those nearest to the waking surface are remembered: but this can be remedied—a greater retention is possible or the power can be developed of going back in memory from dream to dream, from state to state, till the whole is once more before us. A coherent knowledge of sleep-life, though difficult to achieve or to keep established, is possible.

❏

12

From Lucidity to Enlightenment:
Tibetan Dream Yoga

Stephen LaBerge

The first steps toward the dream yogi's goal of awakening involve becoming proficient in "comprehending the nature of the dream state." Once the yogi has become an accomplished dreamer, he proceeds to the next stage, "transmuting the dream content," in which the initial exercise is the following: "If, for example, the dream be about fire, think,' what fear can there be of fire which occurreth in a dream!' Holding to this thought, trample upon the fire. In like manner, tread underfoot whatever be dreamt." After gaining sufficient skill in controlling his reaction to the contents of his lucid dreams, the yogi goes on to more advanced exercises, and by means of these he masters the ability to visit—in his lucid dream—any realm of existence desired.

The next stage of practice is called "realizing the dream state, or dream-content to be *maya* [illusion]." According to Buddhist doctrine, the entire universe of forms, or separate existence, is an illusory appearance or "dream." This should be a familiar idea, since all experiences are necessarily mental representations and, as the subjective products of our brains, are thus of the same nature as dreams.

At the third stage, the dream yogi is advised to practice the transformation of dream content into its opposite. For example, the lucid dreamer should transform the dream, if it be of fire, into water; if it be of small things, into large; if it be one thing, into many, and so on. Thus, the text explains, the lucid dreamer comprehends the nature of dimensions and of plurality and unity.

After becoming "thoroughly proficient" in the art of transforming dream content, the yogi turns his attention to his own dream body: this, he now sees, is just as illusory as any other element of his lucid dream. The fact that the fully lucid dreamer knows he is not his dream body plays a crucial role in self-transformation, as we shall see below.

The fourth and final stage of dream yoga is enigmatically termed "meditating upon the thatness of the dream-state." The text tells us that by means of this meditation, "the dream propensities whence arise whatever is seen in dreams as appearance of deities, are purified." It is, ironically, by means of these "appearances" that the ultimate goal is reached. The yogi is, of course, aware that these "deities" are his own mental images. Bearing this in mind, he is instructed to concentrate in the lucid dream state, focusing on the forms of these deities, and to keep his mind free of thoughts. In the undisturbed quiet of this mental state, the divine forms are said to be "attuned to the non-thought condition of mind; and thereby dawneth the Clear Light, of which the essence is of the voidness."

Thus, one realizes that the appearance of form "is entirely subject to one's will when the mental powers have been efficiently developed" through the practice of the yoga of lucid dreaming. Having learned "that the character of any dream can be changed or transformed by willing that it shall be," the lucid dreamer takes "a step further . . . he learns that form, in the dream state, and all the multitudinous content of dreams, are merely playthings of mind, and, therefore, as unstable as a mirage." A process of generalization "leads him to the knowledge that the essential nature of form and of all things perceived by the senses in the waking state are equally as unreal as their reflexes in the dream state," since both waking and dreaming are states of mind. A final step brings the yogi to "the Great Realization" that nothing within the experience of his mind "can be other than unreal like dreams." In this light, "the Universal Creation . . . and every phenomenal thing therein" are seen to be "but the content of the Supreme Dream."

❑

THE MIND MANIFESTERS: IMPLICATIONS OF PSYCHEDELICS

The mind is its own place, and in itself
Can make a Heaven of Hell, a Hell of Heaven.
JOHN MILTON, *Paradise Lost*

RARELY IN human history has a discovery evoked such a spectacular eruption of hope and hype, love and hate as did the psychedelics. In the exuberant excesses of the sixties, psychedelics were hyped as harbingers of a new age, as psychiatric cure-all's, peace pills, social transformers, aphrodisiacs, and enlightenment in a pill. They were simultaneously vehemently denounced as brain-damaging, psychosis-inducing, life-destroying, and the work of the devil. In short, careful evaluation of the psychedelics was overwhelmed by simplistic, inflammatory, and highly politicized rhetoric.[1]

Unfortunately, this rhetoric avoids the many important yet difficult questions about psychedelics, our culture, and ourselves that these substances raise. Such questions include the nature of the experiences that psychedelics induce, how they induce them, the extent of their benefits and dangers, their potential for research and therapy, the validity of the insights they provide, and what they can tell us about the human mind, brain, pathology, and potential. Then, too, there are social questions about why these substances elicit such intense emotional responses, both pro and con, the many paradoxes inherent in current drug policies, and why there is such wide cross-cultural variation as to which drugs are considered dangerous and which valuable.

Throughout history, diverse groups and cultures have regarded these substances as sacred, and in recent years there has been a growing appreciation of their historical impact.[1,2] Psychedelics appear to have played important roles in several religions, some of which they may have helped initiate, including the shamanic, Vedic, and Greek mystery traditions. In our own time, the psychedelics helped catalyze the phenomena of the sixties, whose effects are still reverberating through Western culture.

Although psychedelics have had an enormous impact on religion, culture, and history, they cannot be defined easily. They have no common chemical structure, their effects are varied, and the mechanisms by which they work their mindboggling effects are little understood. The *Comprehensive Textbook of Psychiatry* points out, "What distinguishes this group . . . is their capacity to reliably induce states of altered perception, thought, and feeling that are not ordinarily experienced except in dreams or at times of religious exaltation."[3] LSD is usually considered the prototype, but many substances with varying effects await research.

Systematic research on the psychological effects of psychedelics was stifled when the drugs became illegal. However, it appears that these powerful substances can be both beneficial and dangerous.

The dangers range from acute to chronic. The most common acute reaction is the classic "bad trip," a nightmare of overwhelming fear. Long-term dangers include the precipitation of psychopathology, including psychosis, in predisposed individuals. Negative reactions occur almost exclusively in individuals who are poorly prepared, in unfavorable environments, use impure substances, or have prior psychopathology.[4,5] With selected subjects in controlled clinical settings, such complications are rare, and psychedelically induced crises can usually be worked through beneficially with the help of an appropriately trained therapist.[4] To date, there is no evidence of permanent brain damage following even long-term LSD use.[5]

In addition to these dangers it appears that psychedelics may also have therapeutic, creative, and religious potential. Although research evidence from controlled outcome studies is modest, case histories suggest significant therapeutic benefits when psychedelics are professionally administered and supervised. Many reports describe dramatic, long-lasting breakthroughs in patients suffering severe disorders that had proved resistant to other therapeutic interventions, and people facing death have found great solace in their experiences.[1,4,6]

Psychedelics also can open the gates of heaven and hell, producing an awesome range of experiences that appear to encompass those of diverse religious traditions and to be extraordinarily intense. Those who have them can feel transformed or even "reborn" and emerge with new philosophies, worldviews, and insights into mind, religion, and reality.

Even the limited research that has been done indicates that the psychedelics may be remarkable research tools for understanding the workings of mind. Though they were first thought to produce psychoses and hence initially called hallucinogens or psychotomimetics (mimicking psychosis), this view is now recognized as incorrect. Rather, they seem to function more as general amplifiers of mental processes that unveil successive levels and structures of the unconscious.[6] They can thereby provide new insight into the nature of the unconscious, psychodynamics, archetypes, psychopathology, and religious experience.

It seems, therefore, that psychedelics may have psychotherapeutic, research, and religious potential and that research should be encouraged rather than stifled. The papers in this chapter address some of the most intriguing questions raised by these substances.

In a famous paper, Huston Smith asks the question, "Do drugs have religious import?" His answers challenge the tendency of many religious scholars to dismiss psychedelically induced religious experiences as false or insignificant. Smith summarizes the five major arguments advanced to suggest that drug experiences can never be truly religious and finds all five wanting.

He concludes that experiences induced by drugs and by religious practices can sometimes be indistinguishable. However, he cautions that "drugs appear to induce religious experiences; it is less evident they can produce religious lives."

One of the most famous drug experiences of all time was that of America's preeminent philosopher and psychologist William James. James experimented with nitrous oxide and the experience changed his views of consciousness and philosophy forever. In "The Varieties of Consciousness: Observations on Nitrous Oxide," he reported an insight into the unity of opposites, and a compelling appreciation of the varieties and importance of alternate states of consciousness.

Early studies of psychedelics suggested that they called forth chaotic explosions of largely incoherent experiences. Yet Stanislav Grof, who is probably the world's most experienced authorized psychedelic researcher, found order in this apparent chaos, namely, patterns of experiences that emerged in orderly, meaningful sequences. After years of painstaking research he was able to piece these patterns together and create new maps of the human unconscious, psychological development, and religious experience.

In "Realms of the Human Unconscious" Grof suggests that the usual sequence of psychedelic experiences reflects an uncovering of progressively deeper layers and structures of the unconscious. This uncovering begins with traditional Freudian psychodynamic experiences, progresses through Rankian birth trauma material and then Jungian archetypal symbols, and may finally culminate in transcendent experiences similar to those described in the great religions. These transcendent experiences can result in a new appreciation of religious traditions, even by people who were previously skeptical of them. This research suggests that the potential for attaining such experiences is latent within us all.

The most profound experiences include reports of infinite consciousness, being and bliss, universal mind, God, or an ineffable void prior to all phenomena and experience. Such experiences show dramatic similarities to the deep spiritual realizations described by such traditions as Taoism, Sufism, Vedanta, Yoga, and Christian mysticism.

Recently, Stanislav and Christina Grof discovered a method, which they call holotropic therapy, of inducing altered states and psychedelic-like experiences without drugs. It consists of a combination of prolonged, intense breathing, music, and bodywork. Case reports suggest that holotropic therapy has significant psychotherapeutic and transformative potential. Of course, a final assessment of both holotropic therapy and therapy using psychedelics awaits carefully controlled research.

13

Do Drugs Have Religious Import?

Huston Smith

Students of religion appear by and large to be dismissing the psychedelic drugs as having little religious relevance, accepting R. C. Zaehner's *Mysticism Sacred and Profane* as having "fully examined and refuted" the religious claims for mescalin, which Aldous Huxley sketched in *The Doors of Perception*. This closing of the case strikes me as premature.

1. DRUGS AND RELIGION VIEWED HISTORICALLY

In his trial-and-error life explorations man almost everywhere has stumbled upon connections between vegetables (eaten or brewed) and actions (yogi breathing exercises, whirling-dervish dances, flagellations) that alter states of consciousness. The instances closest to us in time and space are the peyote of The Native American (Indian) Church and Mexico's 2000 year old "sacred mushrooms." Beyond these neighboring instances lie the *soma* of the Hindus, the *haoma* and hemp of the Zoroastrians, the Dionysus of the Greeks who "everywhere . . . taught men the culture of the vine and the mysteries of his worship and everywhere (was) accepted as a god," the *benzoin* of Southeast Asia, Zen's tea whose fifth cup purifies and whose sixth "calls to the realm of the immortals," the *pituri* of the Australian aborigines, and probably the mystic *kykeon* that was eaten and drunk at the climactic close of the sixth day of the Eleusinian mysteries.[1]

More interesting than the fact that consciousness-changing devices have been linked with religion is the possibility that they actually initiated many of the religious perspectives which, taking root in history, continued after their psychedelic origins were forgotten. Bergson[2] saw the first movement of Hindus and Greeks toward "dynamic religion" as associated with the "divine rapture" found in intoxicating beverages; more recently Robert Graves, Gordon Wasson, and Alan Watts have suggested that most religions arose from such chemically induced theophanies. This is an important hypothesis—one which must surely engage the attention of historians of religion for some time to come.

2. DRUGS AND RELIGION VIEWED PHENOMENOLOGICALLY

Phenomenology attempts a careful description of human experience. The question the drugs pose for the phenomenology of religion, therefore, is whether the experiences they induce differ from religious experiences reached naturally, and if so how.

There are, of course, innumerable drug experiences that have no religious feature; they can be sensual as readily as spiritual, trivial as readily as transforming, capricious as readily as sacramental. If there is one point about which every student of the drugs agrees, it is that there is no such thing as the drug experience per se. Every experience is a mix of three ingredients: drug, set (the psychological make-up of the individual), and setting (the social and physical environment in which it is taken). But given the right set and setting, the drugs can induce religious experiences indistinguishable from experiences that occur spontaneously.

How do we know that the experiences these people have really are religious? We can begin with the fact that they say they are.

But if more rigorous methods are preferred, they exist. At Harvard University Walter Pahnke worked out a typology of religious experience (in this instance of the mystical variety) based on the classic cases of mystical experiences as summarized in Walter Stace's *Mysticism and Philosophy.* He then administered psilocybin to ten theology students and professors in the setting of a Good Friday service. The drug was given "double-blind," meaning that neither Dr. Pahnke nor his subjects knew which ten were getting psilocybin and which ten placebos, to constitute a control group. Subsequently "those subjects who received psilocybin experienced phenomena which were indistinguishable from, if not identical with . . . the categories defined by our typology of mysticism."[3]

Why, in the face of this considerable evidence, does Zaehner hold that drug experiences cannot be authentically religious? There appear to be three reasons:

His own experience was "utterly trivial." This of course proves that not all drug experiences are religious; it does not prove that no drug experiences are religious.

He thinks the experiences of others that appear religious to them are not truly so. Zaehner distinguishes three kinds of mysticism: nature mysticism, in which the soul is united with the natural world; monistic mysticism, in which the soul merges with an impersonal absolute; and theism, in which the soul confronts the living, personal God. He concedes that drugs can induce the first two species of mysticism, but not the supreme instance, the theistic. As proof, he analyzes Huxley's experience as recounted in *The Doors of Perception* to show that it produced at best a blend of nature and monistic mysticism. Even if we were to accept Zaehner's evaluation of the three forms of mysticism, Huxley's case, and indeed Zaehner's entire book, would prove only that not every mystical experience induced by the drugs is theistic. Insofar as Zaehner goes beyond this to imply that drugs do not and cannot induce theistic mysticism, he not only goes beyond the evidence but proceeds in the face of it.

There is a third reason why Zaehner might doubt that drugs can induce genuinely mystical experiences. Zaehner is a Roman Catholic, and Roman Catholic doctrine teaches that mystical rapture is a gift of grace and as such can never be reduced to man's control. This may be true; certainly the empirical evidence cited does not preclude the possibility of a genuine ontological or theological difference between natural and drug-induced religious experiences. At this point, however, we are considering phenomenology rather than ontology, description rather than interpretation, and on this level there is no difference. Descriptively, drug experiences cannot be distinguished from their natural religious counterpart. When the current philosophical authority on mysticism, W. T. Stace, was asked whether the drug experience is similar to the mystical experience, he answered, "It's not a matter of its being similar to mystical experience; it *is* mystical experience."

3. THE DRUGS AND RELIGION VIEWED "RELIGIOUSLY"

Suppose that drugs can induce experiences indistinguishable from religious experiences and that we can respect their reports. Do they shed any light, not (we now ask) on life, but on the nature of the religious life?

One thing they may do is throw religious experience itself into perspective by clarifying its relation to the religious life as a whole. Drugs appear able to induce religious experiences; it is less evident that they can produce religious lives.

Whether chemical substances can be helpful *adjuncts* to faith is another question. The peyote-using Native American Church seems to indicate that they can be; anthropologists give this church a good report, noting among other things that members resist alcohol and alcoholism better than do nonmembers. The conclusion to which evidence currently points would seem to be that chemicals can aid the religious life, but only where set within a context of faith (meaning by this the conviction that what they disclose is true) and discipline (meaning diligent exercise of the will in the attempt to work out the implications of the disclosures for the living of life in the everyday, common-sense world).

□

14

The Varieties of Consciousness:
Observations on Nitrous Oxide

William James

Nitrous oxide and ether, especially nitrous oxide, when sufficiently diluted with air, stimulate the mystical consciousness in an extraordinary degree. Depth beyond depth of truth seems revealed to the inhaler. This truth fades out, however, or escapes, at the moment of coming to; and if any words remain over in which it seemed to clothe itself, they prove to be the veriest nonsense. Nevertheless, the sense of a profound meaning having been there persists; and I know more than one person who is persuaded that in the nitrous oxide trance we have a genuine metaphysical revelation.

Some years ago I myself made some observations on this aspect of nitrous oxide intoxication, and reported them in print. One conclusion was forced upon my mind at that time, and my impression of its truth has ever since remained unshaken. It is that our normal waking consciousness, rational consciousness as we call it, is but one special type of consciousness, whilst all about it, parted from it by the filmiest of screens, there lie potential forms of consciousness entirely different. We may go through life without suspecting their existence; but apply the requisite stimulus, and at a touch they are there in all their completeness, definite types of mentality which probably somewhere have their field of application and adaptation. No account of the universe in its totality can be final which leaves these other forms of consciousness quite disregarded. How to regard them is the question—for they are so discontinuous with ordinary consciousness. Yet they may determine attitudes though they cannot furnish formulas, and open a region though they fail to give a map. At any rate, they forbid a premature closing of our accounts with reality. Looking back on my own experiences, they all converge towards a kind of insight to which I cannot help ascribing some metaphysical significance. The keynote of it is invariably a reconciliation. It is as if the opposites of the world, whose contradictoriness and conflict make all our difficulties and troubles, were melted into unity. Not only do they, as contrasted species, belong to one and the same genus, but *one of the species*, the nobler and better one, *is itself the genus, and so soaks up and absorbs its opposite into itself.* This is a dark saying, I know, when thus expressed in terms of common logic, but I cannot wholly escape from its authority. I feel as if it must mean something, something like what the Hegelian philosophy means, if one could only lay hold of it more clearly. Those who have ears to hear, let them hear; to me the living sense of its reality only comes in the artificial mystic state of mind.

❏

15

Realms of the Human Unconscious:
Observations from LSD Research

Stanislav Grof

A NEW THEORETICAL FRAMEWORK

The concepts presented here are based on my own clinical research of LSD covering a period of seventeen years. My understanding of LSD and my concepts of how it should be used therapeutically underwent fundamental changes during these years of clinical experimentation.

The early years of LSD research were characterized by the so-called "model psychosis" approach. The accidental discovery of LSD and the pioneering research of its effects demonstrated that incredibly minute quantities of this substance could produce dramatic and profound changes in the mental functioning of an individual. Many researchers felt at that time that LSD could mimic the symptoms of schizophrenia and believed that the study of LSD would provide a key to the understanding of this disease as basically a biochemical deviation. Nevertheless, we failed to demonstrate any significant parallels between the phenomenology of the states induced by these drugs and the symptomatology of schizophrenia. Abandoning in theory and practice the "model psychosis" approach, I found it increasingly difficult to share the opinion of the critics who considered the LSD-induced state as simply an unspecific reaction of the brain to a noxious chemical, or "toxic psychosis."

The most astonishing and puzzling aspect of the LSD sessions which I observed in the early years of experimentation was the enormous variability among individuals. I became more and more aware that many of the LSD phenomena seemed to have an interesting psychodynamic meaning and could be understood in psychological terms.

Analysis indicated clearly that the LSD reaction is highly specific for the personality of the subject. Rather than causing an unspecific "toxic psychosis," LSD appeared to be a powerful catalyst of the mental processes activating unconscious material from various deep levels of the personality. Many of the phenomena in these sessions could be understood in psychological and psychodynamic terms; they had a structure not dissimilar to that of dreams. During this detailed analytical scrutiny, it soon became obvious that LSD could become an unrivaled tool for deep personality diagnostics.

At the present time, I consider LSD to be a powerful unspecific amplifier or catalyst of biochemical and physiological processes in the brain. It seems to create a situation of undifferentiated activation that facilitates the emergence of unconscious material from different levels of the personality.

We can delineate for the purpose of our discussion the following four major levels, or types, of LSD experiences and the corresponding areas of the human unconscious: (1) abstract and aesthetic experiences, (2) psychodynamic experiences, (3) perinatal experiences, and (4) transpersonal experiences.

AESTHETIC EXPERIENCES

The aesthetic experiences seem to represent the most superficial level of the LSD experience. They do not reveal the unconscious of the subject and do not have any psychodynamic significance. The most important aspects of these experiences can be explained in physiological terms as a result of chemical stimulation of the sensory organs reflecting their inner structure and functional characteristics.

The following example from an LSD session of a psychiatrist participating in the LSD training program can be used as an illustration:

> I was deeply enmeshed in an abstract world of whirling geometrical forms and exuberant colors that were brighter and more radiant than anything I have ever seen in my life. I was fascinated and mesmerized by this incredible kaleidoscopic show.

PSYCHODYNAMIC EXPERIENCES IN LSD SESSIONS

The experiences belonging to this category originate in the realm of the individual unconscious and in the areas of the personality accessible in usual states of consciousness. They are related to important memories, emotional problems, unresolved conflicts, and repressed material from various life periods of the individual. Most of the phenomena occurring on this level can be interpreted and understood in psychodynamic terms.

The least complicated psychodynamic experiences have the form of actual relivings of emotionally highly relevant events and vivid reenactments of traumatic or unusually pleasant memories from infancy, childhood, or later periods of life. More complicated phenomena in this group represent pictorial concretization of fantasies, dramatization of wishful daydreams, screen memories, and complex mixtures of fantasy and reality. In addition to these, the psychodynamic level involves a variety of experiences that contain important unconscious material appearing in the cryptic form of a symbolic disguise, defensive distortions, and metaphorical allusions.

Psychodynamic experiences are particularly common in individuals who have considerable emotional problems. They are much less important in the sessions of persons who are emotionally stable and whose childhood was relatively uneventful.

The phenomenology of psychodynamic experiences in LSD sessions is to a large extent in agreement with the basic concepts of classical psychoanalysis. If psychodynamic sessions were the only type of LSD experience, the observations from LSD psychotherapy could be considered to be laboratory proof of the basic Freudian premises. The psychosexual dynamics and the fundamental conflicts of the human psyche as described by Freud are manifested with unusual clarity and vividness even in sessions of naive subjects who have never been analyzed, have not read psychoanalytic books, and have not been exposed to other forms of implicit or explicit indoctrination. Under the influence of LSD, such subjects experience regression to childhood and even early infancy, relive various psychosexual traumas and complex sensations related to infantile sexuality, and are confronted with conflicts involving activities in various libidinal zones. They have to face and work through some of the basic psychological problems described by psychoanalysis, such as the Oedipus and Electra complexes, castration anxiety, and penis envy.

In spite of this far-reaching correspondence and congruence, Freudian concepts cannot explain some of the phenomena related to psychodynamic LSD sessions. For a more complete understanding of these sessions and of the consequences they have for the clinical condition of the patient, as well as for the personality structure, a new principle has to be introduced into psychoanalytical thinking. LSD phenomena on this level can be comprehended, and at times predicted, if we think in terms of specific memory constellations, for which I use the name "COEX systems" (systems of condensed experience).

COEX Systems (Systems of Condensed Experience)

A *COEX system* can be defined as a specific constellation of memories consisting of condensed experiences (and related fantasies) from different life periods of the individual. The memories belonging to a particular COEX system have a similar basic theme or contain similar elements and are associated with a strong emotional charge of the same quality. The deepest layers of this system are represented by vivid and colorful memories of experiences from infancy and early childhood. More superficial layers of such a system involve memories of similar experiences from later periods, up to the present life situation. Each COEX system has a basic theme that permeates all its layers and represents their common denominator; the nature of these themes varies considerably from one COEX constellation to another. Various layers of a particular system can, for example, contain all memories of the past exposures of an individual to humiliating and degrading situations that have damaged self-esteem. The experience of emotional deprivation and rejection in various periods of one's development is another common motif of many COEX constellations. Equally frequent are basic themes that depict sex as dangerous or disgusting, and those that involve aggression and violence. Particularly important are COEX systems that epitomize and condense the individual's encounters with situations endangering survival, health, and integrity of the body. The excessive emotional charge which is attached to COEX systems (as indicated by the often powerful abreaction accompanying the unfolding of these systems in LSD sessions) seems to be a summation of the emotions belonging to all the constituent memories of a particular kind.

Individual COEX systems have fixed relations to certain defense mechanisms and are connected with specific clinical symptoms. The detailed interrelations between the individual parts and aspects of COEX systems are in most instances in basic agreement with Freudian thinking; the new element from the theoretical point of view is the concept of the organizing dynamic system integrating the components into a distinct functional unit. The personality structure usually contains a great number of COEX systems. Their character, total number, extent, and intensity varies considerably from one individual to another.

According to the basic quality of the emotional charge, we can differentiate *negative COEX systems* (condensing unpleasant emotional experiences) and *positive COEX systems* (condensing pleasant emotional experiences and positive aspects of an individual's past life). Although there are certain interdependencies and overlappings, separate COEX systems can function relatively autonomously. In a complicated interaction with the environment, they influence selectively the subject's perception of himself and of the world, his feelings and ideation, and even many somatic processes.

Reliving of experiences constituting different levels of the COEX systems is one of the most frequently and constantly observed phenomena in LSD psychotherapy of psychiatric patients. This reliving is rather realistic, vivid, and complex; it is characterized by various convincing indications of regression of the subject to the age when he originally experienced the event in question.

The list of characteristic traumatic experiences that occur as core elements of negative COEX systems covers a wide range of situations that interfere with the security and satisfaction of the child. The oldest core experiences are related to the earliest stage of infancy, the suckling period. Quite frequent is the reliving of oral frustrations related to a rigid feeding schedule, to lack of milk, or to tension, anxiety, nervousness, and lack of love on the part of the nursing mother and her inability to create an emotionally warm, peaceful, and protective atmosphere. Equally frequent seem to be other traumatic experiences from infancy.

The reliving of traumatic childhood experiences is often followed by far-reaching changes in the clinical symptomatology, behavior patterns, values, and attitudes. The powerful transforming effect of the reliving and integration of such memories suggests that a more general dynamic principle is involved.

The most important part of the COEX system seems to be the core experience. It was the first experience of a particular kind that was registered in the brain and laid the foundations for a specific COEX system. The core experience, thus, represents a prototype, a matrix pattern, for the recording of subsequent events of a similar kind in the memory banks. It is not easy to explain why certain kinds of events have such a powerful traumatic effect on the child that they influence psychodynamic development for many years or decades. Psychoanalysts have usually thought in this connection about constitutional and hereditary factors of an unknown nature. LSD research seems to indicate that this specific sensitivity can have important determinants in deeper levels of the unconscious, in functional dynamic matrices that are inborn and transpersonal in nature.

Another important fact might be the dynamic similarity between a particular traumatic incident in childhood and a certain facet of the birth trauma (or perinatal traumatization). In this case, the traumatic impact of a later situation would actually be due to the reactivation of a certain aspect of the psychobiological memory of the birth.

However, whatever the time or number of sessions required, sooner or later the elements of the individual unconscious tend to disappear from the LSD experience and each individual enters the realm of the perinatal and transpersonal phenomena.

PERINATAL EXPERIENCES IN LSD SESSIONS

The basic characteristics of perinatal experiences and their central focus are the problems of biological birth, physical pain and agony, aging, disease and decrepitude, and dying and death. Inevitably, the shattering encounter with these critical aspects of human existence and the deep realization of the frailty and impermanence of man as a biological creature is accompanied by an agonizing existentialist crisis. The individual comes to realize, through these experiences, that no matter what he does in his life, he cannot escape the inevitable: he will have to leave this world bereft of everything that he has accumulated and achieved and to which he has been emotionally attached. The similarity between birth and death—the startling realization that the beginning of life is the same as its end—is the major philosophical issue that accompanies the perinatal experiences. The other important consequence of the shocking emotional and physical encounter with the phenomenon of death is the opening up of areas of spiritual and religious experiences that appear to be an intrinsic part of the human personality and are independent of the individual's cultural and religious background and programming. In my experience, everyone who has reached these levels develops convincing insights into the utmost relevance of the spiritual and religious dimensions in the universal scheme of things. Even hard-core materialists, positivistically oriented scientists, skeptics and cynics, and uncompromising atheists and antireligious crusaders such as Marxist philosophers suddenly became interested in a spiritual search after they confronted these levels in themselves.

In a way that is not quite clear at the present stage of research, the above experiences seem to be related to the circumstances of the biological birth. LSD subjects frequently refer to them quite explicitly as reliving of their own birth trauma. Those who do not make this link and conceptualize their encounter with death and the death-rebirth experience in a purely philosophical and spiritual framework quite regularly show the cluster of physical symptoms described earlier that can best be interpreted as a derivative of the biological birth. They also assume postures and move in complex sequences that bear a striking similarity to those of a child during the various stages of delivery. In addition, these subjects frequently report visions of or identification with embryos, fetuses, and newborn children. Equally common are various authentic neonatal feelings as well as behavior, and visions of female genitals and breasts.

Because of these observations and other clinical evidence, I have labeled the above pheonomena *perinatal experiences*. A causal nexus between the actual biological birth and the unconscious matrices for these experiences still remains to be established. It appears appropriate, however, to refer to this level of the unconscious as Rankian; with some modification, Otto

Rank's conceptual framework is useful for the understanding of the phenomena in question. [1]

Perinatal experiences are a manifestation of a deep level of the unconscious that is clearly beyond the reach of classical Freudian techniques. The phenomena belonging to this category have been neither described in psychoanalytic literature nor taken into consideration in the theoretical speculations of Freudian analysts. Moreover, classical Freudian analysis does not allow for explanation of such experiences and does not offer an adequate conceptual framework for their interpretation.

Perinatal experiences represent a very important intersection between individual psychology and transpersonal psychology or, for that matter, between psychology and psychopathology, on one hand, and religion, on the other. If we think about them as related to the individual birth, they would seem to belong to the framework of individual psychology. Some other aspects, however, give them a very definite transpersonal flavor. The intensity of these experiences transcends anything usually considered to be the experiential limit of the individual. They are frequently accompanied by identification with other persons or with struggling and suffering mankind. Moreover, other types of clearly transpersonal experiences, such as evolutionary memories, elements of the collective unconscious, and certain Jungian archetypes, frequently form an integral part of the perinatal matrices.

Elements of the rich and complex content of LSD sessions reflecting this level of the unconscious seem to appear in four typical clusters, matrices, or experiential patterns. Searching for a simple, logical, and natural conceptualization of this fact, I was struck by the deep parallels between these patterns and the clinical stages of delivery. It proved to be a very useful principle for both theoretical considerations and the practice of LSD psychotherapy to relate the above four categories of phenomena to consecutive stages of the biological birth process and to the experiences of the child in the perinatal period. Therefore, for the sake of brevity, I usually refer to the four major experiential matrices of the Rankian level as *Basic Perinatal Matrices (BPM I—IV)*. It must be re-emphasized that this should be considered at the present stage of knowledge only as a very useful model, not necessarily implying a causal nexus.

The Basic Perinatal Matrices are hypothetical dynamic governing systems that have a function on the Rankian level of the unconscious similar to that of the COEX systems on the Freudian psychodynamic level. They have a specific content of their own, namely, the perinatal phenomena. The latter have two important facets or components: biological and spiritual. The biological aspect of perinatal experiences consists of concrete and rather realistic experiences related to the individual stages of the biological delivery.

Each stage of biological birth appears to have a specific spiritual counterpart: for the undisturbed intrauterine existence it is the experience of
cosmic unity; the onset of the delivery is paralleled by feelings of universal
engulfment; the first clinical stage of delivery, the contractions in a closed
uterine system, corresponds with the experience of "no exit" or hell; the
propulsion through the birth canal in the second clinical stage of the
delivery has its spiritual analogue in the death–rebirth struggle; and
the metaphysical equivalent of the termination of the birth process and of
the events in the third clinical stage of the delivery is the experience of ego
death and rebirth. In addition to this specific content, the basic perinatal
matrices function also as organizing principles for the material from other
levels of the unconscious, namely for the COEX systems, as well as for
some types of transpersonal experiences that occasionally occur simultaneously with perinatal phenomena.

The deep parallel between the physiological activities in the consecutive
stages of biological delivery and the pattern of activities in various ero-
genic zones, in particular that of the genital orgasm, seems to be of great
theoretical significance. It makes it possible to shift the etiological emphasis in the psychogenesis of emotional disorders from sexuality to
perinatal matrices, without denying or negating the validity of many
basic Freudian principles. Even within such an extended framework,
psychoanalytic observations and concepts remain useful for the understanding of occurrences on the psychodynamic level and their mutual
interrelations.

TRANSPERSONAL EXPERIENCES IN LSD SESSIONS

Transpersonal experiences occur only rarely in early sessions of psycholytic therapy; they become quite common in advanced sessions after the
subject has worked through and integrated the material on the psychodynamic and perinatal levels. After the final experience of ego death and
rebirth, transpersonal elements dominate all subsequent LSD sessions of
the individual.

The common denominator of this otherwise rich and ramified group of
phenomena is the feeling of the individual that consciousness expanded
beyond the usual ego boundaries and limitations of time and space.

Embryonal and Fetal Experiences

Vivid, concrete episodes that appear to be memories of specific events
from an individual's intrauterine development are rather common.

As in the case of the reliving of childhood and birth memories, the
authenticity of recaptured intrauterine events is an open question. It

seems, therefore, more appropriate to refer to them as experiences rather than memories. However, on several occasions, I was able to get surprising confirmations by independently questioning the mother or other persons involved.

A researcher studying transpersonal phenomena occurring in LSD sessions has to be prepared for many baffling observations and coincidences that can put to a serious test the existing scientific beliefs and instigate doubts about the validity of some widely accepted and shared basic premises.

Archetypal Experiences and Complex Mythological Sequences

An important group of transpersonal experiences in LSD sessions are phenomena for which C. G. Jung has used the terms primordial images, dominants of the collective unconscious, or archetypes.

In some of the most universal archetypes, the subject can identify with the roles of the Mother, Father, Child, Woman, Man, or Lover. Many highly universalized roles are felt as sacred, as exemplified by the archetypes of the Great Mother, the Terrible Mother, the Earth Mother, Mother Nature, the Great Hermaphrodite, or Cosmic Man. Archetypes representing certain aspects of the subject's personality, such as the Shadow, Animus and Anima, or Persona, are also rather common in advanced LSD sessions.

Not infrequently, unsophisticated subjects have reported stories that strongly resemble ancient mythological themes from Mesopotamia, India, Egypt, Greece, Central America, and other countries of the world. These observations closely parallel C. G. Jung's descriptions of the appearance of relatively unknown but distinctly archetypal themes in the dreams of children and unsophisticated patients, as well as in the manifest symptomatology of some schizophrenics.

We have mentioned elsewhere that as a result of LSD sessions some subjects have developed insights into entire systems of esoteric thought. Thus, individuals unfamiliar with the cabbala have had experiences described in the Zohar and Sepher Yetzirah and have demonstrated a surprising familiarity with cabbalistic symbols. Such new understanding was also observed in regard to various ancient forms of divination, such as the I Ching and Tarot.

Activation of the Chakras and Arousal of the Serpent Power (Kundalini)

Many experiences from transpersonal LSD sessions bear a striking resemblance to phenomena described in various schools of Kundalini yoga as signs of the activation and opening of individual chakras. These parallels do not exist only for experiences of a positive nature; the phenomenology and consequences of mishandled or poorly integrated LSD sessions are very similar to the complications occurring in the course of unsupervised and amateurish Kundalini practices. In general, the chakra system seems to provide very useful maps of consciousness that are of great help in understanding and conceptualizing many unusual experiences in LSD sessions.

Of all the systems of yoga, Kundalini yoga bears the closest resemblance to LSD psychotherapy. Both techniques mediate an instant and enormous release of energy, produce profound and dramatic experiences, and can bring impressive results in a relatively short time. On the other hand, they involve the greatest risk and can be quite dangerous if they are not practiced under careful supervision and responsible guidance.

Consciousness of the Universal Mind

This is one of the most profound and total experiences observed in LSD sessions. Identifying with the consciousness of the Universal Mind, the individual senses that he has experientially encompassed the totality of existence. He feels that he has reached the reality underlying all realities and is confronted with the supreme and ultimate principle that represents all Being. The illusions of matter, space, and time, as well as an infinite number of other subjective realities, have been completely transcended and finally reduced to this one mode of consciousness which is their common source and denominator. This experience is boundless, unfathomable, and ineffable; it is existence itself. Verbal communication and the symbolic structure of our everyday language seem to be a ridiculously inadequate means to capture and convey its nature and quality. The experience of the phenomenal world and what we call usual states of consciousness appear in this context to be only very limited, idiosyncratic, and partial aspects of the over-all consciousness of the Universal Mind.

Discussing experiences of this nature, subjects have frequently commented on the fact that the language of poets, although still highly imperfect, seems to be a more adequate and appropriate tool for this purpose. One understands why so many great seers, prophets, and religious teachers have resorted to poetry, parable, and metaphor in order to share their transcendental visions.

The experience of consciousness of the Universal Mind is closely related to that of cosmic unity but not identical with it. Its important concomitants are intuitive insights into the process of creation of the phenomenal world as we know it and into the Buddhist concept of the wheel of death and rebirth. These can result in a temporary or enduring feeling that the

individual has achieved a global, nonrational, and transrational understanding of the basic ontological and cosmological problems that beset
existence.

The Supracosmic and Metacosmic Void

The last and most paradoxical transpersonal phenomenon to be discussed
in this context is the experience of the supracosmic and metacosmic Void,
of the primordial emptiness, nothingness, and silence, which is the ultimate source and cradle of all existence and the "uncreated and ineffable
Supreme." The terms *supra-* and *metacosmic* used by sophisticated LSD
subjects in this context refer to the fact that this Void appears to be both
supraordinated to and underlying the phenomenal world. It is beyond
time and space, beyond form or any experiential differentiation, and
beyond polarities such as good and evil, light and darkness, stability and
motion, and agony and ecstasy.

No matter how paradoxical it might seem, the Void and the Universal
Mind are perceived as identical and freely interchangeable; they are two
different aspects of the same phenomenon. The Void appears to be emptiness pregnant with form, and the subtle forms of the Universal Mind are
experienced as absolutely empty.

Profound transcendental experiences, such as the activation of the Kundalini or consciousness of the Universal Mind or of the Void, in addition to
having a very beneficial effect on the subject's physical and emotional
well-being, are usually central in creating in him a keen interest in religious, mystical, and philosophical issues, and a strong need to incorporate
the spiritual dimension into his way of life.

Transpersonal Experiences and Contemporary Psychiatry

It certainly is not the first time behavioral scientists and mental health
professionals have been confronted with transpersonal experiences, nor is
the use of psychedelic substances the only framework in which they can
be observed. Many of these experiences have been known for centuries
or millennia. Descriptions of them can be found in the holy scriptures of
all the great religions of the world, as well as in written documents of
countless minor sects, factions, and religious movements. They have also
played a crucial role in the visionary stages of individual saints, mystics,
and religious teachers. Ethnologists and anthropologists have observed
and described them in aboriginal sacred rituals, ecstatic and mystery
religions, indigenous healing practices, and rites of passage of various
cultures. Psychiatrists and psychologists have been seeing transpersonal
phenomena, without identifying and labeling them as such, in their

everyday practice in many psychotic patients, especially schizophrenics. Historians, religionists, anthropologists, and experimental psychiatrists and psychologists have been aware of the existence of a variety of ancient as well as modern techniques that facilitate the occurrence of transpersonal experiences; they are the same procedures that were described earlier as conducive to the emergence of the perinatal elements.

In spite of the frequency of these phenomena and their obvious relevance for many areas of human life, surprisingly few serious attempts have been made in the past to incorporate them into the theory and practice of contemporary psychiatry and psychology. The attitude of most professionals has oscillated among several distinct approaches to these phenomena. Some professionals have been only marginally acquainted with various transpersonal experiences and have more or less ignored them.

For another large group of professionals, transpersonal phenomena are clearly too bizarre to be considered within the framework of variations of normal mental functioning. Any manifestation of this sort is then readily labeled psychotic.

Yet another group of professionals has manifested definite interest in various aspects of the transpersonal realm and made serious attempts at theoretical explanations and conceptualizations. They have not, however, acknowledged the uniqueness of this category or the specific characteristics of such phenomena. In their approach, transpersonal experiences have been explained in terms of old and widely accepted paradigms; in most instances, they are reduced to biographically determined psychodynamic phenomena. Thus, intrauterine experiences (as well as the perinatal elements) appearing in dreams and free associations of many patients are usually treated as mere fantasies; various religious thoughts and feelings are explained from unresolved conflicts with parental authority; experiences of cosmic unity are interpreted as indications of primary infantile narcissism.

At present, there is little doubt in my mind that they represent phenomena *sui generis* which originate in the deep unconscious, in areas that have been unrecognized and unacknowledged by classical Freudian psychoanalysis. I am convinced that they cannot be reduced to the psychodynamic level and adequately explained within the Freudian conceptual framework.

In psycholytic LSD sessions, all my subjects sooner or later transcended the narrow psychodynamic framework and moved into perinatal and transpersonal realms.

PART II

The Farther Reaches of Development

❏

TRANSPERSONAL DIMENSIONS OF DEVELOPMENT

> *The exploration of the highest reaches of human nature and of its ultimate possibilities ... has involved for me the continuous destruction of cherished axioms, the perpetual coping with seeming paradoxes, contradictions, and vagueness, and the occasional collapse around my ears of long-established, firmly believed in, and seemingly unassailable laws of psychology.*
>
> ABRAHAM MASLOW[1]

ALL THINGS change, including ideas about development. Contrary to long-held assumptions, psychological development can continue throughout the lifespan. Motives, emotions, morality, cognition, life tasks, and the sense of identity are all capable of growth in adulthood. It is increasingly clear that conventional adulthood does not represent full psychological maturity. Examples of advanced development include Abraham Maslow's metamotives, Lawrence Kohlberg's postconventional moral thinking, and Ken Wilber's postformal operational cognition. In addition, the world's religious traditions offer maps of contemplative development.

We have, therefore, developmental maps from child, adult, and contemplative sources. Recently, Ken Wilber has integrated these to provide the first "full-spectrum" theory of development. This theory links these three phases into a single spectrum and suggests that the advanced stages of conventional, personal, and psychological development merge into transconventional, transpersonal, and spiritual stages. Although questions remain, and considerable research will be necessary to test and refine this theory, a full spectrum theory holds fascinating implications for understanding normality, pathology, contemplative practices, and human possibilities.

One crucial implication is that what we have considered "normality" is actually a form of arrested development. This idea is not new. Rather, it is a more precise formulation of Abraham Maslow's comment, "What we call normality in psychology is really a psychopathology of the average, so undramatic and so widely spread that we don't even notice it."[1] But if normality is a form of arrested development, then what arrests it? Retarding forces seem to operate within both individuals and society.

Growth involves movement into the unknown and often requires surrendering familiar ways of being. Consequently, we tend to fear growth. The tragic result, as both psychologists and philosophers have recognized, is that we actually deny and defend against our greatness and potential. These metadefenses, as we might call them, have been described in many ways. The humanistic psychiatrist Erich Fromm viewed them as "mechanisms of escape," while Maslow called their net effect "the Jonah complex," after the biblical prophet Jonah, who tried to escape his divine mission. The existential philosopher Kierkegaard described how we seek "tranquilization by the trivial," while others speak of the "repression of the sublime." The crucial point is that our transpersonal potentials do not remain undeveloped merely by accident; rather we actively defend against them.

Defenses against transpersonal development also operate in society. Cultures seem to function not only to educate, but also as collective conspiracies to constrict consciousness. As such they mirror and magnify our individual ambivalence toward transcendence.

One possible mechanism for this social effect on development is "coercion to the biosocial mean," a phenomenon in which social forces compensate for genetic extremes. For example, a person with a strong genetic tendency toward dominance is likely to receive social encouragement for restraint, whereas a submissive person will be encouraged toward assertiveness. Society exerts powerful influences to pull people toward social norms.

This same principle seems to operate on the vertical-developmental dimension. In other words, society may encourage development up to societal norms but hinder development beyond them. Examples of this process might include the frustration and behavior problems of gifted children placed in normal, but to them stultifying, schools. It could also explain the fate of all too many saints and sages who throughout human history have ended up poisoned, crucified, or burned.

The net result is that our latent capacities and geniuses may be covertly suppressed rather than encouraged and expressed. The developmental level of a society may thus set developmental limits for its individuals, no matter how gifted they may be. A classic example of this phenomenon was presented by Aldous Huxley, who asked the question "What would a Cro-Magnon genius look like?" Cro-Magnon people had cranial capacities equal to, or perhaps even slightly greater than, contemporary Homo sapiens. Thus they presumably possessed our potential for psychological, intellectual and religious development. Yet as Huxley pointed out, a Cro-Magnon genius would probably have been a good hunter and gatherer and not much more.

What capacities lie unrecognized within us? What currently unfathomable abilities lie dormant, and what can we do to speed their appearance? These are humbling questions that remind us that for all we know our potentials may exceed our wildest dreams. Plotinus claimed that humankind stands poised midway between the beasts and the gods. Perhaps this is another way of saying that we stand midway on our developmental and evolutionary trajectory to full human potential.

If we harbor undreamed-of possibilities, if normality is actually frozen development, and if much of our individual, social, and global distress reflects this frustrated development, the next question is obvious. How can we overcome these blocks and foster individual and collective maturation? This may be one of the most crucial questions of our time, and the fate of our civilization and planet may depend on it.

As retarding forces operate at both individual and social levels, so too we need individual and social responses. For individuals, practices such as psychotherapy and meditation appear to unfreeze and catalyze development. These approaches are so important that they are discussed in detail in separate chapters.

At the societal level both education and social environment are crucial. Education can provide information about human potentials and transconventional ways of being. Here it will be vital to demonstrate that such possibilities exist, can be realized through specific practices, and are more satisfying than the fleeting gratifications afforded by the obsessive pursuit of "the material triumvirate" of money, sex, and power, so glorified by media and skillfully manipulated by advertising.

The most crucial educational challenges of our time, then, are not those that currently concern most politicians and educators in the West, such as how to raise math scores or foster interest in science. Rather, from global and transpersonal perspectives the key questions of our time are how to make education available worldwide as a cultural resource for fostering lifelong maturation from childhood enrichment to transpersonal development.

It is hard to overestimate the importance of such a transformation of education, since, as H. G. Wells emphasized, "Human history becomes more and more a race between education and catastrophe." From this global, transpersonal perspective it seems possible that eventually, as Lewis Mumford predicted, "Education will constitute the principle business of life."[2]

Another social means of fostering transpersonal development is providing what Abraham Maslow called a eupsychian environment, namely an environment optimal for psychological development. Socially, this means sharing the company of people who value transpersonal growth, who undertake practices to foster it, and who provide an atmosphere of interpersonal safety that allows for defenselessness and experimentation. Historically, such people gathered together in retreats or as religious communities. In modern times they also come together for seminars or workshops or as intentional communities, and support each other through ritual, education, modeling and social reinforcement.

A full spectrum theory of development also has implications for understanding and treating psychopathology. Development can falter and pathology can result at any level. Diagnosis and treatment must therefore take this developmental fact of life into account. For example, there has been considerable confusion over the relative effects and merits of psychotherapy and meditation. Some have proposed meditation as a psychological and spiritual panacea. Meditation may, however, be most effective for transpersonal levels of growth and less effective for people fixated at earlier stages. This makes sense when we remember that contemplative practices have traditionally been employed specifically as catalysts for transpersonal development. Indeed, a transpersonal developmental perspective allows us to recognize that the contemplative core of many religions offers road maps and techniques for inducing transpersonal growth.

While it is sometimes said that diverse practices and traditions are just different roads up the same mountain, it is increasingly clear that various traditions, and groups within traditions, may aim for different developmental levels. Thus there are not only different types, but also different levels, of transpersonal experiences across traditions.

While transpersonal experiences are a goal of the accelerated development that contemplative practices induce, these experiences can themselves accelerate development. Indeed, a single transpersonal experience can be life-changing. For example, the apprentice illumined by the "shaman light" is thereby transformed into a shaman. Likewise, a mystical experience or momentary near-death experience can so transform the mind as to change personality radically.

What are the common characteristics of profound transpersonal experiences? The words vary but people's accounts worldwide agree that a central realization is a penetrating insight into one's nature or identity. That nature is said to be not only transpersonal but transverbal or ineffable, beyond time, space, and limits of any kind, and certainly beyond the power of words or thoughts to encompass. As the Zen master Yasutani Roshi emphasized, "Our true nature is beyond all categories. Whatever you can conceive or imagine is but a fragment of yourself."[3] We may not only be more than we think, but also more than we can think. For as the great Indian philosopher Radhakrishnan said, "The real transcends, surrounds, and overflows our miserable categories."[4]

When words are used, our true nature is traditionally described as infinite, unbounded, Spirit, Geist, Mind, Self, Buddha nature, Atman, the One, or Sat-chit-ananda. The experience of this Spirit, Mind, or One is the source of statements such as the following, which express the mystical core of the great religious traditions.

He and he become one entity. (Abulafia, Judaism)
The Kingdom of Heaven is within you. (Christianity)
Look within, you are the Buddha. (Buddhism)
Atman (individual consciousness) and Brahman (universal consciousness) are one. (Hinduism)
By understanding the Self all this universe is known. (The Upanishads)
He who knows himself knows his Lord. (Mohammed, Islam)
Heaven, earth and human form one body. (Neoconfucianism)

Yet experiences come and go; initial flashes of illumination, no matter how meaningful or profound, eventually fade. There is, then, still another developmental task—to transform a transitory altered state into an enduring altered trait, to extend a peak experience into a plateau experience or, as Huston Smith so eloquently put it, to transform flashes of illumination into abiding light. In more traditional language, the challenge is to transform the Vedantin's nirvikapa samadhi into sahaj samadhi, the TM meditator's transcendental consciousness into cosmic consciousness, the Buddhist's prompted consciousness into unprompted or spontaneous consciousness, and the Christian mystic's rapture into deification. This stabilization of transformed consciousness is variously known as enlightenment, liberation, salvation, wu, moksha, and the end of suffering.

Yet even the stabilization of transformed consciousness is not the final task. When existential questions have been answered and personal suffering alleviated, the suffering of others becomes more compelling and leads to the flowering of compassion. "What a man takes in contemplation," urged Meister Eckhart, "he must pour out in love."[5] Beyond initial illumination and even abiding light lies the challenge of bringing that light back to the world.

For this there are numerous metaphors. For Plato it was reentry into the cave; in the Zen ox-herding pictures it is "entering the marketplace with help bestowing hands"; in Christianity it is "the fruitfulness of the soul" in which the divine marriage of mystical union bears fruit in the world. Joseph Campbell spoke of this final phase as "the hero's return," while the historian Arnold Toynbee described the whole cycle of inner search and outer service as "the cycle of withdrawal and return" and said that it characterized the lives of those who had contributed most to humankind.

Transpersonal development, therefore, involves several steps: seeing through the limitations of convention and recognizing further developmental potentials; undertaking a practice capable of realizing those potentials; experiencing for oneself the flashes of illumination that transform future potentials into present realities; extending flashes of illumination into abiding light, and bringing that light into the world for the benefit of all. Undertaking this process is regarded by the great wisdom traditions as the highest goal and greatest good of human existence.

The essays in this chapter describe several dimensions of transpersonal development. For Abraham Maslow, our desire for such transpersonal experiences was an essential part of human nature, as real, as biologically rooted, and ultimately as important for full human development as basic needs for food and shelter. He argued that failure to recognize and fulfill these transpersonal desires results in psychological distress or "metapathology," whose true nature and origins are rarely recognized. Yet such metapathology may underlie much of the contemporary Western cultural malaise as individuals seek, through the substitute gratification of compulsive consumption, to fill the existential vacuum caused by unappreciated, unfulfilled transpersonal needs. Honoring the transpersonal, religious, philosophical, and aesthetic dimensions of life may be essential for the health and development of both individuals and cultures.

In "The Spectrum of Transpersonal Development," Ken Wilber surveys the world's psychologies and religions, their accounts of the farther reaches of human development, and the major transpersonal stages that can be identified across traditions. In later chapters in this book, he describes the pathologies that can arise at each of these stages and the appropriate therapies.

A common characteristic of higher development is that our identity or ego changes, eventually losing its sense of solidity and separateness and becoming transpersonal. There has been much talk of losing, transcending, or moving beyond ego. Yet the term *ego* is used in many, often poorly defined, ways, and so it is often not clear precisely what is meant by the term or by the idea of *egolessness*. In "The Varieties of Egolessness," Mark Epstein clarifies the ways in which the term *egolessness* is used.

In "Becoming Somebody and Nobody: Psychoanalysis and Buddhism," John Engler provides a developmental comparison of psychoanalysis and Buddhism, psychotherapy and meditation. He contrasts their different views of the self, health, and pathology, and the different disorders and life stages for which they are most helpful.

In "The Pre/Trans Fallacy" Ken Wilber points out that transpersonal experiences have often been confused with early or regressive experiences. Reductionists have dismissed transpersonal experiences as pathological, while "elevationists" have raised infantile, primitive, or pathological experiences to transpersonal status. Wilber describes some of the many forms these pre/trans fallacies can take and the costs they can inflict.

16

The Spectrum of Transpersonal Development

Ken Wilber

1. *Vision-logic.* Numerous psychologists (e.g., Bruner, Flavell, Arieti) have pointed out that there is much evidence for a cognitive structure beyond or higher than Piaget's "formal operational." It has been called "dialectical," "integrative," "creative synthetic," and so forth. I prefer the term "vision-logic." In any case, it appears that whereas the formal mind establishes relationships, vision-logic establishes *networks* of those relationships. Such vision or panoramic logic apprehends a mass network of ideas, how they influence each other and interrelate. It is thus the beginning of truly higher-order synthesizing capacity, of making connections, relating truths, coordinating ideas, integrating concepts. Interestingly, this is almost exactly what Aurobindo called "the higher mind," which "can freely express itself in single ideas, but its most characteristic movement is a mass ideation, a system or totality of truth-seeing at a single view; the relations of idea with idea, of truth with truth." This, obviously, is a highly *integrative* structure; indeed, in my opinion it is the highest integrative structure in the *personal* realm; beyond it lie transpersonal developments.

2. *Psychic.* The psychic level may be thought of as the culmination of vision-logic and visionary insight; it is perhaps best epitomized by the sixth chakra, the "third eye," which is said to mark the beginning or opening of transcendental, transpersonal, or contemplative developments: the individual's cognitive and perceptual capacities apparently become so pluralistic and universal that they begin to "reach beyond" any narrowly personal or individual perspectives and concerns. According to most contemplative traditions, at this level an individual *begins* to learn to very subtly inspect the mind's cognitive and perceptual capacities, and thus to that extent begins to *transcend* them. This is Aurobindo's "illumined mind," the "preliminary stages" of meditation in Hinduism and Buddhism, etc. According to Aurobindo,

> The perceptual power of the inner [psychic] sight is greater and more direct than the perceptual power of thought. As the higher mind [i.e., vision-logic]

brings a greater consciousness into the being than the idea and its power of truth, so the illumined mind [psychic level] brings a still greater consciousness . . . ; it illumines the thought-mind with a direct inner vision.

3. *Subtle*. The subtle level is said to be the seat of actual archetypes, of Platonic Forms, of subtle sounds and audible illuminations (*nada, shabd*), of transcendent insight and absorption. Some traditions, such as Hinduism and Gnosticism, claim that, according to direct phenomenological apprehension, this level is the home of personal deity-form (*ishtadeva* in Hinduism, *yidam* in Mahayana, *demiurge* in Gnosticism, etc.), cognized in a state known as *savikalpa samadhi* in Hinduism. In Theravadin Buddhism, this is the realm of the four "*jhanas* with form," or the four stages of concentrative meditation into archetypal "planes of illumination" or "Brahma realms." In *vipassana* meditation, this is the stage-realm of pseudonirvana, the realm of illumination and rapture and initial transcendental insight. It is Aurobindo's "intuitive mind"; *geburah* and *chesed* in Kabalah, and so on.

4. *Causal*. The causal level is said to be the unmanifest source or transcendental ground of all the lesser structures; the Abyss (Gnosticism), the Void (Mahayana), the Formless (Vedanta). It is realized in a state of consciousness known variously as *nirvikalpa samadhi* (Hinduism), *jnana samadhi* (Vedanta), the eighth of the ten ox-herding pictures (Zen); the seventh and eighth *jhanas*; the stage of effortless insight culminating in *nirvana* (*vipassana*); Aurobindo's "Overmind." Alternatively, this stage is described as a universal and formless Self (Atman), common in and to all beings. Aurobindo: "When the Overmind [causal] descends, the predominance of the centralizing ego-sense is entirely subordinated, lost in largeness of being and finally abolished; a wide cosmic perception and feeling of boundless universal self replaces it . . . an unlimited consciousness of unity which pervades everywhere . . . a being who is in essence one with the Supreme Self."

5. *Ultimate*. Passing fully through the state of cessation or unmanifest causal absorption, consciousness is said finally to re-awaken to its prior and eternal abode as absolute Spirit, radiant and all-pervading, one and many, only and all—the complete integration and identity of manifest Form with the unmanifest Formless. This is classical *sahaj* and *bhava samadhi*; the state of *turiya* (and *turiyatita*), absolute and unqualifiable Consciousness as Such, Aurobindo's "Supermind," Zen's "One Mind," Brahman-Atman, the *Svabhavikakaya*. Strictly speaking, the ultimate is not one level among others, but the reality, condition, or suchness of all levels.

❏

17

Becoming Somebody and Nobody: Psychoanalysis and Buddhism

John H. Engler

Both Buddhist psychology and psychoanalytic object relations theory define the essence of the ego in a similar way: as a process of synthesis and adaptation between the inner life and outer reality, which produces a sense of personal continuity and sameness in the felt experience of being a "self." In both psychologies, then, the sense of "I"—of personal unity and continuity, of being the same "self" in time, in place, and across states of consciousness—is conceived as something that is not innate in personality, not inherent in our psychological or spiritual makeup, but that evolves developmentally out of our experience of objects. The "self" is literally constructed out of our object experience. What we take to be our "self" and feel to be so present and real is actually an internalized image, a composite representation, constructed by a selective and imaginative "re-membering" of past encounters with the object world. In fact, the self is viewed as being constructed anew from moment to moment. But both systems further agree that the self is not ordinarily experienced this way. The sense of self is characterized rather by a feeling of temporal continuity and sameness over time.

The fate of this self is *the* central clinical issue in both psychologies. But the fate of this self is also an issue on which the two psychologies under consideration seem diametrically opposed. From the perspective of psychoanalytic object relations theory, the deepest psychopathological problem is the *lack* of a sense of self. The most severe clinical syndromes—infantile autism, the symbiotic and functional psychoses, the borderline conditions—represent failures, arrests, or regressions in establishing a cohesive, integrated self.

In contrast, from the Buddhist perspective the psychopathological problem is the *presence* of a self and the feeling of selfhood. According to Buddhist diagnosis, the deepest source of suffering is the attempt to preserve a self, an attempt that is viewed as both futile and self-defeating.

The severest form of psychopathology is precisely *attavādupādāna*, the clinging to personal existence.

The therapeutic issue in psychotherapy and psychoanalysis is how to "regrow" a basic sense of self or how to differentiate and integrate a stable, consistent, and enduring self-representation. The therapeutic issue in Buddhism is how to "see through" the illusion or construct of the self. Are the two therapeutic goals mutually exclusive, as they appear to be? Or from a wider perspective might they actually be compatible? Indeed, might one be a precondition of the other? The latter is the view I want to propose. Put very simply, you have to be somebody before you can be nobody.

Buddhism does not have a developmental psychology in the Western sense. It has no theory of child development. What Buddhist psychology and practice appear to do instead is *presuppose* a more or less normal course of development and an intact or "normal" ego. For its practices, it *assumes* a level of personality organization in which object relations development, especially a cohesive and integrated sense of self, is already complete. There is an obvious danger if this assumption of normal selfhood is not understood. Teachers may instruct students in techniques that are designed for a different level of personality organization and these may have adverse effects in some students.

Insight meditation, like psychoanalysis, is an "uncovering" technique, although of course what is uncovered is different. Persons with poorly differentiated and weakly integrated part-object relations cannot tolerate uncovering techniques. Uncovering and interpretation cannot be successful because with faulty self-object differentiation the observing ego cannot take distance from what it observes.

Insight meditation thus presents actual risks to students with this level of functioning. All intensive and/or unstructured therapies present significant dangers to such individuals and run the risk of further fragmenting their already fragile and vulnerable sense of self.

Fortunately, I suspect that in most cases the stringent prerequisites of the practice make it difficult if not impossible for these students to sustain their training. To some extent, a self-selective and self-protective mechanism is probably built in.

Meditation does not address this range of psychopathology, is not designed for it, and is probably contraindicated, even though certain practices may be of some incidental help.

THREE LEVELS OF MENTAL DISORDER

Buddhist diagnosis distinguishes between three different levels of suffering, each springing from a different level of object relations experience. (1) *Dukkha-dukkha* or "ordinary suffering" corresponds to neurotic conflict between impulse and prohibition within a stable self-structure and whole-object relations, as well as to "ordinary human unhappiness," which Freud once said was the exchange for resolution of neurotic suffering. (2) *Dukkha-viparinama* or "suffering caused by change" corresponds to the borderline conditions and the functional psychoses, in which disturbance in the sense of self-continuity, fluctuating drives and affects, contradictory and dissociated ego states, lack of a stable self-structure, and lack of constancy in relations with the object world are the core problem. At this level of personality organization, prior to identity formation and object constancy, change is the deepest and most pervasive threat to the fragile self. (3) *Sankhāra-dukkha* or "suffering as conditioned states" represents, to Western psychiatry, an entirely *new category of psychopathology* that is pervasive at all levels of personality organization, the normal as well as the abnormal. At this level, object-seeking as such is experienced as patho-genic, contradictory as that may sound in terms of present developmental theory. The very attempt to constellate a self and objects that will have some constancy and continuity emerges as the therapeutic problem. The two great achievements in the all-important line of object relations development—identity and object constancy—still represent a point of fixation or arrest. "Normality" appears in this perspective to be a state of arrested development.

The third level of psychopathology is the level of personality organiza-tion and psychopathology that insight meditation is specifically designed to address. This has not been clearly understood by either Buddhist or psychoanalytic psychology, nor by current research paradigms. These two systems have been viewed at worst as competing or at best as alterna-tive treatment modalities for the same range of problems; or else they have been seen as vaguely complementary.

A FULL-SPECTRUM MODEL OF OBJECT RELATIONS DEVELOPMENT

But one has to be somebody before one can be nobody. The issue in personal development is not self *or* no-self, but self *and* no-self. Both a sense of self and insight into the ultimate illusoriness of its apparent continuity and substantiality are necessary achievements. Sanity and complete psychological well-being include both, but in a phase-appropriate developmental sequence. The attempt to bypass the devel-opmental tasks of identity formation and object constancy through a misguided spiritual attempt to "annihilate the ego" has fateful and pathological consequences. This is what many students who are drawn to meditation practice and even some teachers seem to be attempting to do. What is needed, and what has been missing from both clinical and meditative perspectives, is *a developmental psychology that includes the full developmental spectrum.*

According to current clinical thinking, therapy does not treat a disease entity in the older Kraepelinian medical model, but reinstitutes a derailed, arrested, or distorted developmental process. Vipassana addresses the developmental process, which it holds to have been arrested at the object relational level of identity and object constancy, and sets it in motion once again to reach a more ultimate view of the self and reality.

Both a sense of self and a sense of no-self—in that order—seem to be necessary to realize that state of optimal psychological well-being that Freud once described as an "ideal fiction" and the Buddha long before described as "the end of suffering" and the one thing he taught.

❏

18

The Varieties of Egolessness

Mark Epstein

There are now several common misconceptions about the key Buddhist notion of *anatta*, or egolessness. To begin with, many new meditators mistake egolessness for the abandonment of the Freudian ego. Conventional notions of ego, as that which modulates sexual and aggressive strivings, have led many Americans to mistakenly equate egolessness with a kind of primal scream in which the person is finally freed from all limiting constraints. Egolessness is understood here as the equivalent of Wilhelm Reich's orgasmic potency, and the ego is identified as anything that tenses the body, obscures the capacity for pleasurable discharge, or gets in the way of feeling "free." Popularized in the sixties, this view remains deeply embedded in the popular imagination. It sees the route to egolessness as a process of unlearning, of casting off the shackles of civilization and returning to a childlike forthrightness. It also tends to romanticize regression, psychosis, and any uninhibited expression of emotion.

Another popular misconception is that egolessness is some kind of oneness or merger, a forgetting of the self with a simultaneous identification with what lies outside the ego, a trance state or an ecstatic union. Freud described the "oceanic feeling" as a sense of limitless and unbounded oneness with the universe that seeks the "restoration of limitless narcissism" and the "resurrection of infantile helplessness." Thus, egolessness is identified with the infantile state prior to the development of the ego, that is, that of the infant at the breast making no distinction between itself and its mother but rather merged in a symbiotic and undifferentiated union.

This formulation is complicated by the fact that there really are states accessible in meditation that do provide such feelings of harmony, merger, and loss of ego boundaries; but these are not the states that define the (Buddhist) notion of egolessness.

Egolessness is not a return to the feelings of infancy—an experience of undifferentiated bliss or a merger with the mother—even though many people may seek such an experience when they begin to meditate, and even though some may actually find a version of it.

A third and more interpersonal view of egolessness suggests a kind of subjugation of the self to the other. It is as if the idealized merger experience is projected onto interpersonal relationships in what the Gestalt therapists have called "confluence," or loss of interpersonal ego-boundaries. This is really a kind of thinly disguised masochism.

The psychoanalyst Annie Reich, in a classic paper on self-esteem regulation in women, describes this very well. "Femininity," she says, is often "equated with complete annihilation." The only way to recover needed self-esteem is to then merge or fuse with a glorified or idealized other, whose greatness or power she can then incorporate. For both sexes something similar exists in spiritual circles. Meditators with this misunderstanding are vulnerable to a kind of eroticized attachment to teachers, gurus, or other intimates, toward whom they direct their desires to be released "into abandon."

A fourth common misconception, popular in so-called transpersonal circles, stems from a misreading of important papers by Ken Wilber and Jack Engler. The belief here is that egolessness is a developmental stage *beyond* the ego; that the ego must first exist and then be abandoned. This is the flip side of the belief that egolessness precedes the development of the ego—here it is seen as that which succeeds the ego.

This approach implies that the ego, while important developmentally, can in some sense be transcended or left behind. Here we run into an unfortunate mix of vocabulary. The system referred to by these formulations is the Western psychodynamic psychology of ego development. Then there is a jump, or switch, to an Eastern-based, spiritual vocabulary that makes it seem as if the ego that has been formed is the same ego that is being abandoned. Yet listen to the Dalai Lama on this point: "Selflessness is not a case of something that existed in the past becoming nonexistent. Rather, this sort of 'self' is something that never did exist. What is needed is to identify as nonexistent something that always was nonexistent."

It is not ego, in the Freudian sense, that is the actual target of the Buddhist insight. It is, rather, the self-concept, the *representational* component of the ego, the actual internal experience of one's self that is targeted.

What is being transcended here is not the entire ego. Rather, self-representation is revealed as lacking concrete existence. It is not the case of something real being eliminated, but of the essential groundlessness being realized for what it has always been. In the words of the Dalai Lama, "This seemingly solid, concrete, independent, self-instituting I under its own power that *appears* actually does not exist at all."

Meditators with this misunderstanding often feel under pressure to disavow critical aspects of their being that are identified with the "unwholesome ego." Most commonly, sexuality, aggression, critical thinking, or even the active use of the first person pronoun are relinquished, the general idea being that to give these things up or let these things go is to achieve egolessness. Aspects of the self are set up as the enemy and then attempts are made by the meditator to distance oneself from them. But the qualities that are identified as unwholesome are actually empowered by the attempts to repudiate them!

A final misunderstanding of egolessness is one that sees it as a thing in and of itself, a state to be achieved or aspired to. Here, the need to identify something as existing in its own right is manifest, and the belief in the ego as concretely existent is, in some sense, transferred to the belief in egolessness as concretely existent. It is not that the ego disappears, but that the belief in the ego's solidity, the identification with ego's representations, is abandoned in the realization of egolessness.

❑

19

The Pre/Trans Fallacy

Ken Wilber

The concept of ptf (pre/trans fallacy) stems from both developmental philosophy—represented most effectively by Hegel in the West and Aurobindo in the East—and developmental psychology—epitomized by Baldwin and Piaget in the West and kundalini yoga in the East.

If one attempts to look at the world-at-large in such developmental terms, the world itself appears to be evolving in a definite direction, namely, towards higher levels of structural organization, towards greater holism, integration, awareness, consciousness, etc. Indeed, a brief glance at the evolutionary record to date shows a pronounced growth towards increasing complexity and awareness.

Many philosophers and psychologists, looking at this evolutionary course, have concluded that development itself is heading towards noumenon. We are all familiar with Teilhard de Chardin's evolutionary conception of the omega point and with Aurobindo's evolutionary drive towards the supermind, but the same concept was held in the West by such philosophers as Aristotle and Hegel. The "end" of which Hegel speaks is similar to supermind and omega—it is a state of "absolute knowledge" where "Spirit knows itself in the form of Spirit."

Thus history (evolution) was, for Hegel as for the perennial philosophy in general, the process of the self-actualization of Spirit. Significantly, Hegel maintained that this developmental process occurs in three major stages. It begins with nature—the realm of matter and of simple bodily sensations and perceptions. This realm we shall be calling the *prepersonal* or the *subconscient*. Hegel often speaks of subconscient nature (i.e., the prepersonal realm) as a "fall" (*Abfall*)—but it is not that nature is set against Spirit or divorced from Spirit. Rather nature is simply "slumbering Spirit," or "God in His otherness." More specifically, nature is "self-alienated Spirit."

In the second phase of the return of Spirit to Spirit, or of the overcoming of self-alienation, development moves from (prepersonal) nature to what Hegel calls the self-conscious stage. This is the stage of typical egoic or mental awareness—the realm we shall be calling personal, mental, and self-conscious.

Finally, according to Hegel, development culminates in the Absolute, or Spirit's discovery of Spirit as Spirit, a stage/level we shall be calling transpersonal or superconscious.

Note, then, the overall sequence of development: from nature to humanity to divinity, from subconscious to self-conscious to superconscious, from prepersonal to personal to transpersonal. This is represented in Figure 1.

We need only one last theoretical tool. If the movement from the lower to the higher is evolution, then the reverse, the movement from the higher to the lower, is *involution*. (See Figure 2.) Nature became a "fall" or "slumbering God" or "self-alienated Spirit" through the prior process of involution, or the descent and "loss" of the higher in the lower. Call it the "Big Bang," when matter—the lowest realm—was flung into existence out of the Void (*sunyata*). Evolution is the subsequent reversal of the Abfall, the return of Spirit to Spirit via development.

Since development moves from prepersonal to personal to transpersonal, and *since* both prepersonal and transpersonal are, in their own ways, nonpersonal, *then* prepersonal and transpersonal tend to appear similar, even identical, to the untutored eye. In other words, people tend to confuse prepersonal and transpersonal dimensions—and there is the heart of the ptf.

This fallacy has two major forms: the reduction of the transpersonal to the prepersonal, which we call ptf-1, and the elevation of the prepersonal to the transpersonal, or ptf-2. With reference to Figure 1, the point is that if the subtle but drastic differences between A and C are not understood, then the two ends of one's developmental map are collapsed into each

FIGURE 1

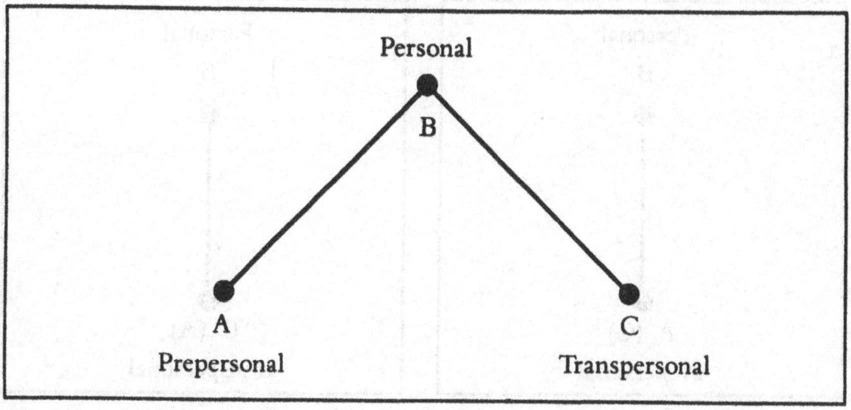

Personal

B

A   C

Prepersonal   Transpersonal

FIGURE 2

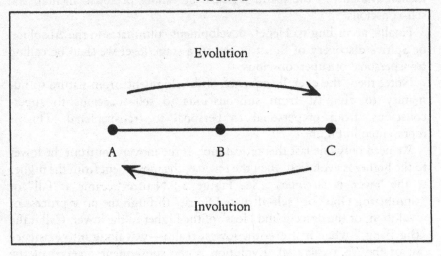

other. In ptf-1, C is collapsed or reduced to A (and thus ceases to exist *as* C)—Figure 3. In ptf-2, A is collapsed or elevated to C (and thus ceases to exist *as* A)—Figure 4. Instead of two legs of development, we get a single axis.

This collapse instantly creates two opposed worldviews. Since the real world still contains A, B, and C, then ptf-1 and ptf-2 will still run into the whole spectrum of existence, but both will necessarily interpret the world in light of their respective deficiencies. Thus, correlative with the two forms of ptf, there are generated two major worldviews, precisely as shown in Figures 3 and 4.

FIGURE 3
The Worldview of Ptf-1

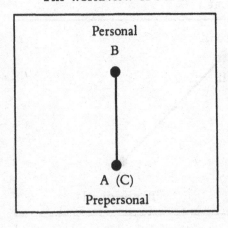

FIGURE 4
The Worldview of Ptf-2

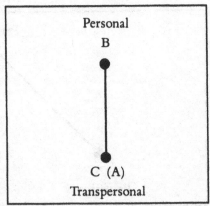

Now both of these worldviews recognize the personal realm, and, moreover, in both views development is thought to have *culminated* in the personal realm.

Worldview one (WV-1) sees development moving from a prepersonal source in nature, through a series of intermediate advances, to a culmination in the "high point" of evolution, that of human rationality. It recognizes no higher source or goal of development, and it vehemently denies the necessity of even mentioning such supposedly "higher" levels. Man is a rational being, and rationality is all that is necessary to comprehend and order the cosmos. It looks very much like science.

WV-2, on the other hand, sees development moving *from* a spiritual source ("in heaven") to a culmination in a "low point" of alienation, that of a sinful humanity or of the individual and personal ego. History is thus the history of a falling down, not a moving up, and mankind (or personal ego) is at the *end* of the fall, just as depicted in Figure 4. It looks a lot like orthodox religion.

Now the difficult and intricate part is that while the pre/trans fallacy itself is simply an error, the two worldviews generated by the two ptfs are half true and half fallacious—and *that* is what has made it so hard to decide on their relative merits. They are true when dealing with the half of development that they have not exalted or reduced, and fallacious when dealing with the half they have so mistreated. To be more specific: Each of these worldviews contains *two* important truths and *two* major errors.

WV-1 is correct in maintaining that (1) we possess a prepersonal, irrational, and subconscious component, which did indeed precede the rational and personal in evolution, and (2) the direction of actual or historical evolution is indeed from the lower to the higher. It is wrong when it (1) denies the existence of a transpersonal component and thus (2) denies that there can be a real moving down or descent from Spirit, an involutionary Abfall from union with and as Godhead.

WV-2 is correct maintaining that (1) there is a transpersonal component to the cosmos, and (2) there is some sense in which we are all "in sin," or living alienated and separated from a supreme identity with Spirit. It is wrong, however, in maintaining that (1) the individual ego, or rational thinking personhood, is the height of alienation from Spirit and wrong in thus maintaining that (2) a true Eden *preceded* the ego in *evolution* (or that the personal ego *caused* original sin).

In fact, as both Hegel and Aurobindo demonstrated, *original alienation*, or the high point of alienation, starts with material nature. Nature, or the prepersonal world, is *already* self-alienated Spirit, without any help whatsoever from the ego; and further, nature is the *greatest* point of alienation from Spirit. The ego (B) is merely the first structure developed enough to self-consciously *recognize* that the world is *already* fallen from Spirit.

WV-2 confuses the real Fall that occurs in involution with a supposed fall that occurred in evolution. It then appears that with the evolutionary rise of ego, Spirit reaches its zenith of alienation, whereas in fact, with the rise of ego, Spirit is half-way back home: It has gone from the prepersonal subconsciousness of nature to the personal self-consciousness of the ego-mind, *on its way to* the transpersonal superconsciousness of Spirit.

With regard to human psychological development, the two major examples of ptf-1 and ptf-2 are, respectively, Freud and Jung. Freud correctly recognized the prepersonal id (A) and the personal ego (B), but he reduced all spiritual and transpersonal experiences (C) to the prepersonal level; transtemporal insights are explained as pretemporal id-impulses; trans-subject/object samadhi is claimed to be a throwback to pre-subject/object narcissism; transpersonal union is interpreted as prepersonal fusion. In every respect, Freud follows WV-1 (Figure 3). WV-1, of course, is not confined to Freud. It is standard, orthodox, unquestioned Western orthodoxy—Piaget to Kohlberg to Loevinger to Arieti.

In my opinion, Jung errs consistently to the opposite side. He correctly and very explicitly recognizes the transpersonal or numinous dimension, but he often fuses or confuses it with prepersonal structures. For Jung, there are only two major realms: the personal and the collective. Jung thus tends to obscure the vast and profound differences between the *lower* collective unconscious and the *higher* collective unconscious; i.e., the prepersonal collective and the transpersonal collective realms. Thus, not only does Jung occasionally end up glorifying certain infantile mythic forms of thought, he also frequently gives a regressive treatment of Spirit. In any event, he and his followers thus tend to recognize only two major realms—ego and Self—and human development is therefore viewed as occurring along an ego-Self axis, which is actually drawn precisely as in Figure 4, with Self at bottom and ego at top. This is pure WV-2, and it is generally accepted by many transpersonal psychologists, even those who disavow Jung.

Incidentally, the Jungians do recognize that development occurs in two major phases: the development and then the transcendence of the ego. So far, so good. However, since they are working more-or-less with only one *actual* leg of development (B-C), they are forced into making that single axis do double duty. Instead of seeing development as going from A to B to C, they see it as going from C to B and then *back* to C. Not unconscious prepersonal to personal to transpersonal, but unconscious transpersonal to personal to transpersonal. Not pre-ego to ego to trans-ego Self, but Self to ego back to Self.

In these types of theories, the prepersonal realm *qua* prepersonal realm seems to get left out. However, what actually happens, behind the theoretical scenes, is simply that the prepersonal realm gets elevated to quasi-transpersonal status. While we can agree that infancy is free of certain conceptual anxieties, that "freedom" is not due, in my opinion, to transpersonal protection but prepersonal ignorance, a point on which Maslow was equally insistent.

The ptf-2 misunderstanding, which devalues ego and/or elevates pre-ego, takes on ominous proportions when it comes to some (but certainly not all) forms of "avant garde" or "human potential" or "humanistic/ transpersonal" psychotherapies. Put simply, the problem is that many, perhaps most, people who seek or need therapy are suffering in large part from *prepersonal* fixations, dissociations, and obsessions, and haven't the ego-strength to transcend those subhuman angers, impulses, and drives which therefore threaten to overwhelm their very existence. Introduced to a purely WV-2 therapist, they are invited to "let go" of the very structure—that of egoic conceptualization and integration—that they are in such desperate need to create and strengthen.

Most neurotics suffer not because of lack of ego-transcendence, but from the prior lack of ego-esteem, and therapy must be, first and foremost, the *facilitator of strong ego-esteem*, and then—but only then—the facilitator of ego-transcendence.

❑

PROBLEMS ON THE PATH: CLINICAL CONCERNS

Without the transcendent and the transpersonal we get sick, violent, and nihilistic, or hopeless and apathetic. We need something "bigger than we are" to be awed by and commit ourselves to in a new naturalistic, empirical, non-churchly sense. Perhaps as Thoreau and Whitman, William James and John Dewey did.

—ABRAHAM MASLOW[1]

THERE IS a widespread fantasy in our culture that transpersonal development brings unalloyed joy and well-being, a soothing combination of relaxation response and benign bliss. Yet in reality transpersonal development, like all development, has its challenges and difficulties. These can emerge at any stage of the path and sometimes can be difficult enough to require clinical treatment.

Historically, transpersonal crises were often treated within a religious context, such as the monastery, but now we are in a new era. Contemplative practices, including previously closely guarded esoteric disciplines, are being practiced by large numbers of lay people. In addition, the development of psychiatry and psychology means that the cultural experts in mental and emotional disorders are now clinicians, not contemplatives. Therefore, for the first time in history, Western psychology and psychiatry are researching and treating significant numbers of transpersonal crises, which are being interpreted within a psychological rather than spiritual context. This novel situation offers considerable benefits and considerable risks.

The benefits: Many advances of Western psychology and psychiatry now can be used to understand and treat transpersonal crises. Therapists are specifically trained to deal with psychological difficulties and can utilize a wide range of new diagnostic, research, and therapeutic skills.

The risks: Most Western therapists know very little about transpersonal practices and crises. Moreover, many are philosophical materialists who at best deny the value of transpersonal experiences and at worst regard them as signs of serious pathology.

Diagnostically there are two dangers, both reflecting different aspects of what Ken Wilber has called "the pre/trans fallacy." One is reductionistic: failing to recognize a transpersonal crisis and instead viewing it as purely pathological. For example, people who have had near-death experiences, which are usually powerfully beatific and beneficial, sometimes have been diagnosed as psychotic, tranquilized, and on rare occasions have even been forcibly hospitalized. The opposite error is "elevationistic": to mistake a serious pathology such as schizophrenia for a transpersonal process.

Distinguishing prepersonal regressions from transpersonal progressions is not always easy. The precise criteria for doing so are only now being developed, and the task is complicated by the existence of hybrid forms in which both transpersonal and pathological elements co-exist.[2] However, misdiagnoses of either type can have tragic results. Diagnostic errors lead to therapeutic errors and unrecognized transpersonal crises may be inappropriately treated by a kind of psychopharmacological suppression of the sublime.

The ideal goal is a sensitive integration of ancient and contemplative wisdom with modern clinical and scientific skills. This is a major clinical challenge and opportunity for transpersonal psychology.

THE VARIETIES OF TRANSPERSONAL DIFFICULTIES

Transpersonal difficulties can be grouped into three categories. In the first, transpersonal experiences emerge in the midst of severe pathology. The second kind is developmental and may either initiate or complicate higher development. In contrast, the third type of difficulty stems from a lack of transpersonal experience.

In the first kind, transpersonal experiences erupt unexpectedly in the midst of severe pathology such as psychoses. One way of understanding this is that when normal cognitive functions disintegrate, the psyche can be flooded with elements from all parts of the unconscious, high and low, pathological and transcendent. The term "psychotic disorders with mystical features" has been suggested for these crises.[2] Appropriate treatment and outcome depend on the nature and severity of the pathology.

In the second kind, what initially appears to be pure pathology can turn out to be a potentially beneficial developmental crisis. It is rarely appreciated that psychological crises, even psychoses, sometimes can function as growth experiences that result in greater psychological and spiritual well-being. Over two thousand years ago, Socrates declared that "our greatest blessings come to us by way of madness provided the madness is given us by divine gift."[2] More recently the eminent psychiatrist Menninger observed that "some patients have a mental illness and then get well and then get weller! I mean they get better than they ever were. . . . this is an extraordinary and little realized truth."[2]

The general process is one of temporary psychological disturbance followed by resolution and repair to a higher level of functioning than before the initial crisis. From this perspective what seemed at the time to be a crisis of disturbance and disease later can be reinterpreted as a stage of development and growth. Such crises have been given many names, each of which illuminates some aspect of the process. For example, growth-producing disturbances have been described as "positive disintegrations," "creative illnesses," "regenerative processes," and "renewals." When such crises are specifically associated with mystical or transpersonal experiences, they have been described as "divine illnesses," "mystical experiences with psychotic features," "spiritual emergencies," "spiritual emergences," "metanoiac voyages," "visionary states" and "transpersonal crises."[2,3]

If these crises are successfully negotiated, then the disorganization and turmoil may turn out to be the means by which constricting outdated life habits are cast off. Old beliefs, goals, identities, and life-styles may be reassessed and more life-affirming modes adopted. It seems that psychological pain and confusion can be symptoms of psychological disease and decline on the one hand, or of developmental transition and growth on the other. The outcome depends in part on whether they are appropriately diagnosed and treated.

This is *not* to say that all psychological distress is a developmental crisis or that all developmental crises, even transpersonal ones, will be successfully navigated and result in greater growth and well-being. Clearly, some people can be left impaired. One of the challenges facing transpersonal psychology is to identify and help people at risk from developmental crises and those practices that can precipitate them.

These crises can be precipitated by stress or spurred by psychological or spiritual practices. They also can occur spontaneously, expressing inner forces that compel development, whether the individual wants it or not. These developmental forces have been described by such terms as the drives for individuation, self-actualization, and self-transcendence. Their result is a dynamic tension between the forces of growth and the seductiveness of the familiar, between the pull of transcendence and the inertia of routine. John Weir Perry, a Jungian analyst, observed:

> Spirit [is] constantly striving for release from its entrapment in routine or conventional mental structures. Spiritual work is the attempt to liberate this dynamic energy, which must break free of its suffocation in old forms. . . .
>
> During a person's developmental process, if this work of releasing spirit becomes imperative but is not undertaken voluntarily with knowledge of the goal and with considerable effort, then the psyche is apt to take over and overwhelm the conscious personality. . . . The individuating psyche abhors stasis as nature abhors a vacuum.[4]

In other words, rather than tolerate stagnation, the psyche actually may create crises that force development. A classic example is the shamanic initiation crisis, which catapults shamans into their careers. Western researchers long dismissed these initiation crises as hysteria, epilepsy, or schizophrenia. Now they can be recognized as initial transpersonal crises or spiritual emergences. Tribal cultures have long recognized them as such and assume that they occur in people suited to become shamans.[3]

Psychological crises can not only initiate but also complicate transpersonal development. These complications are usually of three types: the eruption of unresolved early psychological issues; problems associated with specific stages of contemplative practice; and interpersonal difficulties.

Unresolved early psychological issues can emerge at any stage of the path as defenses soften and awareness illuminates successively deeper layers of the unconscious. Uncovering traumatic material initially may be experienced as painful and problematic, but in the long run it can be cathartic and a stepping stone for further progress.

Contemplative traditions have evolved sophisticated maps of transpersonal development and its difficulties. Now that all traditions are available, for the first time in history we can begin to make cross-cultural maps of developmental stages, difficulties, and appropriate therapies. This is what Ken Wilber has begun to do with his "spectrum of pathologies."

Interpersonal difficulties also can occur. Beginning a spiritual practice and joining a community of practitioners can create difficulties relating to the new community as well as to family and friends who may disparage the practice. Some spiritual groups and leaders can be very demanding, even pathologically so. Issues such as autonomy, boundaries, personal responsibility, assertion, surrender, and balance require sensitive discernment.

The third kind of problem is associated with *not* having transpersonal experiences. In the long run this may exact a far greater toll. This lack can result from people's ignorance of the possibility of transpersonal experiences or from their deliberate attempt to suppress them.

These ideas have a long history. In tribal cultures those who declined the call to shamanism were thought to be at risk for sickness, madness, or death.[3] Joseph Campbell called this kind of avoidance "the refusal of the call" and pointed out that the world's myths warn that it exacts a heavy toll. This is the basis of Maslow's claim that "if you deliberately plan to be less than you are capable of being, then I warn you that you will be deeply unhappy for the rest of your life."[5]

Growing evidence suggests that lack of transpersonal experience may underlie a significant part of contemporary individual, cultural, and global pathology. Maslow described this as metapathology resulting from the failure to satisfy meta (transpersonal) motives and needs. As discussed in the development section of this book, a lack of transpersonal experience and its resultant metapathology may underlie diverse psychological and social disturbances. These may range from the midlife crises faced by countless individuals whose lives are devoid of meaning to the global crises that reflect the insatiable consumption by millions of such people.

It is also possible that hunger for transpersonal experiences may play a significant but largely unrecognized role in the etiology and treatment of specific clinical disorders. For example, addiction has many causes—biological, social, and psychological—and of late much attention has been given to its biological roots.

Whatever its biological bases, however, addictive craving also may be in part a substitute gratification for transpersonal experiences. Carl Jung described it as "the equivalent, on a low level, of the spiritual thirst of our being for wholeness, expressed in medieval language: the union with God."[6]

This idea of substitute gratification is the heart of what Ken Wilber calls the Atman project, by which the fundamental human drive to regain awareness of our true nature, Atman, is displaced by the craving for objects and experiences. As Wilber puts it, "When applied to the separate self, the intuition that one *is* the All is perverted into the desire to *possess* All. In place of *being* everything, one merely desires to *have* everything. That is the basis of substitute gratifications, and that is the insatiable thirst lying in the soul of all separate selves."[7] But since we can never get enough of what we don't really want, any substitute—be it money, sex, power, or prestige—results in inevitable frustration and suffering.

If addictive craving can reflect a lack of transpersonal experience, it follows that supplying such experiences might be therapeutic. Support for this view comes from several sources. There are many accounts of people—including Bill W., the founder of Alcoholics Anonymous—whose craving ceased when transpersonal experiences began.

Transpersonal practices such as meditation may reduce consumption of both legal and illegal drugs.[8] The success of treatment programs with an explicit spiritual orientation, such as the twelve-step recovery groups, suggests that spirituality can be an important healing factor for some people. However, it must be remembered that spiritually oriented programs can be offputting to other people, some of whom have formed an alternative "Secular Organization for Sobriety." Moreover, contrary to widespread beliefs, there is no evidence that A.A. has a higher cure rate than other treatments, although it certainly reaches more people and is cost-effective.[9]

A transpersonal perspective suggests that addiction may be a much more pervasive source of suffering and pathology than most people previously appreciated. As psychiatrist Arthur Deikman put it, "It is hard to find a neurotic symptom or a human vice that cannot be traced to the desire to possess or the fear of loss."[10] Of course, this is hardly a new insight, being one of the central claims of the world's wisdom traditions, which argue that

You are deceived by your addiction to and desire for sensuous objects,
As is the moth by the flame of a lamp.[11]

The Buddha summarized the situation succinctly in the second noble truth, which states, "The cause of suffering is craving."

A transpersonal perspective may therefore shed light on the nature, cause, and treatment of addiction. It suggests that addiction to food and drugs—which is more or less the extent of addiction recognized by Western society and mainstream psychology—may be merely the tip of a far more profound and pervasive dynamic. Addiction may underlie a vast range of human suffering. It may be universal rather than individual in frequency, existential rather than only circumstantial in origin, ontological rather than only psychological in its foundation. If this is the case, any enduring cure may need to be existential and transpersonal as well as pharmacological and behavioral.

In summary, a transpersonal perspective offers new diagnostic, etiological, and therapeutic insights into a variety of clinical issues. Diagnostically, it recognizes a number of new (to Western psychologists) clinical syndromes and warns against misdiagnosing and pathologizing them by forcing them into traditional diagnostic categories. Etiologically, it suggests that transpersonal causative factors may have been overlooked in disorders such as addiction and spiritual emergencies. Therapeutically, it argues that transpersonal crises may be potentially beneficial if worked with psychotherapeutically rather than pathologized and aborted. Finally, it suggests that the failure to recognize and satisfy our transpersonal nature and needs may underlie much of the individual, cultural, and global suffering that surrounds us.

The papers in this chapter span the range of transpersonal clinical problems. First are two essays by Christina and Stanislav Grof. In their classic paper "Spiritual Emergency: The Understanding and Treatment of Transpersonal Crises," which marked the founding of a new clinical field, they review the varieties, causes, and treatments of transpersonal crises. In "Addiction as Spiritual Emergency" they examine ways in which addiction can mask, or lead to, a spiritual emergency and the implications for understanding and treating addictions.

There is a disastrously widespread belief that spiritual teachers are entirely free of the neuroses that bedevil the rest of us. While transpersonal experiences and development may remove, or at least attenuate, some psychopathology, it remains unclear which dimensions of personality and pathology are transformed and which remain untouched and problematic. Here, then, is a major field for future transpersonal research. Georg Feuerstein examines these issues in "The Shadow of the Enlightened Guru." Finally, in "The Spectrum of Pathologies," Ken Wilber reviews the difficulties that can arise at specific stages of transpersonal development.

❏

20

Spiritual Emergency: The Understanding and Treatment of Transpersonal Crises

Christina Grof and Stanislav Grof

There exists increasing evidence that many individuals experiencing episodes of nonordinary states of consciousness are undergoing an evolutionary crisis rather than suffering from a mental disease. The recognition of this fact has important practical and theoretical consequences. If properly understood and treated as difficult stages in a natural developmental process, these experiences—spiritual emergencies or transpersonal crises—can result in emotional and psychosomatic healing, creative problem-solving, personality transformation, and consciousness evolution. This fact is reflected in the term "spiritual emergency," which suggests a crisis, but also suggests the potential for rising to a higher state of being.

Traditional psychiatry does not recognize the difference between mystical and psychotic experiences. All unusual states of consciousness are essentially seen as pathological. There is no acknowledgment that any dramatic experiential states involving changes of consciousness could be potentially therapeutic and transformative. Psychiatry thus routinely and indiscriminately uses controlling and suppressive approaches to terminate such experiences. However, in the case of transpersonal crises, insensitive use of repressive measures can lead to chronicity and long-term dependence on tranquilizing medication or other pharmaceuticals with ensuing serious side effects and impoverishment of personality. It seems, therefore, extremely important to clarify theoretically the concept of transpersonal crises and to develop comprehensive and effective approaches to their treatment.

Spiritual emergencies (transpersonal crises) can occur spontaneously without any precipitating factors, or they can be triggered by emotional stress, physical exertion, disease, accident, intense sexual experience, childbirth, psychedelic drugs, or various meditative practices.

Supportive evidence for the concept of spiritual emergency can be drawn from a variety of fields: history, anthropology, comparative religion, clinical psychiatry, modern consciousness research, psychedelic therapy, Jungian psychology, new experiential psychotherapies, and many others.

It is important to emphasize that not every experience of unusual states of consciousness and intense perceptual, emotional, cognitive, and psychosomatic changes falls into the category of spiritual emergency. Many mental disorders are directly related to brain dysfunctions or diseases of other organs and systems of the body. A good medical and psychiatric examination is, therefore, a necessary prerequisite for any alternative therapeutic considerations. Even purely psychological work with people whose problems are not primarily of a medical nature can result in difficulties that require medical considerations. Here belong, for example, a concern for proper nutrition, supply of minerals and vitamins, adequate rest, and prevention of dehydration.

The following are the important criteria suggesting that a person might be experiencing a spiritual emergency and can be offered alternative treatment:

1. Episodes of unusual experiences that involve changes in consciousness and in perceptual, emotional, cognitive, and psychosomatic

functioning, in which there is a significant transpersonal emphasis in the process, such as dramatic death and (re)birth sequences, mythological and archetypal phenomena.
2. Absence of a gross organic brain disorder.
3. Absence of a physical disease of another organ or system which is responsible for the mental disorder.
4. Reasonably good general somatic and cardiovascular condition allowing the client to safely endure physical and emotional stress frequently associated with the experiential work and with the uncovering strategy.
5. The ability to see the condition as an inner psychological process and approach it in an internalized way; the capacity to form an adequate working relationship.
6. Absence of a long history of conventional psychiatric treatment and hospitalization, which generally tends to make the application of the new approaches much more difficult.

FORMS OF SPIRITUAL EMERGENCY

All forms of transpersonal crisis can be seen as dynamic exteriorizations of deep unconscious and superconscious realms of the human psyche, which form one indivisible, multidimensional continuum without any clear boundaries. It is, therefore, obvious that a sharp demarcation of various types of spiritual emergency is in practice not possible.

However, we feel that it is possible and useful to distinguish several major experiential patterns which are particularly frequent. Although they often overlap, each has characteristic features

1. Awakening of the serpent power (Kundalini)
2. Shamanic journey
3. Psychological renewal through activation of the central archetype
4. Psychic opening
5. Emergence of a karmic pattern
6. Possession states

Awakening of the Serpent Power (Kundalini)

According to the Hindu and Buddhist Tantric schools, Kundalini is the creative energy of the universe and is female in nature. In her external aspect, she is manifest in the phenomenal world. In her internal aspect, she lies dormant at the base of the human spine; in this form, she is traditionally symbolically represented as a serpent coiled three-and-a-half times. Activated by spiritual practice, by contact with a guru, or spontaneously, it rises in the form of active energy, or *Shakti*, up the conduits in the subtle body called *nadis*, opening, clearing, and lighting the psychic centers, or *chakras*.

Although not without dangers and pitfalls, the arousal of Kundalini is seen, in general, as potentially conducive to psychosomatic healing, positive restructuring of the personality, and consciousness evolution. However, because of its extraordinary power, the scriptures treat this process very seriously and recommend the guidance of an experienced teacher for people involved in it.

Kundalini awakening can be accompanied by dramatic physical and psychological manifestations called *kriyas*. The most striking among these are powerful sensations of heat and energy streaming up the spine, associated with tremors, spasms, violent shaking, and complex twisting movements. Quite common also is involuntary laughing or crying, chanting of mantras or songs, talking in tongues, emitting of vocal noises and animal sounds, and assuming spontaneous yogic gestures (*mudras*) and postures (*asanas*).

The individual can see geometric patterns, bright radiant lights, and complex visions of saints, deities, demons, and entire mythological sequences. Acoustic phenomena include a variety of sounds. The emotional manifestations of Kundalini awakening range from ecstasy, orgastic raptures, and states of indescribable peace and tranquillity, to waves of depression, anxiety, and agitation bordering on feelings of insanity and/or death.

The process of Kundalini awakening can simulate many psychiatric disorders and medical problems. Intimate knowledge of the Kundalini syndrome is essential for the clinician to make a correct differential diagnosis.

Shamanic Journey

Transpersonal crises of this type bear a deep resemblance to what the anthropologists have described as the *shamanic* or *initiatory illness*. It is a dramatic episode of a nonordinary state of consciousness that marks the beginning of the career of many shamans.

The core experience of the shamanic journey is a profound encounter with death and subsequent rebirth. Initiatory dreams and visions include a descent into the underworld under the guidance of ancestral spirits, attacks by demons, exposure to unimaginable emotional and physical tortures, and finally complete annihilation. This is then typically followed by sequences of rebirth and ascent to supernal realms. Although there exist considerable variations in the details of these ordeals among different tribes and individual shamans, they all share the general atmosphere of horror and inhuman suffering.

In the experiences of individuals whose transpersonal crises have strong shamanic features, there is great emphasis on physical suffering and encounter with death followed by rebirth and elements of ascent or magical flight. They also typically sense a special connection with the elements of nature. It is also not unusual to feel an upsurge of extraordinary powers and impulses to heal.

A good integration of the "shamanic illness" and adequate functioning in everyday life are indispensable conditions for being accepted as a shaman. Like the initiatory crisis, the transpersonal episodes of a shamanic type, if properly supported, can lead to good adjustment and superior functioning in certain areas.

Psychological Renewal Through Activation of the Central Archetype

This type of transpersonal crisis has been explored by the Jungian analyst John Weir Perry. In his clinical work with young psychotic patients, if sensitive support was provided, the nature of the psychopathological development was drastically transformed and what resulted was emotional healing, psychological renewal, and deep transformation of the patients' personalities.

Individuals in this type of crisis experience themselves as being in the middle of the world process or being the center of all things, which Perry attributes to the activation of what he calls the *central archetype*. They are preoccupied with death and the themes of ritual killing, martyrdom, crucifixion, and afterlife. Another important theme is the return to beginnings of the world, to creation, the original paradisean state, or the first ancestor.

These experiences typically focus on some cataclysmic clash of opposite forces on a global or even cosmic level that has the quality of a sacred combat, or in the mundane form of protagonists—capitalists and communists, Americans and Russians, the white and yellow races, or secret societies against the rest of the world. The archetypal form of this conflict involves the forces of light and darkness, Christ and Antichrist or the Devil, Armageddon, and the Apocalypse.

A characteristic element of this process is preoccupation with the reversal of opposites. This is expressed particularly strongly in the sexual area. It involves intense misgiving with regard to the opposite sex, homosexual wishes or panic, and fear of the other sex or gender reversal. These problems find their resolution typically in the theme of the union of opposites, particularly the Sacred Marriage (hierosgamos). This union is of a mythological nature, an archetypal fusion of the feminine and masculine aspects of one's personality.

This process culminates in an apotheosis, an experience of being raised to a highly exalted status. This is often associated with a sense of new birth or rebirth, the other side of the all-important theme of death.

Perry's work clearly demonstrates the paramount significance of the archetypal process reenacted in this type of transpersonal crisis and the need to treat these states with respect. Properly understood and supported, they have healing and transformative potential. They can lead to a positive restructuring of personality and to a psychological and spiritual renewal.

Psychic Opening

A transpersonal crisis of this type is characterized by a striking accumulation of instances of extrasensory perception (ESP) and other parapsychological manifestations. In acute phases of such a process, the individual can literally be flooded by extraordinary paranormal occurrences. Among these are various forms of out-of-the-body experiences.

Many spiritual traditions describe emergence of paranormal abilities as a common and particularly tricky stage of consciousness evolution. It is considered essential not to become fascinated by the new abilities and interpret them in terms of one's own uniqueness. The danger of what Jung called "inflation of the ego" is probably greater here than with any other type of spiritual crisis.

However, in our culture, which tends to accept uncritically the pragmatically successful but simplistic worldview of mechanistic science, the opposite danger might be even more relevant. In this situation, many people tend to interpret experiences of telepathy, clairvoyance, or synchronicity as signs of self-deception or even insanity, because contemporary science denies the possibility of their existence.

Emergence of a Karmic Pattern

In a fully developed form of this type of transpersonal crisis, the individual experiences dramatic sequences that seem to be occurring in a different temporal or spatial context, in another historical period and another country. These experiences can be quite realistic and are accompanied by strong negative or positive emotions and intense physical sensations. The person involved typically has a convinced feeling of retrieving these events from memory, reliving episodes from his or her own previous incarnations. In addition, specific aspects of such sequences suddenly seem to throw a new light on various emotional, psychosomatic, and interpersonal problems of the person's present life, which were previously obscure and incomprehensible.

Full experience and good integration of past life sequences typically have dramatic therapeutic effects. Emotional, psychosomatic, and interpersonal problems can be drastically alleviated or disappear after a powerful karmic sequence. For this reason, therapists should recognize this phenomenon and utilize it, irrespective of their own belief system or the historical truth of such sequences.

Possession States

This transpersonal crisis can occur in the context of experiential psychotherapy, psychedelic treatment, or as a spontaneous development in the life of the individual.

Whether this archetype of evil emerges in a working session or in the conditions of everyday life, the individual typically identifies the energy involved as demonic and tries to suppress it by all means. A latent pattern of this kind can underlie serious psychopathology such as suicidal depression, murderous aggression, impulses for antisocial behavior, or craving for alcohol and drugs. Such manifestations often alienate relatives, friends, and even professionals.

The resolution of this problem requires support from people who are not afraid of the uncanny nature of the experiences and who can facilitate full emergence and exteriorization of the archetypal pattern.

The resolution often happens after dramatic sequences of choking, projectile vomiting, or frantic motor behavior with temporary loss of control. With good support, experiences of this kind can be extremely liberating and therapeutic. Recently, the interest of professionals in this phenomenon was rekindled by the study of multiple personalities.

THERAPEUTIC ASSISTANCE IN TRANSPERSONAL CRISES

The first and most important task for the facilitator working with individuals in transpersonal crises is to establish a good trusting relationship with the client. On this basis it is then possible to mediate a new understanding of the process the client is involved in and to convey respect for its healing and transforming nature. This approach is diametrically opposed to the traditional psychiatric strategy that uses pathological labels and an indiscriminate suppressive approach for all nonordinary states of consciousness. The basic principle of the new strategy is to support the process and to cooperate with it in order to utilize its positive potential.

It is of critical importance for the positive outcome of transpersonal crises that the client recognizes the intrapsychic nature of the unusual experiences.

The degree of help that is needed depends on the nature, depth, and intensity of the process. Some individuals are bewildered and puzzled by their experiences but can operate in everyday life to some extent. In situations like this, a new understanding, recommendation of pertinent literature, and occasional supportive discussions facilitating integration of unusual experiences might be sufficient.

The general strategy here is to create situations in the everyday life where it is possible to fully confront the emerging material, such as periods of meditation or introspective experiencing facilitated by music. This seems to clear the remaining time in everyday life from the intrusion of unconscious elements. Conversely, it is possible to use techniques that slow down the process, if the circumstances require full attendance to practical tasks. Among these are heavier diet, drinking of beverages containing large amounts of sugar or honey, intense physical exercise such as jogging, hiking, swimming, or garden work, avoidance of stressful and over-stimulating situations, discontinuation of any spiritual practice, and in the extreme, occasional use of minor tranquilizers as a temporary measure.

If the process is so intense that it interferes with everyday life, even if the above measures have been tried, it might be necessary to offer regular experiential sessions, where the process is facilitated with the use of various uncovering techniques that have been developed by humanistic and trans-personal psychologies, or by different spiritual traditions of the world. Of these, Gestalt practice, psychosynthesis, Jungian active imagination and mandala drawing, certain neo-Reichian approaches, focused body work, and the use of music and expressive movement seem to be particularly useful.

In all the stages of the process, artistic expression, such as mandala drawing, psychodrama, expressive dancing and movement, and creative writing can be extremely useful.

❏

21

Addiction as Spiritual Emergency

Christina Grof and Stanislav Grof

It is possible that for many people, behind the craving for drugs or alcohol is the craving for transcendence or wholeness. If this is so, then drug and alcohol dependency, as well as the multitude of other kinds of addiction, may be in many cases forms of spiritual emergency. Addiction differs from other forms of transformative crisis in that the spiritual dimension is often obscured by the apparent destructive and self-destructive nature of the disease. In other varieties of spiritual emergencies, people encounter problems because of spiritual or mystical states of mind. In contrast, during addiction many difficulties occur because the quest for the deeper dimensions within is not being carried out.

Alcoholics and other addicts describe their decline into the depths of addiction as "spiritual bankruptcy" or "soul sickness," and the healing of their impoverished soul as "rebirth." Since many spiritual emergencies follow this same trajectory, many lessons in assistance during transformation crises can be learned from successful alcohol and drug-abuse treatment programs.

For many people, behind the craving for drugs, alcohol, or other addictions is the craving for the Higher Self or God. Many recovering people will talk about their restless search for some unknown missing piece in their lives and will describe their vain pursuit of a multitude of substances, foods, relationships, possessions, or powerful positions in an effort to fulfill their unrewarded craving. In retrospect, they acknowledge that there was a tragic confusion, a misperception that told them that the answers lay outside themselves.

Some even describe the first drink or drug as their first spiritual experience, a state in which individual boundaries are melted and everyday pain disappears, taking them into a state of pseudo-unity, as acknowledged by William James in the following passage from *The Varieties of Religious Experience*:

> The sway of alcohol over mankind is unquestionably due to its power to stimulate the mystical faculties of human nature, usually crushed to earth by the cold facts and dry criticisms of the sober hour.

After hitting bottom with their disease and becoming part of a spiritual recovery program, recovering addicts will exclaim, "This is what I was looking for!" Their newfound clarity and connection with a Higher Power and with other human beings offers them the unitive state that they had been seeking, and the insatiable yearning diminishes.

For many people, drug and alcohol dependency and other addictions are forms of spiritual emergency. As with many other forms of spiritual emergency, the journey of the addict or alcoholic to the bottom and into recovery is often an ego-death and rebirth process.

During the ego death, whether it occurs in an episode of spontaneous spiritual awakening or at the bottom of an individual's drinking career, everything that one is or was—all relationships and reference points, all rationalizations and protections—collapse, and the person is left naked, with nothing but the core of his or her being.

From this state of absolute, terrifying surrender, there is nowhere to go but up. As part of the rebirth that follows this devastating death, one easily opens to a spiritually oriented existence during which the practice of service becomes an essential impulse. Many people are surprised to find a constant, unending benevolent source within that offers them strength and guidance. They develop the insight that life without spirituality is trivial and unfulfilling.

The key to this redemption has been the complete surrender of the illusion that one is in control of one's life and the acceptance of help from a Higher Power.

Bill Wilson, the cofounder of Alcoholics Anonymous, spoke and wrote eloquently about alcoholism and the need for the spiritual dimension in recovery. Wilson's transformation began in a hospital room, where, desperately sick, he received medical treatment after one of his many binges. His biographer writes:

> Now, there was nothing ahead but death or madness. This was the finish, the jumping-off place. "The terrifying darkness had become complete," Bill said. . . . In his helplessness and desperation, Bill cried out, "I'll do anything, anything at all!" He had reached . . . a state of complete, absolute surrender. . . . He cried, "If there be a God, let Him show Himself!"
>
> [Wilson's words follow:] "Suddenly, my room blazed with an indescribably white light. I was seized with an ecstasy beyond description . . . I stood upon [the summit of a mountain], where a great wind blew. A wind, not of air, but of spirit. In great, clean strength, it blew right through me. Then came the blazing thought, 'You are a free man.' . . . [A] great peace stole over me and . . . I became acutely conscious of a Presence which seemed like a veritable sea of living spirit. I lay on the shores of a new world. . . . For the first time, I felt that I really belonged. I knew that I was loved and could love in return."

Bill Wilson never drank again.

❏
22

The Shadow of the Enlightened Guru

Georg Feuerstein

That the personality of enlightened beings and advanced mystics remains largely intact is obvious when one examines biographies and autobiographies of adepts, past and present. Each one manifests specific psychological qualities, as determined by his or her genetics and life history. Some are inclined toward passivity, others are spectacularly dynamic. Some are gentle, others fierce. Some have no interest in learning, others are great scholars. What these awakened beings have in common is that they no longer identify with the personality complex, however it may be configured, but live out of the identity of the Self. Enlightenment, then, consists in the transcendence of the ego-habit, but enlightment does *not* obliterate the personality.

[This] raises the crucial question of whether enlightenment also leaves untouched traits that in the unenlightened individual might be called neurotic. I believe that this is so. If they are true teachers, their overriding purpose can be expected to be the communication of the transcendental Reality. Yet, their behavior is, in the outside world, always a matter of personal style. Devotees, of course, like to think that their ideal guru is free from whims and that apparent idiosyncrasies must be for the sake of teaching others. But a moment's reflection would show this to be based in fantasy and projection.

The personality of the adept is, to be sure, oriented toward self-transcendence rather than self-fulfillment. However, it is characteristically not on a self-actualizing trajectory. I use *self-actualization* here in a more restricted sense than it was intended by Abraham Maslow: as the intention toward realizing psychic wholeness based on the integration of the shadow. The shadow, in Jungian terms, is the dark aspect of the personality, the aggregate of repressed materials.

The traditional spiritual paths are by and large grounded in the vertical ideal of liberation *from* the conditioning of the body-mind. Therefore, they focus on what is conceived to be the ultimate good—transcendental

Being. This spiritual single-mindedness jars the human psyche out of focus: its personal concerns become insignificant and its structures are viewed as something to be transcended as quickly as possible rather than transformed. Of course, all self-transcending methods involve a degree of self-transformation. But, as a rule, this does not entail a concerted effort to work with the shadow and accomplish psychic integration. This may explain why so many mystics and adepts are highly eccentric and authoritarian and appear socially to have weakly integrated personalities.

Unlike transcendence, integration occurs in the horizontal plane. It extends the ideal of wholeness to the conditional personality and its social nexus. Yet, integration makes sense only when the conditional personality and the conditional world are not treated as irrevocable opponents of the ultimate Reality but are valued as manifestations of it. Having discovered the Divine in the depths of his or her own soul, the adept must then find the Divine in all life.

❑

23

The Spectrum of Pathologies

Ken Wilber

PSYCHIC DISORDERS

By "psychic pathology" I mean specifically all the spiritual crises and pathologies that may (1) awaken *spontaneously*; (2) invade any of the lower levels of development during periods of severe stress (e.g., psychotic episodes); and (3) beset the *beginning* practitioner of a contemplative discipline.

1. Spontaneous

The most dramatic psychic pathology occurs in the spontaneous and usually unsought awakening of spiritual-psychic energies or capacities. At best, these crises are annoying; at worst, they can be devastating. The awakening of Kundalini, for instance, can be psychological dynamite.

2. Psychotic-like Episodes

One of the most puzzling aspects of transient schizophrenic breaks or psychotic-like episodes is that they often channel rather profound spiritual insights, but they do so through a self-structure that is neurotic, borderline, or even frankly psychotic (particularly paranoid schizophrenic).

3. Beginning Practitioner

Psychic pathologies besetting the novitiate include:

a. *Psychic inflation.* The universal-transpersonal energies and insights of the psychic level are exclusively applied to the individual ego, with extremely unbalancing results (particularly if there are narcissistic residues).

b. *Structural imbalance due to faulty practice of the spiritual technique.* This is particularly common in the paths of purification and purgation; in Kriya and Charya Yoga, and in the more subtle techniques, such as mantrayana. It usually manifests in mild, free-floating anxiety, or in psychosomatic conversion symptoms (headaches, minor heart arrhythmia, intestinal discomfort, etc.).

c. *The Dark Night of the Soul.* Once experience of the Divine begins to fade (which it initially does), the soul may suffer a profound abandonment depression (*not* to be confused with borderline, neurotic, or existential depression).

d. *Split life-goals.* For example, "Do I stay in the world or retreat to meditation?" This can be extremely painful and psychologically paralyzing. It expresses one form of a profound splitting between upper and lower self-needs.

e. *"Pseudo-duhkha."* In certain paths of meditation (e.g., Vipassana), the early phase of awareness training brings a growing realization of the painful nature of manifest existence itself. Where this realization becomes overwhelming we speak of "pseudo-duhkha." Pseudo-duhkha is often the result of residual existential, psychoneurotic, or, more often, residual borderline contamination. The individual does not gain an understanding of the sourness of life; he or she simply goes sour on life.

f. *Pranic disorders.* This refers to a misdirection of Kundalini energy in the early stages of its arousal. Various psychic (pranic) channels are over- or underdeveloped, crossed, or prematurely opened, e.g., "windhorse" (*rlung*) disorders in Tibetan Buddhism. Pranic disorders are usually caused by improper visualization and concentration. Dramatic psychosomatic symptoms are usually prevalent, including barely controllable muscle spasms, violent headache, breathing difficulty, etc.

g. *"Yogic illness" (Aurobindo).* This disorder, according to Aurobindo, results when the development of the higher or psychic levels of consciousness puts an undue strain on the physical-emotional body, resulting (according to Aurobindo) in everything from allergies to intestinal problems to heart disorders.

SUBTLE DISORDERS

The emergence of the subtle basic structure of consciousness brings with it the possibility of subtle level self-development: a new mode of self, with new object-relations, new motivations, new forms of life, new forms of death—and new forms of possible pathology.

The two vulnerable points concern: (1) the differentiation-separation-transcendence of the previous mental-psychic dimension, and (2) the identification-integration-consolidation of the subtle-archetypal self and its object relations. Apparently, this pathology occurs most often in intermediate-to-advanced meditators. Some of its many forms:

1. Integration-Identification Failure

The subtle basic structure—which is conceived and perceived by different paths as a Being, a Force, an Insight, a Deity-Form, or a self-luminous Presence (all of which, for simplicity's sake, are referred to as Archetypal Presence or Awareness)—is first apprehended, to put it metaphorically, "above and behind" mental-psychic consciousness. Eventually, as contemplation deepens, the self differentiates from its psychic moorings and ascends to an intuited-identification with that Ground, Insight, Archetypal Presence or Awareness. Gradually we realize that the Divine Form or Presence is our own archetype, an image of our own essential nature. This Identity arises concomitantly with a stable *witnessing* of the object relations of subtle consciousness—infinite space, audible illuminations (*nada*), Brahma realms of ascended knowledge. A *failure* to realize this Prior Identity-Awareness, *after* the practitioner is in fact structurally capable of it, is the central defining pathology of these syndromes, because it constitutes, at that point, a fracture between self and Archetype; in Christian terms, a pathology of the soul.

This fracture arises for one basic reason: to identify with and as Archetypal Presence or Awareness demands the *death* of the mental-psychic self. Rather than suffer this humiliation, the self *contracts* on its own separate being, thus fracturing the higher and prior archetypal identity.

2. Pseudo-nirvana

This is simply the mistaking of subtle or archetypal forms, illuminations, raptures, ecstasies, insights, or absorptions for final liberation. This is not a pathology unless one is in fact pursuing causal or ultimate levels of consciousness, in which case the *entire* subtle realm and all its experiences, if clung to, are considered pathological, "makyo," subtle illusions—Zen actually calls it the "Zen sickness."

3. Pseudo-realization

This is the subtle-level equivalent of pseudo-duhkha on the psychic. As Vipassana meditation proceeds into the subtle levels of awareness, a stage of insight called "realization" arises. *Every* content of consciousness appears terrifying, oppressive, disgusting, painful, and loathesome; there is extreme physical pain and intense mental-psychic discomfort. However, this is not the pathology of this stage, but is *normalcy* at this stage, which involves an intense insight into the ultimately unsatisfactory nature of phenomena when viewed apart from noumenon. This intense pain and revulsion acts as the motivation to transcend all conceivable manifestation in nirvanic absorption. The pseudo-realization pathology occurs when that process fails to quicken and the soul is stranded on the shores of its own agony. It does seem that this pathology, in deep structure form, is identical to what was previously called a failure to engage Archetypal Awareness and its stable witnessing of all subtle-level object relations.

CAUSAL DISORDERS

The last major fulcrum of self-development has, for its two branches, the Formless or Unmanifest, and the entire world of Form, or the Manifest Realm. Normal development involves their proper differentiation (in the causal) and their final integration (in the ultimate). Pathology, on the other hand, results from miscarriages in either of these two crucial movements.

1. Failure of Differentiation

An inability to accept the final death of the archetypal self (which is simply the subtlest level of the separate-self sense) locks consciousness into an attachment to some aspect of the manifest realm. The Great Death never occurs, and thus Formless Consciousness fails to differentiate from or transcend the manifest realm, blocked by the subtlest contracting, grasping, seeking, or desiring; the final block: desire for liberation.

2. Failure to Integrate, or Arhat's Disease

Consciousness manages to differentiate itself from *all* objects of consciousness, or the entire manifest realm, to the extent that no objects even arise in awareness (*jnana samadhi, nirvikalpa samadhi, nirvana*). Although this is the "final" goal of some paths, in fact a subtle disjuncture, dualism, or tension now exists in consciousness, namely, between the manifest and the unmanifest realms. Only as this disjuncture is penetrated does the manifest realm arise as a modification of Consciousness, not a distraction from it. This is classic *sahaj-bhava samadhi*. I have read no text, nor heard of any sage, that speaks of a level beyond this.

❑

THE QUEST FOR WHOLENESS:
TRANSPERSONAL THERAPIES

*Psychotherapy is the art, science and practice of studying
the nature of consciousness and of what may reduce or
facilitate it.*

—JAMES BUGENTAL[1]

PYCHOTHERAPIES REFLECT underlying assumptions about human nature that guide the choice of therapeutic goals and techniques. Since the transpersonal view of human nature is so encompassing, its view of therapy is similarly broad. Consequently, most transpersonal therapists assume that no one therapeutic strategy or technique can address all psychological problems, dimensions, or levels. Different therapies and techniques are therefore usually regarded as potentially complementary rather than necessarily conflictual. Each makes a unique contribution, and the therapeutic task is to recognize the strengths, limits, and optimal area of application of each approach. Transpersonal therapists therefore seek to blend the best of mainstream work with transpersonal perspectives and techniques, drawing on each as appropriate to match the unique needs of individual clients.

Since transpersonal therapy is so inclusive, training for it needs to be similarly inclusive. There has been an understandable reluctance to establish standards in a young, growing field that encourages diversity, experimentation, and transconventional values. As the field grows, however, so does the need for clinical training guidelines, and the following guidelines are therefore offered as a basis for discussion. They include conventional training and accreditation, transpersonal training, experiential work in psychotherapy and a transpersonal discipline, and ethical standards.

Conventional training requires a degree in a mental health discipline and clinical licensing. Transpersonal clinical training requires knowledge of transpersonal theory, diagnostic issues, therapies, and supervised clinical work. A good knowledge of spiritual issues and problems is essential. Such issues arise commonly in the course of psychotherapy, but very few therapists are trained to deal with them.[2]

The ability to do in-depth psychological and transpersonal work with clients depends on the depth of the therapist's own explorations. Therefore, for transpersonal therapists, undergoing their own in-depth, transpersonally oriented psychotherapy and long-term practice of transersonal disciplines such as yoga or meditation are invaluable. Ideally, such disciplines are part of a lifetime practice of deepening transpersonal exploration.

Ethical criteria include conventional professional standards. However, these serve as a starting point rather than a final goal, since exceptional ethical sensitivity is essential for fostering transpersonal growth.

These are obviously demanding requirements, perhaps more demanding than those of any other school of psychotherapy. But just as transpersonal growth demands much of those who seek it, so too it demands much of those who would foster it in others. To help others transform we must first transform ourselves. In the words of the Buddha:

> To straighten the crooked
> You must first do a harder thing—
> Straighten yourself.[3]

In psychotherapy in general, and particularly in transpersonal psychotherapy, the therapeutic relationship is the medium in which healing occurs. Theoretical study, clinical training, and inner exploration are the means by which the capacity to be a healing presence is refined. This process of refinement is the therapist's life-long task and a gift to clients. For as Ram Dass says:

> What one person has to offer to another,
> is their own being, nothing more, nothing less.[4]

In this section Ken Wilber continues his survey of the spectrum of transpersonal development and pathology with "The Spectrum of Therapies," in which he outlines therapeutic approaches to problems at each of the major transpersonal stages. Frances Vaughan provides an overview of transpersonal psychotherapy, while Bryan Wittine identifies its underlying core assumptions. Finally, Michael Murphy calls for the creation of "integral practices" that draw from diverse therapies and disciplines and foster a balanced development of body, heart, and mind.

24

The Spectrum of Therapies

Ken Wilber

PSYCHIC PATHOLOGY

Contemplative development in general possesses three broad levels or stages (beginning, intermediate, and advanced); different tasks and capacities emerge at each level; different distortions, pathologies, or disorders may therefore occur at each level; and these distortions or pathologies may best be treated by different types of "spiritual" therapy (some of which may also benefit from adjunct conventional therapies).

1. Spontaneous

For pathology resulting from spontaneous and unsought awakening of spiritual-psychic energies or insights, there seem to be only two general treatment modalities: the individual must either "ride it out," sometimes under the care of a conventional psychiatrist who may interpret it as a borderline or psychotic break and prescribe medication, which often freezes the process and prevents any further reparative developments; or the individual can *consciously* engage this process by taking up a contemplative discipline. If the spontaneous awakening is of the kundalini itself, the Path of Yogis is most appropriate, and for a specific reason: Paths which aim for the higher subtle and causal realms contain very little explicit teachings on the stages of psychic-kundalini awakening (e.g., one will look in vain through the texts of Zen, Eckhart, St. John of the Cross, etc., for any mention or understanding of kundalini). If at all possible, the individual should be put in touch with a qualified yogic adept, who can work, if desired, in conjunction with a more conventional therapist.

2. Psychotic-like

For genuinely psychotic or psychotic-like episodes with periodic but distorted spiritual components, Jungian therapy may be suggested. A contemplative discipline is usually contraindicated; these disciplines demand a sturdy ego which the psychotic or borderline does not possess. After a sufficient period of structure-building, the individual may wish to engage in the less strenuous contemplative paths (e.g., mantrayana).

3. Beginning Practitioner

a. *Psychic inflation.* This can often be handled with a subtler version of "optimal disillusionment," a continual separation of psychic fact from narcissistic fantasies. If this repeatedly fails, it is usually because a psychic insight has reactivated a narcissistic-borderline or even psychotic residue. At that point, meditation should usually be stopped immediately and, if necessary, structure-building engaged (either psychoanalytic or Jungian). If the individual responds to these, and eventually can understand the how and why of his psychic inflation, meditation can usually be resumed.

b. *Structural imbalance (due to faulty practice of the spiritual technique).* The individual should verify this with the meditation teacher; these imbalances, which are not uncommon, point up how extremely important it is to undertake contemplative disciplines only under guidance of a qualified master.

c. *Dark Night of the Soul.* Reading accounts of how others have weathered this phase can be very helpful. In periods of profound despair, the soul may break into petitionary, as opposed to contemplative, prayer (to Jesus, Mary, Kwannon, Allah, etc.); this need not be discouraged—it is prayer to one's own higher Archetype. The Dark Night literature contains virtually no cases of it leading to suicide (in sharp contrast to existential or borderline depressions, for example). It is as if the depression of the Dark Night had a "higher" or "purgatorial" or "intelligent" purpose—and this, of course, is exactly the claim of contemplatives.

d. *Split-life goals.* It is important (particularly in our society, and particularly at this point in evolution) that one's spiritual practice be integrated into daily life and work (as a bodhisattvic endeavor). In my opinion, the path of ascetic withdrawal all too often introduces a profound split between the upper and lower dimensions of existence, and, in general, confuses suppression of earthly life with transcendence of earthly life.

e. *Pseudo-duhkha.* The teacher is sometimes the worst person to consult in these particular cases. Spiritual teachers generally have no knowledge of the dynamics of borderline or psychoneurotic disorders, and their advice may be "Intensify your effort!" which is precisely what triggered the problem in the first place. In most cases, the meditator should cease all meditation for a few months.

f. *Pranic disorders.* These disorders are notorious for inducing hysterical-like conversion symptoms which, if left untreated, may induce genuine psychosomatic disease. They are best handled in conjunction with the yogic meditation teacher (and a physician if needed).

g. *Yogic illness.* The best "cure" is also the best prevention: strengthening and purifying the physical-emotional body: exercise, lactovegetarian diet, restricted intake of caffeine, sugar, nicotine, and social drugs.

SUBTLE PATHOLOGY

1. Integration-Identification Failure

The author is not aware of any treatment modality for this pathology except to engage (or intensify) the path of subtle-level contemplation, which, at this point, usually *begins* to involve some form of *inquiry*, overt or covert, into the *contraction* that constitutes the separate-self sense. It is said to be an actual *seeing* of that contraction, which is blocking subtle or archetypal awareness, and *not* a direct attempt to identify with archetypal awareness itself, that constitutes the therapeutic treatment.

2. Pseudo-nirvana

Many of the most sophisticated contemplative traditions have numerous "checking routines" that help the practitioner review the ecstatic, luminous, blissful, and "tempting" subtle experiences and thus eventually gain a distancing or nonattached stance towards this archetypal level.

3. Pseudo-realization

Unlike pseudo-duhkha, which usually demands a halting of meditation, there is usually no cure for pseudo-realization except more meditation. The only thing more painful than continuing meditation is failing to continue meditation. Zen refers to this particular type of "Zen sickness" as being like "swallowing a red-hot iron ball"; it is apparently one of the few *disorders* for which one can *therapeutically* say, "Intensify your efforts!"

With most subtle-level pathologies, it apparently is not too late for adjunct psychotherapy, if, and only if, the therapist is sympathetic towards, and reasonably knowledgeable about, transcendental or spiritual concerns. The psychotherapeutic freeing of repressed emotional energies, for example, might be the crucial boost needed to negotiate subtle-level integration.

CAUSAL PATHOLOGY

1. Failure to Differentiate

This final differentiation or detachment (i.e., from all manifest form) involves a subtle but momentous collaboration of the student and the teacher. The student, in the final and root form of the separate-self sense (archetypal self), is still resisting the final and total dissolution of the separate-self sense. The student and teacher "together," through an "effortless effort," release this stance. This "fall" into formless, unmanifest cessation or emptiness breaks all exclusive attachment to manifest forms and destinies, and Consciousness as Such (or Absolute Subjectivity) differentiates itself from all objects, high or low, and from all archetypal tendencies or root contractions (klesas, vasanas, etc.). Repetition of this "fall"—or repeated "movement" from manifest to unmanifest and back again—"burns" the root inclinations and desires for contracted and separated modes of self existence.

2. Failure to Integrate

This "ultimate pathology"—a failure to integrate the manifest and unmanifest realms—results when the root klesas and vasanas (or archetypal forms and inclinations) are seen *only* as defilements and not also as the means of *expression* or manifestation of unobstructed Wisdom (absolute Spirit or Being). The overcoming of this disjunction and the reunion or reintegration of emptiness-form and wisdom, *is* the "supreme path," the path of "ordinary mind" (Maha Ati), "open eyes" (Free John), and "everyday mind" (Ch'an)—wherein all phenomena, high or low, exactly as they find themselves, are seen as already perfect expressions and seals of the naturally enlightened mind.

□
25

Healing and Wholeness: Transpersonal Psychotherapy

Frances Vaughan

Transpersonal psychotherapy is a healing endeavor that aims at the integration of physical, emotional, mental, and spiritual aspects of well-being. Its goals include the classic ones of normal healthy functioning. The healing potential of transpersonal experiences is affirmed, and spiritual issues are explored from a psychological perspective. Some transpersonal therapists consider caring for the soul to be a major task of psychotherapy.

A transpersonal therapist may employ traditional therapeutic techniques as well as methods derived from spiritual disciplines, such as meditation and mind training. The client may be encouraged to attend to mind-body processes and explore the inner life of the psyche in depth, leading to the discovery of a wealth of inner resources and an innate capacity for self-healing.

In transpersonal therapy, consciousness is both the instrument and the object of change. The work aims not only at changing behavior and the contents of consciousness, but also at developing awareness of consciousness itself as the *context* of experience. Ideally, a transpersonal approach aims at awakening from the consensus trance that perpetuates illusion. Since consciousness is often constricted by egocentric identifications, questions of identity and self-concept may also be explored. Finally, the relationship of the person to society and the natural environment is viewed as an integral part of psychological maturation.

A useful distinction can be made between the *context* of therapy established by the beliefs and values of the therapist; the *content* of therapy, consisting of the client's experience; and the *process* in which both therapist and client participate and through which healing occurs.

A transpersonal context in psychotherapy is established by the therapist who affirms the importance of spiritual issues for psychological health. A therapist who has personally explored the transpersonal domain, experientially as well as intellectually, will therefore be better equipped to assist others who are exploring transpersonal frontiers. Hence, in addition to modeling authenticity as any good therapist may be expected to do, the transpersonal therapist must be willing to attend to his or her own inner work and spiritual practice.

A transpersonal orientation does not invalidate other approaches, any of which may be relevant to different people at different times. It does, however, call for a more expanded context than is usually constructed by conventional approaches. It allows a more inclusive vision of possibility in which a person can let go of the past and live more fully in the present. In light of the perennial wisdom of spiritual teachings, it affirms the possibility of living in harmony with others and the environment, less driven by fear and greed, and motivated by compassion and a sense of purpose.

A transpersonal context implies that the therapist is aware of the centrality of consciousness and perception in determining the outcome of therapy. For example, the healing potential of the therapeutic relationship may be enhanced when the client is perceived by the therapist as potentially creative rather than simply reactive to external circumstances. As the client gradually shifts from being self-identified as a victim to taking a more responsible and creative stance that is based on a realization of personal freedom, the work may focus increasingly on transpersonal issues.

Transpersonal psychotherapy does not focus exclusively on problem solving per se. Like the fisherman who teaches the hungry person how to fish rather than simply providing a fish, the therapist encourages the client to develop a variety of inner resources and problem-solving skills. The therapist also recognizes that there is no one method or technique that will necessarily result in healing for everyone.

The content of transpersonal therapy is the life experience of the client. Since clients with spiritual concerns tend to seek out transpersonal therapists, some of the content may be mythical, archetypal, personal, or transpersonal. When the content is explicitly transpersonal, i.e., when the client is attempting to make sense out of transpersonal experiences, the transpersonal therapist affirms the healing potential of such experiences and does not pathologize, discount, or invalidate them. Conventional approaches that tend to devalue such experiences can contribute to their repression and to subsequent disturbances.[1] This is one reason why it is helpful for transpersonal therapists to be identified in the community.

Carl Jung was one of the first psychotherapists to recognize the value of transpersonal experience. He said, "The fact is that the approach to the numinous is the real therapy and inasmuch as you attain to the numinous experience you are released from the curse of pathology."[2] He also wrote, in a letter to Bill W., the founder of Alcoholics Anonymous, that the "craving for alcohol was the equivalent, on a low level, of the spiritual thirst of our being for wholeness." Recovery from addiction is therefore facilitated by religious experience or "a higher education of the mind beyond the confines of mere rationalism."[3]

Although transpersonal experiences are potentially healing, their effects are often temporary unless an effort is made to stabilize the insight gained. The task of psychotherapy therefore goes beyond the induction of such experiences to the task of integrating them effectively into everyday life. As behaviors, values, and attitudes begin to change, dramatic breakthroughs may evolve into awareness that transforms the quality of subjective experience and personal relationships.

From a transpersonal perspective, wholeness implies a harmonious integration of physical, emotional, mental, and spiritual aspects of well-being as well as social responsibility. While other therapies address physical, emotional, mental, and social concerns, the spiritual dimension tends to be overlooked.

Following is a brief summary of some methods commonly associated with transpersonal therapy that may be applied at any level of development. They can all be used to assist clients to open to inner experience and to develop inner resources.

Physical health. In addition to cultivating awareness of how psychological health is affected by habits of diet and exercise, transpersonal psychotherapy may include bodywork such as bioenergetics, hatha yoga, t'ai chi ch'uan, aikido, biofeedback, sensory awareness, and movement therapy, to name a few. These disciplines train awareness by focusing attention on subtle physical sensations, and some focus specifically on mind-body integration and self-mastery. Some of them release emotional blocks and habitual patterns of tension, enabling a person to feel more relaxed and free.[4]

Emotional catharsis. The release of emotional blocks, whatever the method, is essential for healing the wounds of the past and freeing a person to live fully in the present. Transpersonal exploration through various methods such as breathwork, guided imagery, and dreams can have a powerful effect on emotional healing. One of the most effective methods for emotional catharsis in a transpersonal context is holotropic breathing, developed by Stanislav and Christina Grof.

Cognitive reattribution. By learning to think differently about experience and to shift perception of painful events, a person can learn to see difficulties as learning experiences and release shame, guilt, and anger associated with the past in order to experience greater freedom in the present. Given the opportunity, the psyche can learn to see both self and world with compassion.

Existential questions. At times of crisis, confronting existential questions of value, meaning, and choice can lead to transpersonal exploration. Although some psychotherapists consider spirituality an illusory palliative for the painful realities of human existence, there is no doubt that the proximity of death raises spiritual issues that are beyond the scope of conventional clinical training. The widespread denial of death in Western culture reflects an equally widespread denial of transpersonal realities.

Many people find themselves terrified of the dark and skeptical of the light. The task of the transpersonal therapist, then, is to assist clients in facing their fears and discovering a source of wisdom in themselves.

Imagery and dreamwork. These methods include techniques such as dream analysis, active imagination, Gestalt dialogue, and the hypnotic induction of altered states. They may be used for building ego strength or exploring transpersonal dimensions of the psyche. Transpersonal work does not depend on the technique, but on how it is used.

For example, if the therapist does not have a transpersonal orientation, the transpersonal potentials of dreamwork tend to be overlooked. A traditional psychoanalyst, for instance, may overlook the fact that dreams can be more than the royal road to the personal unconscious, that they have been an important source of revelation and inspiration in the world's religious traditions and can provide access to transpersonal realms.

Meditation. Meditation can enhance appreciation of the spiritual dimension of life and be a helpful adjunct to therapy. Different types of meditation have different effects, but most tend to increase self-awareness and sensitivity to how the mind works. Concentration practices that focus and calm the mind are sometimes useful in treating anxiety. Insight practice, on the other hand, can be particularly useful for uncovering repressed memories and other unconscious material.

Disidentification. By cutting through the contents of consciousness such as feelings, thoughts, and fantasies, meditation enables the practitioner to differentiate consciousness from its contents, thereby assisting the process of disidentification, which is central to transpersonal work. Whereas the ego tends to be predominantly identified with emotions, roles, and relationships, transcendence of ego is facilitated by disidentifying from the personality and personal history.

When the client is ready for it, disidentification exercises (e.g., "I have thoughts, but I am not my thoughts; I have emotions, but I am not my emotions; I have a body, but I am not my body") affirm identification with pure awareness, and the capacity for directing and utilizing psychological processes without becoming exclusively identified with any one of them.

Confession. The therapeutic relationship provides a contemporary version of the confessional for many people who have become alienated from formal religion. Any trustworthy therapist can serve the function of confessor by providing a safe place where the darkest secret places in the psyche may be explored. Healing occurs when the rejected, disowned aspects of the self are accepted and reintegrated into a larger vision of wholeness.

Altered states of consciousness. The use of techniques such as music, fasting, drumming, chanting, dancing or ingesting drugs to alter consciousness is as old as recorded history. The use of altered states in hypnotherapy and deep relaxation is familiar to most clinicians. The investigation of other nondrug methods for altering consciousness has been pioneered by transpersonal researchers such as Stanislav and Christina Grof (holotropic breathwork), Elmer and Alyce Green (biofeedback), and Michael Harner (shamanic drumming). Their work indicates that some altered states can have powerful therapeutic effects. Hence transpersonal therapists have sought to work with such states, as appropriate, in psychotherapy.

In practice, the transpersonal clinician may work with any number of different processes, depending on what is appropriate for a particular client. Since many clients who seek transpersonal therapists are already on a spiritual path, practitioners are often called upon to deal with specifically spiritual issues. This makes it necessary for the therapist to distinguish healthy spirituality from spiritual practices that mask psychological problems.

Transpersonal psychotherapy is often presumed to be most suitable for relatively healthy, growth-oriented clients. According to Seymour Boorstein,[5] a psychoanalytically trained transpersonal psychiatrist, transpersonal techniques can also be helpful in treating some severely disturbed individuals, since accessing the spiritual part of one's nature can provide a source of inner nourishment. He cautions, however, that sometimes individuals may come into therapy misusing certain practices such as meditation to avoid relationship or mask pathology. In such cases the therapist may counsel against these practices.

A pitfall for therapists in general is the tendency to impose their own beliefs on their clients, either consciously or unconsciously. Maintaining a detached attitude may be particularly challenging for a therapist who has recently discovered a rewarding spiritual practice. A commitment to assist the client to discover his or her own path rather than recommending a particular system is important. If the goal is to become aware of transpersonal dimensions of consciousness, there is no conflict between the process of psychotherapy and the process of spiritual growth.

The words of the Buddha in the Kalamas Sutra seem relevant for anyone working in this field:

> Do not believe in what you have heard; do not believe in traditions because they have been handed down for many generations; do not believe anything because it is rumored and spoken of by many; do not believe merely because the written statement of some old sage is produced; do not believe in conjectures; do not believe merely in the authority of your teachers and elders. After observation and analysis, when it agrees with reason and it is conducive to the good and benefit of one and all, then accept it and live up to it.[6]

❏

26

Assumptions of Transpersonal Psychotherapy

Bryan Wittine

The Greeks had a word, *pou sto*, meaning a place to stand, a ground, base, or set of principles from which to operate. The purpose of this paper is to suggest a *pou sto* for the practice of transpersonal psychotherapy.

It is common knowledge that the beliefs and state of mind of the therapist—both conscious and unconscious—determine to a great extent the nature of the therapy and, in particular, its outcome. Therefore, I believe it will be useful to make explicit some of the fundamental assumptions held by many transpersonal therapists.

As I see it, transpersonal therapy is an approach to healing/growth that aims to bridge the Western psychological tradition, including psychoanalytic and existential psychological perspectives, and the world's perennial philosophy. What differentiates transpersonal therapy from other orientations is neither technique nor the presenting problems of clients but the spiritual perspective of the therapist.

A transpersonal approach seeks to help clients integrate the transcendental or spiritual and personal dimensions of existence, to help them fulfill their unique, creative individuality while pointing toward their rootedness in the nontemporal, formless, depth dimension of being.

The following five postulates are an attempt to weave Western psychology and the perennial wisdom. They form a *pou sto* for transpersonally oriented clinical work. I suggest transpersonal psychotherapy affirms: (a) the need for healing/growth on all levels of the spectrum of identity—egoic, existential, and transpersonal; (b) the therapist's unfolding awareness of the Self, or deep center of Being, and his or her spiritual perspective on life as central to the therapeutic process; (c) the process of awakening from a lesser to a greater identity; (d) the healing, restorative nature of inner awareness and intuition; and (e) the transformative potential in the therapeutic relationship not only for the client but for the therapist as well.

Postulate 1

Transpersonal Psychotherapy is an approach to healing/growth that addresses all levels of the spectrum of identity—Egoic, Existential, and Transpersonal

"Who am I?" and "What am I?" are the central questions addressed in the field of psychology. The quest to find answers to these eternal questions is as ancient as the questions themselves.

And the answer? Wilber, one of transpersonal psychology's most influential and prolific exponents, suggests it depends entirely upon where we are identified in a spectrum of identity. Our identification is determined by where we draw the boundary line between what we identify as "I" and what we exclude as "not-I."

I emphasize three levels, dimensions, or bands in this spectrum—the egoic, existential, and transpersonal—extending from the strictly isolated and individual to the wholly inclusive and universal. I view them as interpenetrating levels in a "hierarchy of wholes." The higher dimensions go beyond, yet include, the lower.

Our mental-egoic identity is a whole constellation of concepts, images, self- and object representations, identifications, subpersonalities, and coping and defense mechanisms associated with the feeling of being separate persons, different from all other persons.

As I see it, one primary task of transpersonal psychotherapy is identical to that of many other Western psychotherapies: to facilitate the emergence and development of a stable, cohesive egoic identity when this is needed by the client. Many individuals come to therapy needing a clearer sense of who they are as separate, distinct individuals. Their self-identity can be described as preegoic. They are identified almost entirely with certain acceptable aspects of their total selves (what Jung called the *persona*) and deny, repress, or project their unacceptable aspects (Jung's *shadow*).

Thus work at the egoic level builds boundaries, integrates polarizations, replaces nonfunctional concepts of self and other, and modifies character structure so clients can interact with others and the world in a more fulfilling way.

Once individuals have developed a more cohesive egoic identity, they can embark on a process that takes them further on the journey of self-discovery, that of unfolding their existential self, or their true inner individuality.

In general, it seems to me clients unfold the inherent potentialities of their existential self as they confront what Bugental terms the existential givens or the conditions of being human. As human beings, we are embodied, finite, capable of making choices and taking action, and separate from, but related to, others. Each human being is subject to these conditions of existence.

The fact of our embodiment means we are subject to youth, maturity, and age, to continual change, to illness and health, to all the joys and anxieties of being physical and dwelling on planet earth. Because we are embodied, we are also finite. Nothing embodied is permanent. The one certainty of our earthly life is that it will end; the greatest uncertainty is when.

In my own clinical practice, I often find that as clients encounter these givens, they become more aware of themselves, other people, and the world. They begin to prize authenticity and gradually make their outer behavior and communication congruent with their inner thoughts and feelings. They come to treasure a way of life ruled by the dictates of their "alive center," the existential self, and less by the need for approval or direction from outside authority.

The task of transpersonal psychotherapy at this level is to help loosen the hold of the rigidified mental ego so that the dharma of the individual may come forth. Clients gradually liberate their energies from the superstructure of their conditioned mental-egoic identity and put them in the direction of actualizing the skills, talents, and functions that are uniquely their own.

In transpersonal psychology, it is assumed our mental-egoic and existential selves are incomplete. When our identity is primarily egoic, we are identified with a mental conception of who we and the world are, a conception determined substantially by the self- and object representations formed through interactions with primary care-givers during childhood. In the vernacular, we are "living in our heads" and split off from our intrinsic individuality and our physical bodies. When our identity is existential, we have begun to confront and accept the givens of human life—that we are embodied, finite, free, and related—but we are still individuals and therefore at the same time separate from others, the environment, and the universe. According to the perennial philosophy, we cannot be truly whole until we awaken to the wholeness of a deeper level of identity, the Self.

The perennial philosophy tells us that we come from (or are grounded in) the One Self, that we are estranged from or unaware of our origin, and can return, not by learning something new, but by remembering our true identity. Each historically conditioned religion has its own way of saying this.

In the course of psychotherapy, some clients begin to recognize a profound truth: No matter how great they will ever become, how much they will ever possess, and whatever they will ultimately accomplish, still they will never be fulfilled. The first of the four noble truths of Buddhism—the impermanence, pain, and insubstantiality of embodied existence—becomes starkly, even shockingly felt. As a result, prompted by an inner imperative, their attention begins to turn to spiritual questions.

Transpersonal experiences sometimes occur in my practice of psychotherapy when the client incorporates one or more of the existential givens into his or her being, or in a very profound way penetrates beneath a well-entrenched defensive pattern. These individuals quite naturally begin to consider their relationship to God, ultimate Mystery, their place in the evolutionary scheme of things, life after death, and spiritual disciplines.

One final point before leaving Postulate 1. It is essential to keep in mind that the egoic, existential, and transpersonal levels of identity are interpenetrating levels in a "hierarchy of wholes." Because these levels are interpenetrating, *the life concerns of clients can involve all levels simultaneously.* This point is often underemphasized in hierarchical and developmental models of human functioning but becomes apparent when one applies these models to clinical work.

POSTULATE 2

Transpersonal psychotherapy recognizes the therapist's unfolding awareness of the Self and his or her spiritual worldview as central in shaping the nature, process, and outcome of therapy.

As I see it, therapy can be considered transpersonal insofar as the therapist seeks to realize the Self, the deep center of Being.

Insofar as we view our clients egoically, we tend to see them as separate individuals different from ourselves. Insofar as we awaken to transpersonal identity, however, we also experience our essential unity with all human beings and living things. In the eyes of a therapist on a path of self-realization, therefore, the person seated opposite the therapist is not just a constellation of personal characteristics; he or she also becomes an individualized expression of the Self we share.

What are the implications of this viewpoint? I believe there is something very important in this principle, but it is frustratingly out of grasp unless the therapist has begun to awaken to his or her deep center of Being. Essentially, it is this: More than anything else, our clients need to be seen and felt as the Self they truly are, which is no different than the true Self we are. As I see it, through this recognition of the client's and our own true identity we hold an expanded vision of who the client is and what he or she is capable of. If our frame for holding the client is broad, the client is aided to relinquish some of the crippling egoic self- and world constructs and beliefs that underlie his or her presenting and ongoing concerns and to enlarge his or her sense of identity. Recognition of the client's true nature, inner light and beauty, creativeness, power, and dignity, through eyes that are accepting, appreciative, and unconditionally loving—all of which Assagioli contends are attributes of the Self—is the heart of healing in transpersonal psychotherapy.

Vaughan speaks of something akin to this as "healing awareness."

POSTULATE 3

Transpersonal psychotherapy is a process of awakening from a lesser to a greater identity.

According to *A Course in Miracles*, "What you think you are is a belief to be undone." In the perennial philosophy, self-identity and sense of the world at the egoic and existential levels in the spectrum of identity are viewed as arising from our thoughts and beliefs. In transpersonal therapy, healing involves the realization of a greater identity that comes to light when we relinquish our unquestioned conceptions of self and world.

By gradually relinquishing our exclusive identification with our pre-egoic identity, we can awaken to our egoic identity; by relinquishing our exclusive identification with our limited egoic self- and world structure, we can deepen to our existential identity; by relinquishing our exclusive identification with our embodied individual self-sense, we can eventually transcend to our true identity as the Self, the origin and source of all our experience. With each transcendence of who we thought we were, we come closer to who we are, until ultimately, paradoxically, we come home to the Self we never left.

This postulate has important implications for the conduct of transpersonal therapy. As therapists, we do not necessarily use specific practices to help clients have transpersonal experiences. Rather, following the metaphor of the proverbial onion that is gradually unwound, we compassionately yet persistently help our clients identify and let go of those self-definitions and patterns of living that are impeding enhanced self-awareness and the emergence of a greater identity.

If, in the course of therapy, the resistances and defenses of the lesser identity are gradually relinquished, clients are likely to enter a "dark night" or crisis of awakening. They become acutely aware that their old way of life has little to offer, that its cost in terms of aliveness and creativity is enormous. St. John of the Cross called a similar transition the dark night of the senses and characterized it as a normal stage in spiritual growth when a spiritual seeker, having tired of the "things of the senses," cannot yet depend upon consolation from the "things of God."

It takes both an open heart and great skill to guide a client through this crisis of awakening. It is imperative that therapists realize *this is a healing crisis, not a pathological one*. The client is falling apart; however, this crisis also heralds the birth of a new person. I believe one of our greatest functions as therapists is to act as midwives to this birth.

As therapists, we must be prepared to remain psychologically present and supportive with our clients during this experience of giving birth. The most basic preparation we can have is to have undergone our own dark nights and, through them, to have learned that birth follows death.

POSTULATE 4

Transpersonal psychotherapy facilitates the process of awakening by enhancing inner awareness and intuition.

According to the perennial philosophy the truth lies within, and salvation comes by expanding our inward awareness. To turn attention inward and "self-ward" and become more fully aware of our inner realms is a natural human capacity transpersonal psychotherapy makes full use of. Learning to live directly from an inner center and from one's internal sense of things is in itself restorative and healing. However, in most of us, this capacity is blunted.

To develop intuition and know the intrinsic wisdom of our deeper wellsprings, we must relinquish the dominance of our judging, analyzing mind and shift our attention away from its exclusive focus on the objective world. We must become more aware of our interiors. Many, if not most, human beings can access deeper levels of inner wisdom and intuit within themselves whatever they need to make their lives more the way they really want them to be, if they will only turn inward. As Perls (1969) noted, "Awareness per se—by and of itself—can be curative."

POSTULATE 5

In transpersonal psychotherapy, the therapeutic relationship is a vehicle for the process of awakening in both client and therapist.

As I see it, transpersonal psychotherapy differs from other therapeutic approaches in the kind of attention it gives to the relationship between therapist and client. This relationship can be seen not only as a vehicle for the client's awakening but for the therapist's as well. Every person who comes to transpersonal therapy also offers us an opportunity to heal our own wounds and to realize more fully our own authenticity. In their healing, we are also healed; in our healing, they too are healed.

CLOSING REMARKS

I believe transpersonal therapists have yet to clarify the *pou sto* of their orientation. It is essential for transpersonal therapists to be explicit about the principles and assumptions to which they subscribe and out of which they interact with their clients, for our beliefs and assumptions about clients and the process of psychotherapy stamp irrevocably how we interact with them, what we expect them to do in therapy, and the outcome of the therapeutic journey.

As transpersonal therapists, we must be explicit in our assumptions if we are to contribute to a comprehensive approach that addresses the whole human being—ego, existential, and spiritual.

❏
27

Integral Practices: Body, Heart, and Mind

Michael Murphy

We need to develop *integral practices*, which I define as transformative practices that address the somatic, affective, cognitive, volitional, and transpersonal dimensions of human nature in a comprehensive way. Creating integral practices in the modern world is a bit like assembling a jigsaw puzzle whose assorted pieces are culled from all parts of the world. We find intimations of this whole-person education among the Greek philosophers and its continued presence among Renaissance thinkers. We also find the idea of wholeness in Zen Buddhism and in the *Yoga Sutras* of Patanjali, in which the spiritual aspirant acquires ethical virtues, then disciplines the body, vital energies and mental processes before undertaking meditative practices that lead to union with God.

While drawing on the time-tested practices of the past, such as Yoga, Zen, and Judeo-Christian mysticism, we need not be limited by the achievements of the past. To integrate the personal and transpersonal dimensions of life, we draw on the wisdom of modern psychology and on transpersonal psychologies such as Psychosynthesis. When we add to these "ingredients" practices and insights from the martial arts, somatics, and modern sports research, we can build the transformative disciplines appropriate to our age.

Indeed, most traditional spiritual programs don't translate well when imported uncritically into our modern culture. In this age of great religious reinvention, we need discrimination and wisdom to synthesize the best of the old and the new to forge modern yogas.

Every practice and every teacher promotes a certain set of virtues, while others are either neglected or suppressed. For example, ascetic contemplative practices typically fail to appreciate the body's genius for transformation, the glory of interpersonal relationship, and the need for individuation and creativity (which are frequently interpreted as assertions of the ego). Transformative therapies generally suffer from a one-sidedness that reflects their founders' biases. Consider Gestalt Therapy, which put a big premium on openness, honesty, courage, and risk-taking, while remaining weak on empathy and kindness. While some martial arts, such as aikido, come close to being integral practices, most focus physically and meditatively but fall short on the interpersonal dimension of life.

In general, then, transformative practices can subvert our wholeness by emphasizing certain virtues over others. And the belief systems that undergird these approaches by and large determine which aspects of reality will be honored and encouraged and which will be ignored and suppressed. If you view the world as *maya* or illusion, your focus may become profoundly otherworldly. If, on the other hand, you view personal integration as the highest goal worth pursuing, you may suppress your capacity for transcendence. That's why I call for integral practices that balance, integrate, and express our many-sided nature.

We create them through judicious personal experimentation, guided by the wisdom of the past but fueled by an adventurous spirit. You can make a conscious attempt to yoke whatever physical practices you do, such as martial arts, t'ai chi, hatha yoga, jogging, or sports, with whatever interpersonal and transpersonal practices you do on a regular basis. If you're involved in daily meditation, for example, consider some form of physical exercise to strengthen your musculature and nervous system. If you're involved in psychotherapy or Psychosynthesis, consider introducing a somatic component in your therapy to ground intellectual insights and emotional releases in your body.

Our metanormal abilities stand a better chance of flowering if integral practice receives institutional support. Wherever communal life has embraced a transformative life-style—such as in Hassidism, whose religious rituals enrich all aspects of life—practice is extended and deepened. We need to design social structures that reinforce our transformative practices. If you're at home, create a support group of friends who inspire practice, otherwise even with the best intentions, you may fall prey to the inertia of your old conditioned habits. We need each other to grow.

The unfoldment of humanity's stupendous potential is uncertain. It's touch and go: It might happen, it might not, depending on the long-term choices we make in dealing with the global crisis.

Look at what confronts us today—an epidemic of drug addiction, gratuitous violence and a life-style of overconsumption, all of which imperil our inner life and the world's ecological health. We have a choice: We can anesthetize ourselves and remain addicted to external activities, or we can rechannel our energies into integral practices that offer creative alternatives to the social and ecological problems we confront at home and at work. If we focus on inner development and bring forth our extraordinary capacities, we can learn to live more lightly on the Earth, conserve the world's precious resources, and find meaning and delight through an inner-directed, more compassionate approach to life.

PART III

❏

Foundations and Applications

❏

SCIENCE, TECHNOLOGY, AND TRANSCENDENCE

In envisioning the way things are, there is no better place to begin than with modern science. Equally, there is no worse place to end. . . . science dominates the modern mind. Through and through, from premises to conclusions, the contemporary mind is science ridden. Its sway is the stronger because we are unaware of its extent.

—HUSTON SMITH[1]

THE RISE of science and technology has shaped the course of culture and history for several centuries. Technological miracles—from microsurgery to space shuttles—are the most obvious signs, but science and technology also exert subtle yet powerful and pervasive effects on our thinking. Our views of what we are, of the mind and reality, of our relationship to the world and to each other all have been affected in far-reaching ways.

The technologies, values, and worldviews fostered by science have been enormously beneficial in many ways, but have also created problems that lie at the core of our contemporary cultural, global, and religious crises. The dangers of technologies such as nuclear weapons are obvious while the dangers of certain scientific values and philosophies are more subtle. But consider scientism and its philosophy of logical positivism. Their central belief is that only what science and technology can observe and measure can be regarded as valid knowledge. The result is a truncated vision of ourselves and our world because the subtler dimensions of life and meaning are overlooked or viewed reductionistically as mere epiphenomena of biological existence. As Huston Smith put it, higher dimensions such as "values, life meanings, purposes and qualities slip through science like sea slips through the nets of fishermen."[1]

Nobel laureate Alfred North Whitehead pointed out, however, that, "This position on the part of the scientist was pure bluff."[2] After all, if someone claims that science alone can provide valid data, then one is entitled to ask, "What is your scientific proof of this?" The answer is "None."

Even if this position was pure bluff, it was for a long time a successful bluff that reduced our view of nature, in Whitehead's words, to "a dull affair, soundless, scentless, colorless; merely the hurrying of material, endlessly, meaninglessly."[2] According to this view there was no room for meaning, purpose, consciousness, or spirit. The result was what Lewis Mumford described as "a disqualified universe" and what sociologist Max Weber called "the disenchantment of the world."

Of course, human beings were also disenchanted and diminished. Beginning with the seventeenth-century philosopher Thomas Hobbes, humans were increasingly regarded as merely sophisticated machines. Twentieth-century versions of this view see us as, for example, the "stimulus-response machines" of behaviorists, the "wet computers" of artificial intelligence, or what sociobiologists describe as "only DNA's way of making more DNA" and "survival machines—robot vehicles blindly programmed to preserve the selfish molecules known as genes."[3] Needless to say, mind was similarly deflated and among sociobiologists, for example, it is regarded as merely "an epiphenomenon of the neuronal machinery of the brain."[3]

It follows, of course, that transcendental experiences and religions have been dismissed as, for example, projections of unrealized potentials (Feuerbach), expressions of infantile wishes (Freud), or symptoms of medical disturbances. William James aptly labeled this position "medical materialism" and wrote:

> Medical materialism finishes up St. Paul by calling his vision on the road to Damascus a discharging lesion of the occipital cortex, he being an epileptic. It knocks out St. Theresa as an hysteric, St. Frances of Assisi as an hereditary degenerate.[4]

Medical materialism is still alive and well. Consider the Nobel Prize winner Francis Crick's recent suggestion that belief in the existence of God might be due to dangerous mutant molecules that he named "theotoxins."

So in addition to providing enormous benefits, science and technology have fostered worldviews that have disenchanted and diminished our views of the world, humankind, the mind, and transpersonal experiences. Yet the second half of the twentieth century saw a partial turnaround in which the supposedly necessary connection between science and disenchantment was broken for both philosophical and scientific reasons.

Philosophically, the two strongest advocates of disenchantment, namely scientism and logical positivism, were found wanting. In addition, the philosophical movements of postmodernism and constructivism forced us to recognize that our interpretations and worldviews are conditioned and constructed by social factors such as language, historical period, race, gender, social class, and the dominant cultural ideology. A worldview, then, is not only a description of the way things "really are," but also a construction or projection. The result is that the disenchanted worldview, so often thought to follow logically from science, can now be seen, in part, as a culturally conditioned choice. As such it is only one of several possible worldviews consistent with science and is neither proved nor required by science.[5]

This recognition is vital to the transpersonal enterprise. Consequently researchers have given considerable attention to the nature of science and its appropriate relationship to transpersonal studies. Transpersonally oriented researchers also have done significant experimental work, and some of their many studies are described in the sections on meditation and lucid dreaming. The following papers contain some of their most significant ideas relating to the nature and impact of science and technology.

One of the most impactful ideas was Charles Tart's suggestion that the scope of scientific inquiry could be extended by developing what he called "State-Specific Sciences." He suggested training scientists to function in altered states as participant-observers to report on their experiences. Tart argued that owing to the state-specific nature of such experiences and knowledge, we may need a number of separate but complementary state-specific sciences.

"Different Views from Different States" consists of two letters written by Gordon Globus in response to Charles Tart. These must surely be among the most unusual and remarkable responses ever written to a scientific paper, for the two letters were written in two different states of consciousness and come to diametrically opposite conclusions about the validity of Tart's hypothesis. Here we have the unique situation of a respected researcher denying the need or usefulness of state-specific sciences while in his ordinary state, yet finding the suggestion appropriate while in an altered state. This is compelling support for the power of state-dependent phenomena. Interestingly, the journal *Science* declined to publish the letters.

Ken Wilber argues for the necessity of complementing the sensory observations of science with philosophical and contemplative approaches. In his paper "Eye to Eye: Science and Transpersonal Psychology," he begins by pointing to traditional distinctions between three distinct "eyes of knowledge" or ways of knowing: the empirical (sensory) mode, the rational mode of logic and philosophy, and the contemplative mode of contemplation/meditation. Each of these has its own domain of data and its own means for assessing the validity of its data, and each only partly overlaps the other. Wilber suggests that transpersonal disciplines are uniquely able to employ all three modes of knowledge. Thereby they may create a more comprehensive, integrated, and balanced discipline uniquely committed and able to investigate the biological, psychological, social, and spiritual dimensions of humankind through appropriate use of science, philosophy, and contemplation.

In "Science and Mysticism," physicist Fritjof Capra echoes this theme of complementarity. He suggests that neither scientific observation nor mystical insight can be reduced to or comprehended by the other, but that each offers essential benefits and together they yield a fuller vision of the world than either could alone.

The birth of transpersonal anthropology marks the extension of the transpersonal perspective into another discipline, and this new field is summarized by Charles Laughlin, John McManus, and Jon Shearer. Hopefully future years will see the birth of other disciplines such as transpersonal philosophy and politics.

In the second half of the twentieth century something wholly unexpected emerged that further challenged the connection between science and disenchantment, excited enormous interest in transpersonal phenomena, and affected the culture in ways that are still being felt. That was the discovery of technologies that induce transcendent experiences. Examples include psychedelics, which induce a variety of powerful altered states; biofeedback, which validated yogic claims for voluntary control of the autonomic nervous system; resuscitation technology, which multiplied by several orders of magnitude the number of people having near-death experiences; and space travel, which evoked transpersonal experiences in both astronauts and cosmonauts. The net result has been a dramatic increase in the number of people having powerful transpersonal experiences, and the collective impact on individual lives and the culture as a whole has yet to be fully appreciated or understood.

For example, most astronauts and cosmonauts have been engineers or test pilots schooled in emotional control and detachment. Yet all of them have been awed by the stunning beauty of the earth framed by the black infinity of space. "No one," said cosmonaut Oleg Makarov, "has been able to restrain his heartfelt wonder at the sight of the enthralling panorama of the earth."[6]

Some were so impacted that they had powerful transpersonal experiences. The two most common types have been called "the overview effect" and "the universal insight." The overview effect is a sense of the unity, interdependence, and fragility of life on earth; "the universal insight," is a sense of the unity and interconnection of all things.[7] Amplified by the media, these experiences are impacting and transforming our collective consciousness, and space travel yet may prove to be an important milestone and catalyst of human evolution.

In his paper "The Near-Death Experience," Ken Ring offers a clear, broad-ranging summary of the nature and implication of such experiences. The more we learn about these experiences, the more mysterious they become and no single explanation—biological, psychological, or spiritual—has proved adequate. What is clear is that they are remarkably powerful, meaningful, and transformative. Survivors show a dramatically heightened appreciation of life, love, learning, and concern for others. Since millions have now been so affected, Ring wonders if their psychological transformations could catalyze a collective transformation in our culture. The impact of transcendence-inducing technologies on our culture and consciousness may be only beginning.

28

Different Views from Different States

Gordon Globus

June 30, 1972
Editors of *Science*
American Association for the Advancement of Science

Dear Sirs:

It is commendable that *Science* has published Tart's controversial article, "States of Consciousness and State-Specific Sciences." Tart rightfully has emphasized the importance of scientific investigation into altered states of consciousness (ASCs). It is hard to imagine a moment in scientific history when science has lagged so far behind the culture at large that even otherwise ordinary students recognize the irrelevance of the few behavorial studies on psychedelic drugs. Unfortunately, Tart's philosophy of science perspective is so narrow, and his views on the relations among "state-specific sciences" so radical, that his discussion is liable to be dismissed by those toward whom it is directed, i.e., the "straight" scientific establishment reading the paper in an ordinary state of consciousness.

The discussion of the "public nature of observation" as one basic rule of the scientific method is quite beside the issue. Tart is correct in indicating that "observations must be public in that they must be replicable by any properly trained observer." However, in addition to replicability, the observations must be equally accessible to all observers. The methodological problem with respect to ASCs is precisely that the subject has a special access to his own consciousness that no other observer has.

This is the fundamental problem in investigating ASCs and is aside from difficulties in describing complex ASCs, the training of the observer, or his "innate characteristics."

Until empirical investigation proves otherwise, it would seem most justifiable and parsimonious to develop one science for all states of consciousness—ordinary and extraordinary—rather than following the dubious path of a science (and scientists) for each state of consciousness.

Gordon G. Globus, M.D.

July 10, 1972
Editors of *Science*
American Association for the Advancement of Science

Dear Sirs:

This letter is in response to my previous letter, which was critical of Tart's recent discussion on altered states of consciousness (ASCs). I happened to recall Tart's paper while in an ASC and—to my great amazement—his proposal that a science specific to a given ASC may be independent of sciences specific to other ASCs now seems quite correct to me. *I therefore immediately drafted this letter while remaining in the ASC.*

It is quite apparent to me at this moment that I do not appreciate in the ordinary state of consciousness just what the ASC is like. The peak of the ASC takes me quite by surprise as I forget what a unique experience it is until I am in it again. It seems clear to me that if I were to talk with a person in an ordinary state, he could not appreciate my unique experience at this moment; nor, I now predict, will I fully appreciate it when I again regain the ordinary state.

I am struck, then, by the extraordinary paradox that Tart's proposal for state-specific sciences seems absurd to me in an ordinary state but quite correct in terms of my "incorrigible experience" while in an ASC. I have retained my critical stance toward all other issues in Tart's paper with which I previously disagreed.

ADDED IN PROOF: Again in an ordinary state, I would argue in favor of one science for all states of consciousness and trust that there is an explanation for my experience that while in an ASC, the ASC seems clearly incomprehensible to an ordinary state. It seems obvious to me that I can remember what occurred in the ASC, but I can't remember it in the way I experienced it at that time, i.e., the memory is not veridical. There seems no way to retrieve completely the experience in the ASC without entering again the ASC, which supports Tart's thesis. But available scientific data on "state-dependent learning" easily can explain this phenomenon.

It seems to me, then, that at an experiential level Tart may have a sound point in favor of state-specific science, but that at a conceptual level a single science still can encompass all states of consciousness. In any case, the difference in my letters, written in both ordinary and altered states of consciousness, supports scientific interest in these intriguing phenomena.

Gordon G. Globus, M.D.

❑
29

Eye to Eye: Science and Transpersonal

Psychology

Ken Wilber

It is probably true that the single greatest issue today facing transpersonal psychology is its relation to empirical science. The burning issue is *not* the scope of transpersonal psychology, not its subject matter, not its methodology—not its premises, not its conclusions, and not its sources—because, according to modern thinking, *all* of those are purely secondary issues compared with whether or not transpersonal psychology itself is *valid* in the first place. That is, whether it is an *empirical science*. For, the argument goes, if transpersonal psychology is not an empirical science, then it has no valid epistemology, no valid means of acquiring knowledge. There is no use trying to figure out the range or scope or methods of knowledge of the new and "higher" field of transpersonal psychology until you can demonstrate that you *have* actual knowledge of any sort to begin with.

I would like, then, to examine briefly the nature of science, the nature of transpersonal psychology, and the relationship between them.

THREE EYES OF THE SOUL

St. Bonaventure, a favorite philosopher of the mystics, taught that men and women have at least three modes of attaining knowledge—"three eyes," as he put it: the *eye of flesh*, by which we perceive the external world of space, time, and objects; the *eye of reason*, by which we attain a knowledge of philosophy, logic, and the mind itself; and the *eye of contemplation*, by which we rise to a knowledge of transcendent realities.

Now that particular wording—eye of flesh, mind, and contemplation—is Christian; but similar ideas can be found in every major school of traditional psychology, philosophy, and religion. The "three eyes" of a human being correspond, in fact, to the three major realms of being described by the perennial philosophy, which are the gross (flesh and material), the subtle (mental and animic), and the causal (transcendent and contemplative). These realms have been described extensively elsewhere, and I wish here only to point to their unanimity among traditional psychologists and philosophers.[1,2,3]

To extend on Bonaventure's insights, we moderns might say that the eye of flesh participates in a select world of shared sensory experience, which it partially creates and partially discloses. This is the "gross realm," the realm of space, time, and matter. It is the realm *shared* by all those possessing a similar eye of flesh. This is basic sensorimotor intelligence— object constancy—the eye of flesh. It is the *empirical eye*, the eye of sensory experience. It should be said, at the start, that I am using the term "empirical" as it is employed in philosophy: capable of detection by the five human senses or their extensions.

The eye of reason, or, more generally, the eye of mind, participates in a world of ideas, images, logic, and concepts. Because so much of modern thought is based solely on the empirical eye, the eye of flesh, it is important to remember that the mental eye *cannot* be reduced to the fleshy eye. The mental field includes but transcends the sensory field. Although the eye of mind relies upon the eye of flesh for much of its information, not all mental knowledge comes strictly from fleshy knowledge, nor does it deal solely with objects of the flesh. Our knowledge is *not* entirely empirical and fleshy. The truth of a logical deduction is based on internal consistency, it is not based on its relation to sensory objects.

The eye of contemplation is to the eye of reason as the eye of reason is to the eye of flesh. Just as reason transcends flesh, so contemplation transcends reason. Just as reason cannot be reduced to, nor derived from, fleshy knowledge, so contemplation cannot be reduced to nor derived from reason. Where the eye of reason is trans-empirical, the eye of contemplation is trans-rational, trans-logical, and trans-mental.

Let us simply assume that all men and women possess an eye of flesh, an eye of reason, and an eye of contemplation; that each eye has its own objects of knowledge (sensory, mental, and transcendental); that a higher eye cannot be reduced to nor explained in terms of a lower eye; that each eye is valid and useful in its own field but commits a fallacy when it attempts, by itself, to fully grasp higher or lower realms.

The only point I wish here to emphasize is that when one eye tries to usurp the role of any of the other eyes, a category mistake occurs. And it can occur in any direction: the eye of contemplation is as ill-equipped to disclose the facts of the eye of flesh as the eye of flesh is incapable of grasping the truths of the eye of contemplation. Sensation, reason, and contemplation disclose their own truths in their own realms, and any time one eye tries to see for another eye, blurred vision results.

Now that type of category error has been *the* great problem for almost every major religion. The point is that Buddhism and Christianity and other religions contained, at their summit, ultimate insights into ultimate reality, but these trans-verbal insights were invariably all mixed up with rational truths and empirical facts. Humankind had not, as it were, yet learned to differentiate and separate the eyes of flesh, reason, and contemplation. And because (for example) revelation was confused with logic and with empirical fact, and all three were presented as *one truth*, then two things happened: the philosophers came in and destroyed the rational side of religion, and science came in and destroyed the empirical side. . . . From that point on, spirituality in the West was dismantled, and only philosophy and science remained.

Within a century, however, philosophy as a rational system—a system based on the eye of mind—was in its own turn decimated, and decimated by the new scientific empiricism. At that point, human knowledge was *reduced* to only the eye of flesh. Gone was the contemplative eye; gone the mental eye—and mankind restricted its means of valid knowledge to the eye of flesh.

For science became scientism. It did not just speak for the eye of flesh, but for the eye of mind and for the eye of contemplation as well. In so doing, it fell prey to precisely the same category mistakes that it discovered in dogmatic theology, and for which it made religion dearly pay. The scienticians tried to force science, with its eye of flesh, to work for all three eyes. And that is a category error. And for that not only science but the world has paid dearly.

Thus, in effect, the sole criterion of truth came to be the scientific criterion, that is to say, a sensorimotor test by the eye of flesh based on measurement. And yet here is the real point: "This position on the part of the scientists was . . . pure bluff"[4] of the part playing the whole. The eye of flesh came to say, what it can't see does not exist; whereas what it should have said was, what it can't see it can't see.

A "HIGHER" SCIENCE

Is it not possible that scientists themselves have defined the scientific method in a too narrow fashion? Could a more expanded science be applied to the realm of the mind's eye and the realm of the eye of flesh? Is science *tied* to the eye of flesh, or can it expand into the eye of mind and contemplation? Is state-specific science—science occurring on higher states of consciousness—a possibility or a well-intentioned mistake?

Charles Tart believes that the scientific method has been unnecessarily and arbitrarily limited to the eye of flesh by a "physicalistic bias,"[5] the assumption that only material entities are worth studying. The scientific method itself, he feels, can be freed from its materialistic accretions and applied to higher states of consciousness and being (and that is the concept of state-specific sciences). He thus concludes that "the essence of scientific method is perfectly compatible with the study of various altered states of consciousness."

My opinion is twofold: First, Tart has defined science in such a broad fashion that it can apply to all sorts of endeavors. And, second, the tighter and firmer we make his propositions, in order to avoid that difficulty, then the less they apply to higher states of consciousness and the more they return to the old physicalistic science.

If this is so, then it seems that the scientific method is not well suited to the higher states of being and consciousness, but rather must remain basically what it has always been: the best method yet devised to discover the facts of the realm of the eye of flesh. My own opinion is that Tart, in his pioneering attempts to legitimize the *existence* of higher states of consciousness, has inadvertently applied lower-state-specific criteria to the higher states in general.

Empirical/physical research conducted by the eye of flesh or its extensions will always be important *adjuncts* to transpersonal psychology, but they will never form its core, which alone is concerned with the eye of contemplation. Transpersonal psychology is a state-specific enterprise (not science), which—because it transcends the eye of flesh and the eye of reason—is free to use both; the former in scientific-empiric studies, the latter in philosophical/psychological inquiry. But it cannot be grasped or defined by either.

THE PROBLEM OF PROOF

It is important to realize that scientific knowledge is not the only form of knowledge; it is simply a refined eye of flesh, and there exists beyond it mental knowledge and contemplative knowledge. Thus, the fact that transpersonal psychology is not a science doesn't mean that it is invalid, emotional, nonverifiable, antireason, noncognitive, and meaningless. Transpersonal psychologists tend to panic when it is said that transpersonal psychology is not a science, because the scienticians have taught us that "nonscientific" means "not verifiable." But if transpersonal psychology is nonscientific, how *can* it be verified?

This seems to be a problem because we do not see that all knowledge is essentially similar in structure. That is, all knowledge consists of three basic components:

1. *An instrumental or injunctive wing:* This is a set of instructions, simple or complex, internal or external. All have the form: "If you want to see this, do this."
2. *An illuminative wing:* This is an illuminative *seeing* by the particular eye of knowledge evoked by the injunctive wing. Besides being self-illuminative, it leads to the possibility of:
3. *A communal wing:* This is the actual sharing of the illuminative seeing with others who are using the same eye. If the shared vision is agreed upon by others, this constitutes a communal proof of true seeing.

Those are the basic wings of any type of true knowledge using any eye. Knowledge does become more complicated when one eye tries to match its knowledge with a higher or lower eye, but these basic wings underlie even that complication. In other words, the injunctive strand demands that, for whatever type of knowledge, *the appropriate eye must be trained until it can be adequate to its illumination.* This is true in art, in science, in philosophy, in contemplation. It is true, in fact, for all valid forms of knowledge.

Now, if a person refuses to train a particular eye (flesh, mental, contemplative), then it is equivalent to refusing to look, and we are justified in disregarding this person's opinions and excluding him from our vote as to communal proof. Someone who refuses to learn geometry cannot be allowed to vote on the truth of the Pythagorean theorem; someone who refuses to learn contemplation cannot be allowed to vote on the truth of Buddha-nature.

It is my own feeling that the most important thing transpersonal psychology can do is try to avoid the category errors: confusing the eye of flesh with the eye of mind with the eye of contemplation (or, in the more detailed models, such as the Vedanta, avoid confusing any of the six levels). When someone asks, "Where is your empirical proof for transcendence?" we need not panic. We explain the instrumental methods for our knowledge and invite him or her to check it out personally. Should that person accept, and complete the injunctive wing, then that person is capable of becoming part of the community of those whose eye is adequate to the transcendent realm. Prior to that time, that person is inadequate to form an opinion about transpersonal concerns. We are then no more obliged to account to that person than is a physicist to one who refuses to learn mathematics.

In the meantime, the transpersonal psychologist should attempt to avoid category mistakes. He or she should not present transcendent insights as if they were empirical scientific facts, because those facts *cannot be scientifically verified*, and therefore the entire field will quickly gain the reputation of being full of nonsensical statements. A transpersonal psychologist is free to use the eye of flesh (scientifically) in gathering adjunct data; and a transpersonal psychologist is free to use the mind's eye to coordinate, clarify, criticize, and synthesize. But none of these realms should be confused with each other, and especially none of them should be confused with the realm of contemplation. Especially the eyes of flesh and reason should not think they have "proven" the Transcendent, circumscribed the Transcendent, or even adequately described the Transcendent. To the extent the transpersonal psychologist commits those errors, then the more the entire field faces the fate of the medieval theologist: it becomes psuedo-science and pseudo-philosophy, and is thereby destroyed by real scientists and real philosophers—and rightly so.

Transpersonal psychology is in an extraordinarily favorable position: it can preserve for itself the utterly unique position of possessing a balanced yet complete approach to reality—one which can include the eye of flesh and the eye of reason and the eye of contemplation. And I think that the history of thought will eventually prove that to do more than that is impossible, to do less than that, disastrous.

❏

30

Science and Mysticism

Fritjof Capra

Is modern science, with all its sophisticated machinery, merely rediscovering ancient wisdom, known to the Eastern sages for thousands of years? Should physicists, therefore, abandon the scientific method and begin to meditate? Or can there be a mutual influence between science and mysticism—perhaps even a synthesis?

I think that all these questions have to be answered in the negative. I see science and mysticism as two complementary manifestations of the human mind, of its rational and intuitive faculties. The modern physicist experiences the world through an extreme specialization of the rational mind; the mystic through an extreme specialization of the intuitive mind.

The two approaches are entirely different and involve far more than a certain view of the physical world. However, they are 'complementary', as we have learned to say in physics. Neither is comprehended in the other, nor can either of them be reduced to the other, but both of them are necessary, supplementing one another for a fuller understanding of the world. To paraphrase an old Chinese saying, mystics understand the roots of the *Tao* but not its branches; scientists understand its branches but not its roots. Science does not need mysticism and mysticism does not need science; but humans need both. Mystical experience is necessary to understand the deepest nature of things, and science is essential for modern life. What we need, therefore, is not a synthesis but a dynamic interplay between mystical intuition and scientific analysis.

❑

31

Transpersonal Anthropology

Charles D. Laughlin, Jr., John McManus, and Jon Shearer

Although never integrated under a single rubric like transpersonalism, anthropological research involving alternate phases of consciousness has been extensive and has, in fact, provided much of the cross-cultural material upon which transpersonal theoretical work in other disciplines has been grounded.

A society may inhibit access to and integration of experience by systematically ignoring or negatively sanctioning the phase of consciousness under which the experience is derived. We, for instance, live in a relatively *monophasic* society: that is, a society that narrowly confines experience and knowledge to a narrow range of phenomenological phases. For our culture generally, the only phases of consciousness appropriate to the accrual of information about the world are those acceptable as "normal waking consciousness."

Of immense anthropological significance is the fact that most human societies operate upon multiple realities, experienced directly by some or all group members through *polyphasic consciousness*. Most societies require integration of experiences (Maslow's "unitive consciousness") derived from two or more alternative phases (e.g., integration of waking, meditative, and dream consciousness in Tibetan tantrism). It is quite possible to argue that failure to integrate polyphasic experience may result in psychopathology. Development of unitive consciousness requires adequate transmission of information across phase warps, a process we have termed *cross-phasing*.

Societies that recognize the salience of experiences derived in alternate phases of consciousness tend to socially modulate the information flow between phases: (1) by controlling phase warps via ritual (e.g., dream incubation, public dance, and ingestion of drugs under socially controlled conditions, societal stipulation of techniques to be used in attaining an alternate phase, etc.), and (2) by providing a system of polyphasic symbols around which information about experience may be organized and shunted across warps as required for integration. Failure to realize the cross-phasing function of symbolism has often resulted in the failure to comprehend certain wide-spread cultural elements. For instance, anthropologists have from time to time wondered if the shaman can really believe in the efficacy of his cures when he knows he is using sleight-of-hand techniques. This seeming paradox evaporates when we realize that therapeutic theater in the waking phase may provide the elements of direct and therapeutic experience in alternate phases (say, dreams or trance).

With very few exceptions, the work of most anthropologists reflects an ethnocentric bias toward monophasia. This appears quite ironic when considering that anthropology is probably the oldest transpersonal discipline to be found among the sciences. Whereas most anthropologists would not hesitate to record descriptions of transpersonal experiences offered by informants, few have found it necessary to hazard entry into the phase of consciousness whence the experiences are phenomenologically obtained. The difference here is theoretically and methodologically crucial, for the loss of intuitive insight on the part of monophasic anthropologists into how multiple realities are integrated has been a major hindrance to the formation of a sophisticated theory of consciousness and culture.

For one thing, we are slowly coming to see that there exist real, direct experiences somewhere behind many seemingly (to us anthropologists) bizarre beliefs, myths, legends, and "superstitions." We must examine carefully the possibility that our informants, or those from whom they learn, have indeed experienced a reality which gives rise to the tradition we are examining.

For another thing, we are beginning to realize that speech events and other modes of symbolic communication are *not* cognition, but rather simplified expressions of cognitive events at best. Thus, for the mono-phasic fieldworker there exist severe constraints to vicarious participation in alternate phases of consciousness. Finally, many of the questions being asked by transpersonalists today require participant observation in its grandest sense. The demand is for anthropologists insightful and courageous enough to enter the direct experience of multiple realities, armed only with the host culture's hermeneutic, and return to describe their phenomenology first hand. In other words, the demand upon anthropology today is to produce what Tart has called "state-specific scientists."

A number of advantages to producing a cadre of full-blown transpersonalists in anthropology is already implied by our discussion thus far, but there might be some value in making this explicit. First, the transpersonal anthropologist would be equipped and able to ascertain the degree of cross-phasing inherent in many cultural institutions. That is, he or she would seek to master activities in one phase of consciousness designed to catalyze experiences in other phases of consciousness. The anthropologist might as a consequence participate in "possession ceremonies," or in a Balinese Kris dance, become a shaman's apprentice and seek a guide in trance, or seek divinatory guidance as a dreamer. In a real sense, the transpersonal anthropologist's activities in this respect are but extensions of the method of participant observation. Once the liabilities inherent in monophasia are completely understood by anthropologists, there really can be no alternative to a transpersonal orientation.

Second, transpersonal anthropologists will be able to explore the polyphasic phenomenology underlying the *cosmologies* of non-Western peoples. It is an interesting paradox that the systems view that environmentalists have striven so hard to inculcate in the decision-making process of modern social planning seems to be present and quite normal in the thinking of many so-called primitive peoples. It is our hunch that transpersonal experiences gained through polyphasic consciousness are a major ingredient in the generation and reinforcement of the systemic features of cosmologies everywhere—if not direct experience gained by all members of the group, at least that gained and communicated by an adept few (the shamans, the creators and transformers of myth). It is through transpersonal experience, after all, that humanity is potentially able to directly experience the essential unity of all phenomenal reality, is able to experience the dissolution of the personal ego and participation as an element in a greater being (Buber's *I-Thou*, the Buddhist's 'absorption'), is able to expand his knowledge of reality by transcending the barriers of corporeal existence and traveling to realms beyond the limits imposed by his immediate operational environment.

Third, as Roszak, Teilhard de Chardin, and Weil among others have claimed, there seems to exist in mankind an innate drive to seek transpersonal experience. This claim is borne out by the culturally universal trend towards altering the "natural" flow of consciousness by socially prescribed techniques, conditions, and drugs. We agree with Carl Jung's hypothesis that this drive is no more nor less than the organism seeking structural unity by integrating the personal ego and the true self. The primordial means by which humanity seems to facilitate integration of conscious and unconscious aspects of the organism would seem to be via the organizational principles of symbolism, experienced in alternate phases of consciousness.

Our society is presently in the throes of a spiritual transformation going from a period of virtual repudiation of transpersonal experience—including rituals and techniques designed to elicit such experience, and the hermeneutic systems that lead to and lend meaning to such experience—to a helter-skelter sampling of every conceivable approach to attainment of transpersonal experience, from psychedelic drugs and "psychogismology" to East Indian *gurus*.

The mediating role of transpersonal anthropology in this scramble could be useful, and might affect the course of events in at least three ways: (1) The potential exists right now for the construction of a neurocognitively, psychologically, and cross-culturally sophisticated body of theory explaining the nature of transpersonal experience. This would necessarily involve unearthing the operating structures mediating consciousness and the elements and relations given coherence by consciousness. Such a theory would explain how various techniques lead to various experiences, as well as how cultural elements are involved. (2) From a bulwark of theory, the transpersonal anthropologist could participate in and evaluate various programs, both indigenous and borrowed, for altering consciousness, and thus act as a quality control agent, pointing up effective programs and exposing charlatans. (3) It is conceivable that a field of applied transpersonal anthropology could develop to the extent that the anthropologist becomes the shaman to guide others, both professional and non-professional, in their quest for uniting consciousness through polyphasia. It is more likely, however, that the anthropologist will find his or her most attentive audience among the healing professions, particularly medicine and clinical psychology. In any case, cross-cultural familiarity with the methods and means of attaining transpersonal experience and unitive consciousness would give the anthropologist an even more important role as "culture broker."

Obviously there are pitfalls inherent in the transpersonalist-as-expert formula. These are the dangers always attendant upon professionally legitimized egos: "I know and you don't!" When we speak here of the professional transpersonal anthropologist, we are not referring to someone who has had a few "wow" acid experiences. Rather, we are referring to seasoned and disciplined investigators of alternative phases of consciousness with years of experience behind them who have, at least to some minimal degree, won through to the realization of the very structures of experience in their own being. Obviously the process of apprenticeship becomes crucial to the transpersonal movement.

THE TRAINING OF TRANSPERSONAL ANTHROPOLOGISTS

Not every student of anthropology could or should be trained as a transpersonalist. First, confrontation with transpersonal experience does not leave the transpersonalist unchanged. In fact, such experiences can be quite dangerous to the psychological well-being of a person, especially if unguided by an experienced adept or shaman. This is perhaps most evident if one conceives of transpersonal experiences as excursions into the unconscious.

The potential transpersonal anthropologist, then, should be an individual with a strong and durable, but flexible, ego structure, an individual who is capable of confronting novelty without danger of severe trauma, and preferably an individual who is to some extent familiar with transpersonal experience.

What we need, at least for a start, are highly capable, abstract thinkers who can remain scientists while at the same time participating fully in polyphasic explorations. As many ethnographers have learned over the generations, it is not easy to maintain a long-term stance as it were with a foot in two different worlds. Yet we are in need of individuals who can develop the means of communicating phase-specific phenomenology in a scientifically rigorous way, and the techniques for testing scientific models of polyphasic events.

A candidate for specialization in transpersonal anthropology might receive the normal round of orthodox training with the addition of specialized instruction and guidance designed to further familiarize him or her with the varieties of transpersonal experience. We would suggest that such exceptional training begin with a period of intensive transpersonal psychotherapy as well as other approaches.

After completion of initial self-exploration, the student could then begin a lengthy period of transpersonal exploration under the supervision of competent guides. The range of techniques and experiences would vary with the inclination of the student and the talent available for guidance, but could be as diverse as controlled psychedelic experience, intense meditation involving lengthy retreats, hypnotherapy and psychoanalysis (particularly of a Jungian bent), dream incubation and exploration. The results of these various explorations into polyphasic consciousness could be processed and formalized in the context of a seminar involving at least one experienced transpersonalist as instructor and perhaps all of the transpersonal anthropology students in the program.

In this seminar, individuals would be encouraged to formulate means of communicating to others the scientifically relevant aspects of their experiences, thus developing the conceptual tools to be later used in the field. They might also confront and evaluate the various theoretical approaches available in the literature that purport to explain transpersonal experience and polyphasic consciousness. At every juncture, of course, individuals exhibiting debilitating levels of psychological stress should be encouraged to withdraw from transpersonal training and follow a more orthodox course in anthropology.

Not all of our emphasis, naturally, should be placed upon producing transpersonal anthropologists. All field researchers should be sensitized to the problems inherent in the study of polyphasic societies so that they will not fail, through ignorance of their monophasic bias, to collect relevant data.

❏

32

The Near-Death Experience

Kenneth Ring

What is it exactly that someone experiences who reports having survived an NDE? Perhaps the best way to grasp this (through the written word) is for you to imagine that this is something that is happening to you. There are, however, two important qualifications. First, though they tend to follow a single common pattern, near-death experiences vary greatly in terms of the number of experiential elements that serve to define the prototypic pattern. In short, some are more complete than others. Second, as one gets deeper into the experience, there are several different "branches" that one may follow after experiencing the basic NDE "stem." For our purposes, you should imagine a fairly full NDE, which will progress along one of the most common branches.

Probably the first sensation would be a feeling of extreme peace and tremendous well-being. You'd feel no pain—nor indeed any bodily sensation of any kind. You might be aware of a kind of crystalline, pure silence unlike anything you'd ever experienced before. You would probably have the direct awareness that whatever this was, you were absolutely safe and secure in this all-pervading atmosphere of peace.

Then you'd begin to have a kind of visual awareness of your environment. The first thing you'd notice is that while you—the real you—appear to be watching everything from above, your *body* is "down there" surrounded by a knot of concerned individuals. Indeed, you have never felt better in your life—your perception is extremely vivid and clear, your mind seems to be functioning in a hyper-lucid fashion and you are feeling more fully alive than you can ever remember.

Suddenly your attention is drawn to an inviting, velvety blackness and you find yourself moving through this blackness—without a body but with an unmistakable sense of motion—and, as you do, you are aware that this blackness has the configuration of a tunnel.

As you approach the end of the tunnel, you become aware of a pinpoint of light. This light quickly grows bigger and brighter and becomes more effulgent. It is an extremely brilliant light—golden-white—but it absolutely does not hurt your eyes at all. You've never experienced a light like this—it seems to be sourceless and to cover the entire vista before you. As you move closer to the light you begin to be overwhelmed with the most powerful waves of what can only be described as pure love, which seem to penetrate to the very core of your being. There are no thoughts at all now—only total immersion in this light. All time stops; this is eternity, this is perfection—you are home again in the light.

In the midst of this timeless perfection, however, you become aware that somehow associated with this light there is a definite *presence*. It is not a person, but it is a *being* of some kind, a form you cannot see but to whose consciousness your own mind seems linked. The presence informs you that you must make a decision whether to remain here or to go back. Even as this thought is communicated to you, you are suddenly seeing as though in a million simultaneous yet precise and sharp images, everything that has ever happened to you in your life. There is no sense of judgment but as this patterned fabric of your life unravels before you, you grasp the essential meaning of your life and you see with absolute clarity that you must go back, that your family, especially your children, needs you.

That's the last bit of transcendental awareness you have. The next thing you know is that you are in excruciating pain in an intensive care unit, unable to talk but able to remember every last detail of what happened to you.

What is clear to you is that this was no dream or hallucination. Nor was it something that you simply imagined. This was compellingly real and absolutely objective: it was more real than life itself. You wish you could talk to somebody about it, but who could understand, even if you found words adequate to describe it? All you know is that this is the most profound thing that has ever happened to you and that your life—and your understanding of life—will never again be the same.

So much for a fairly common *deep* near-death experience and its immediate aftermath. In any event, this is what many people have said "it is like to die." Of course, the bare recital of such an experience only raises a multitude of empirical and interpretative questions; it does not provide any firm answers (except, possibly, to those who have the experience) concerning what occurs at death, much less what, if anything, takes place *after* biological death. However, considerable research has recently been conducted into these experiences.

PARAMETERS AND INTERPRETATIONS OF THE NDE

How often does it actually occur? If one were to take one hundred consecutive cases of patients who clinically died, how many of the survivors would relate NDEs?

Early research (Ring, 1980; Sabom, 1982) suggested that the answer might be about 40 percent, and this estimate has also been supported by the results of a Gallup poll (Gallup, 1982). Most people remember nothing as a result of a near-death crisis, but a very high percentage of those who claim to have some conscious recall report experiences that conform, at least in part, to the prototypic NDE we've already considered. A scattered number will report idiosyncratic experiences that usually seem to be hallucinatory in character; likewise, a tiny fraction of all cases appear to be negative experiences.

Another question that is often asked is, does the way one nearly dies affect the experience? Overall, the pattern seems quite clear-cut: by whatever means a person comes close to death, once the NDE begins to unfold, it is essentially invariant and has the form described earlier. In addition, research on suicide-related NDEs has shown that these experiences likewise tend to conform to the prototypic pattern.

If situational variables do not significantly influence the experience, what about personal characteristics? Are certain people more likely to have such an experience because of social background, personality, prior beliefs, or even prior knowledge of near-death experiences? Once again, the research to date is consistent in finding that individual and social factors appear to play a minimal role. Demographic variables such as gender, race, social class, or education, for example, have been shown not to be connected with NDE incidence and form. Similarly, it is evident that there is no particular kind of person—defined by psychological attributes—who is especially likely to have a near-death experience. Atheists and agnostics are no less likely to recount prototypic near-death experiences than religious people, though their interpretation of the experience is apt to be different. Finally, prior knowledge does not seem to increase the probability of having one.

When we come to the question—and it is an all-important one—of *universality*, we must admit that this is an area of research that is still lamentably underdeveloped. Nevertheless, it seems that despite some degree of cultural variation, there may be certain universal constants such as the out-of-body experience, the passage through a realm of darkness toward a brilliantly illuminated area, and the encounter with "celestial" beings.

Finally, we must address the issue of the general interpretation of the NDE. There exist a plethora of theories and a minimum of consensus about them. These theories tend to fall into three broad classes: biological, psychological, and transcendental, though many interpretations do not confine themselves to a single perspective. The biological theories tend to be reductionistic and antisurvival in tone whereas those with transcendental emphases tend to be empirically untestable but compatible with a survivalistic interpretation. Naturally, the psychological theories are intermediate in most respects.

A decade of research on the near-death experience has utterly failed to produce any kind of generally accepted interpretation. Moreover, I have recently tried to show (Ring, 1984) that the surrounding interpretative issues are even more complex than many theorists have apparently appreciated.

The larger significance of the near-death experience turns not so much on either the phenomenology or the parameters of the experience but on its *transformative* effects. For it is precisely these effects that afford us a means of merging it with certain broad evolutionary currents that seem to be propelling humanity toward the next stage of its collective development. To understand the basis of this linkage, we must now explore the ways in which a near-death experience tends to change the lives, conduct, and character of those who survive it.

TRANSFORMATIVE EFFECTS OF NDE

The most recent work in near-death studies has been increasingly focused on the after-effects of the NDE, and it is concordant in revealing a very provocative set of findings. First, it appears that just as the near-death experience itself seems to adhere to a common pattern of transcendental elements, so also there seems to be a consistent pattern of transformative after-effects. Second, this pattern of changes tends to be so highly positive and specific in its effects that it is possible to interpret it as indicative of *a generalized awakening of higher human potential*. To see how this could be so, and to lay the groundwork for its possible evolutionary significance, let us now review the findings of my own study (Ring, 1984).

This investigation examined three broad categories of after-effects: (1) changes in self-concept and personal values; (2) changes in religious or spiritual orientation; and (3) changes in psychic awareness. What, then, is the psychological portrait that can be drawn from this study?

First, in the realm of personal values, people emerge from this experience with a heightened *appreciation of life*, which often takes the form not only of a greater responsiveness to its natural beauty but also of a pronounced tendency to be focused intently on the present moment. Concern over past grievances and worries about future problems tend to diminish. As a result, these people are able to be more fully present to life now, in the moment, so that an enhanced attentiveness to their environment and a freshness of perception follow naturally. They also possess a greater appreciation of themselves in the sense that they have greater *feelings of self-worth* generally. In most cases, it is not that they show signs of ego inflation, but rather that they are able to come to a kind of acceptance of themselves as they are, which they will sometimes attribute to the tremendous sense of affirmation they received "from the Light."

Perhaps one of the most evident changes that follows a near-death experience is an *increased concern for the welfare of others*. This is a very broad and important domain with many different aspects to it. Here I will only be able to briefly summarize its principal modes of expression—increased tolerance, patience, and compassion for others, and especially an increased ability to express love. Indeed, after a near-death experience, people tend to emphasize the importance of sharing love as the primary value in life. In addition, they seem to feel a stronger desire to help others and claim to have more insight into human problems and more understanding of other human beings. Finally, they seem to demonstrate an unconditional acceptance of others, possibly because they have been able to accept themselves in this way. In a sense, one might characterize all these changes as exemplifying a *greater appreciation of others* and, as such, it may represent still another facet of what appears to be a general appreciation factor that the near-death experience itself serves to intensify.

In other values there is a clear and consistent decline. For example, the importance placed on material things, on success for its own sake, and on the need to make a good impression on others, all diminish. In general, people-oriented values rise while concern over material success plummets.

These people tend to seek a deeper understanding of life, especially its spiritual or religious aspects. They tend to become involved in a search for increased self-understanding as well, and appear more inclined to join organizations or engage in reading or other activities that will be conducive to achieving these ends.

Statements by close friends and family members tend to provide support for the behavioral changes these people describe in themselves.

Moving to the area of religious and spiritual changes, it will come as no surprise to learn that there are far-reaching after-effects here, too. In general, however, such changes tend to follow a particular form to which the term *universalistic* might most appropriately be applied. In characterizing this universalistic orientation, it will be helpful to distinguish a number of different components that together make up the model spiritual world-view of those who have experienced a near-death crisis.

First, there is a tendency to describe themselves as more spiritual, not necessarily more religious. By this they appear to signify that they have experienced a deep inward change in their spiritual awareness, but not one that made them more outwardly religious in their behavior. They claim to feel, for example, much closer to God than they had before, but the formal, more external aspects of religious worship often appear to have weakened in importance. They are also more likely to express an unconditional belief in "life after death" for everyone and to endorse the conviction that not only will there be some form of post-mortem existence, but that "the Light" will be there for everyone at death, regardless of one's beliefs (or lack of them) about what happens at death.

A greater openness to the idea of re-incarnation is often expressed.

Finally, the near-death experience draws people to a belief in the idea known to students of comparative religion as "the transcendent unity of religions," the notion that underlying all the world's greatest religious traditions there is a single and shared transcendent vision of the Divine.

Not only my findings but those of others (Greyson, 1983; Kohr, 1983) tend to support the hypothesis that the near-death experience serves to trigger an increase in psychic sensitivity and development. For example, they claim to have had more telepathic and clairvoyant experiences, more precognitive experiences (especially in dreams), greater awareness of synchronicities, more out-of-body experiences, and a generally increased susceptibility to what parapsychologists call "psi-conducive states of consciousness" (that is, psychological states which seem to facilitate the occurrence of psychic phenomena).

Having now reviewed the findings on some of the major after-effects of near-death experiences, we must seek a coherent framework to place them in. I believe it is possible and plausible to regard the near-death experience as playing a critical *catalytic* role in personal development. Specifically, it seems to serve as a catalyst to promote the *spiritual awakening and growth* of the individual because of its power to thrust one into a transcendental state of consciousness whose impact is to trigger a release of a universal "inner programming" of higher human potentials. There may be in each of us a latent spiritual core that is set to manifest in a particular form if only it can be activated by a powerful enough stimulus. A near-death experience certainly tends to stimulate a *radical spiritual transformation* in the life of the individual, which affects self-concept, relations to others, view of the world *and* worldview, as well as mode of psychological and psychic functioning. But how does any of this—profound as these changes may be—speak to the weighty issues of human evolution and planetary transformation?

IMPLICATIONS OF THE NDE FOR HUMAN EVOLUTION AND PLANETARY TRANSFORMATION

I believe only a very partial understanding of the significance of the near-death experience can be attained from a strictly psychological perspective, i.e., one that concentrates on the *individual's* experience and its effects upon him. A more complete appreciation is available, however, if we shift the level of analysis from the individual plane to the sociological.

Recall, first of all, that it has already been projected that perhaps as many as *eight million* adult Americans have experienced this phenomenon—and we know that American children also report such experiences. Although we do not have even a crude estimate of how many people in the whole world may have had this experience, it certainly does not seem unreasonable to assume that additional millions outside the United States must also have had them. But the point is not simply that many millions will know this experience for themselves but also *how the NDE will transform them afterward.*

The radical spiritual transformation which often follows a near-death experience is by no means unique to that experience alone. Rather, as Grof has recently implied, transcendental experiences, however they may come about, tend to induce similar patterns of spiritual change in individuals who undergo them. In short, the near-death experience is only *one* means to catalyze a spiritual transformation.

With resuscitation technology likely to improve and to spread in use around the globe, it appears inevitable that many more millions will undergo and survive near-death experiences and thus be transformed according to this archetypal pattern.

May it be that this high rate of transcendental experience *collectively represents an evolutionary thrust toward higher consciousness for humanity at large*? Could it be that the near-death experience is itself an *evolutionary mechanism* that has the effect of jump-stepping individuals into the next stage of human development by unlocking previously dormant spiritual potentials? Indeed, are we seeing in these people, as they mutate from their former personalities into more loving and compassionate individuals, the prototype of a new, more spiritually advanced strain of the human species striving to come into being? Do these people represent the "early maturers" of a new breed of humanity emerging in our time—an evolutionary bridge to the next shore in our progression as a species, a "missing link" in our midst? These are heady and provocative questions, but they are not entirely speculative ones.

I am not one who foresees the emergence of a new, cooperative planetary culture as a necessary consequence of the kind of evolutionary shift in consciousness I detect. Rather, I see that shift as a potential of the human species that is beginning to manifest, but whether it takes hold and transforms the earth depends on many factors; not least is the extent to which many of us consciously align with these trends and seek to awaken. Clearly, nothing in the collective human potential emerging from the spawning grounds of transcendental experiences precludes the possibility of our planet's self-destructing.

At the same time this recent curious phenomenon—the near-death experience—seems to be holding out a powerful message of hope to humanity that even, and perhaps especially, in its darkest moments, the Light comes to show us the way onward. It is up to each of us whether we shall have the courage and the wisdom to follow where it beckons.

SECTION NINE

❑

THE PHILOSOPHY OF TRANSCENDENCE

Philosophy is to be studied, not for the sake of any definite answers to its questions, since no definite answers can, as a rule, be known to be true, but rather for the sake of the questions themselves, because these questions enlarge our conception of what is possible, enrich our intellectual imagination and diminish the dogmatic assurance which closes the mind against speculation; but above all because, through the greatness of the universe which philosophy contemplates, the mind is also rendered great, and becomes capable of that union with the universe which constitutes its highest good.

—BERTRAND RUSSELL[1]

ALL DISCIPLINES rest on a network of philosophical assumptions about the nature of life and reality. These fundamental assumptions play a potent, but often unconscious, role in determining our beliefs about mind and human nature. For example, the materialist who believes that matter is the primary constituent of reality and that life and consciousness are merely curious accidents will regard mind and human nature very differently from the person who believes that consciousness is primary and life is its purposeful creation. For the materialist, people and minds may be endlessly fascinating but are at bottom merely machines devoid of significance and ultimately reducible to neuronal fireworks and chemical combinations. For the idealist, on the other hand, people and minds may be part of a universal consciousness and partake of its boundless significance.

Likewise, persons who value contemplation and the vast range of transpersonal experiences it offers probably come to conclusions about mind and consciousness very different from those of logical positivists who trust only science. In other words, our assumptions about the mind reflect our assumptions about the universe; psychology mirrors philosophy.

Yet these philosophical assumptions are rarely investigated. As Ken Wilber lamented, "Most orthodox psychologists, under the delusion that they are empirical scientists, think that they can ignore philosophy, whereas in fact their empirical-analytical psychology rests on extensive systems of hidden metaphysics and arbitrary epistemic assumptions. At the very least, hidden metaphysics is bad metaphysics (just as unconsciousness motivation is often pathological)."[2]

In "Transpersonal Worldviews: Historical and Philosophical Reflections," Robert McDermott points out that transpersonal psychology has given insufficient attention to philosophical assumptions and implications. A transpersonal philosophy adequate to support the transpersonal movement has yet to be articulated. McDermott also suggests that transpersonalism may be able to learn a great deal from related philosophical movements such as romanticism and American transcendentalism.

There have been some efforts to link transpersonal psychology to the perennial philosophy—that common core of philosophical and psychological wisdom at the heart of the great religious traditions. Parts of transpersonal psychology may represent a contemporary rediscovery and description of certain psychological dimensions of the perennial philosophy. The perennial philosophy, in turn, may provide part of a philosophical framework on which to build this new discipline.

Aldous Huxley, who did more than anyone else to popularize the term, pointed out that aspects of the perennial philosophy emerged "in every region of the world, and in its fully developed forms it has a place in every one of the higher religions."[3] Indeed, "It has, in one form or another, been the dominant official philosophy of the larger part of civilized mankind throughout most of its history."[4]

In his essay Huxley describes four central claims of the perennial philosophy: the world and all its creatures are expressions of an underlying divine reality; by appropriate training humans can come to know this reality; and they can recognize their unity with this divine ground. Finally, this recognition of the divine ground as our true nature is the highest goal of human existence.

According to the perennial philosophy the fundamental nature or substrate of reality is spirit or consciousness, also known as Brahman, Tao, or God. This fundamental reality is beyond all qualities, descriptions, and concepts. In "The Great Chain of Being," Ken Wilber points out that this fundamental reality also manifests or projects itself as the universe. This universe is said to be organized or layered in an ontological hierarchy, or better, holoarchy. This holoarchy of being that constitutes the great chain ranges from matter through increasingly subtle realms of mind, soul, and spirit. Different traditions use different terms to describe it, but the general assumptions are the same.

In a materialistic culture human beings usually identify only with the physical and mental levels of the great chain. Through appropriate training, however, we can expand our sense of identity to include the spiritual realm and this movement constitutes development.

For Wilber the major problem of contemporary philosophy and psychology is that in their infatuation with science, which focuses on the investigation of matter, philosophers and psychologists too have largely restricted their investigations to matter. Philosophy and psychology, therefore, have ignored or even denied the existence of the more subtle levels of the great chain. The result has been a constriction of the scope and significance of these disciplines and our vision of reality.

While the perennial philosophy and great chain of being are powerful ideas, Donald Rothberg has cautioned that they are not widely accepted in mainstream psychology and philosophy. Though many transpersonal psychologists find the perennial philosophy attractive, crucial questions have yet to be answered. These include whether it successfully identifies common structures underlying different philosophical and religious traditions, whether the model can be shown to be valid, and how the perennial philosophy can best be understood and expressed in contemporary terms.[5] These criticisms need to be carefully considered and incorporated in transpersonal thinking.

In "Hidden Wisdom," Roger Walsh points out that the world's traditional transpersonal philosophies and psychologies are multistate disciplines developed in, and descriptive of, multiple states of consciousness. Contemplative training for accessing these states may therefore be essential for understanding and constructing transpersonal disciplines.

The crucial conclusion is this: Without contemplative training we may overlook the most profound wisdom contained in transpersonal philosophies and psychologies, and yet be completely unaware that this wisdom exists and that we have overlooked it. The result is an entirely unsuspected but tragically impoverished view of transpersonal disciplines, of reality, and of ourselves.

33

Transpersonal Worldviews: Historical and Philosophical Reflections

Robert A. McDermott

This essay is an attempt to show that the assumptions that underlie emerging transpersonal disciplines presuppose an essentially philosophical worldview. Transpersonal psychology, which is surely the "home base" of the various meanings of transpersonalism, evolved from humanistic psychology primarily because of differences that are broadly philosophical, or at least involve a difference of worldview, not merely a difference within a specific discipline.

In the first half of this essay, I will try to show that the salient philosophical characteristics of transpersonalism are evident in the double transition from mainline academic psychology to humanistic psychology and from humanistic to transpersonal psychology. Building on this development, the second part of this essay will attempt to move transpersonalism, of whatever form, toward a more constructive and articulate philosophical position. Specifically, I will suggest that a transpersonal worldview, or transpersonalism, is more intelligible and significant within the context of Romanticism and would realize a greater potential if it were to cultivate the participatory epistemology variously espoused in the nineteenth century by Goethe, Coleridge, and Emerson and in the early twentieth century by William James, Rudolf Steiner, and recently in nascent form in the writings of transpersonal psychologists.

EMERGENCE OF TRANSPERSONAL WORLDVIEWS

This essay assumes that contemporary Western thought, particularly in North America and Western Europe, is slowly but definitely moving toward the creation of a new paradigm—a new set of dominant assumptions. Eventually these assumptions will replace the Newtonian-mechanistic-materialistic worldview that has dominated Western thought

206

since the seventeenth century and will in time become so fundamental that they too will serve as the unconscious presuppositions for subsequent thought and cultural expression.

While it would be premature and presumptuous to claim that the new paradigm would be known as or characterized by transpersonalism, it is not too much to claim that transpersonal psychology exhibits some of the essential marks of a larger development to an emerging paradigm. Transpersonal psychology originated recently and modestly—in fact, from a small group of psychologists in the San Francisco Bay Area who wanted to distinguish their psychological theories and practices from humanistic psychology. It is generally well known, and nevertheless worth repeating, that Abraham Maslow, Anthony Sutich, and Stanislav Grof had been the primary founders of the humanistic psychology movement, and then in collaboration with colleagues initiated a new organization and movement for which Stanislav Grof provided the name "transpersonal."

Transpersonal psychologists had lived happily in the community of humanistic psychology for approximately a decade before they began to focus less on what they held in common with the humanistic worldview—a need to break the hold of a dehumanizing reductionism—and more on all that remains omitted from the humanistic conception of human experience. From many sides came reports of experiences, therapies, and sources of insight that collectively affirm realities far beyond the humanistic worldview. Without needing to reject what is affirmed in the humanistic perspective, the transpersonalist tends to emphasize the extraordinary, the "trans," whether with respect to the intimacy of the relation between the individual and the cosmos, or altered states of consciousness, or the relevance of mystical and shamanic disciplines. All of these interests involve significant epistemological and ontological judgments.

Humanistic psychology, like humanistic philosophy, opposes the naturalistic/positivist reduction of the cosmos and the individual to an impersonal mechanism. All varieties of humanism oppose the prevalent rejection of distinctively human values and aspirations. Against a worldview that sees the human, and particularly the individual, as a by-product of mindless material forces, "humanistic" affirms a universe in and through which the human being is capable of generating and sharing distinctively human meanings and values. Transpersonal psychologists affirm all that humanistic psychology stands for in contrast to the depersonalization of modern Western scientific thinking, but they also insist, with William James, that "the human being is continuous with Something More."

For transpersonalism to be understood it will need to be defined in relation to the family resemblances it shares with traditional and contemporary like-minded worldviews. Aristotle taught that a definition must include an account of the edges as well as the essential; to define is to delimit. In the case of transpersonalism, we need first to find its core, and then to find its edges in relation to humanistic psychology, Asian psychologies, and spiritual philosophies such as Vedanta, yoga, or Taoism. To describe or to characterize a multidisciplinary perspective necessarily lands us in a consideration of presuppositions and underlying principles—in short, philosophical considerations.

Since psychology separated from its philosophical moorings at the end of the nineteenth century, virtually all psychological schools and movements have made enormous implicit philosophical assumptions. Transpersonal psychology is no exception. The essays in this book assume positions (and exclude others) concerning the nature of the cosmos, society, and the individual; the reality of spirit and soul (or psyche); varieties of transformative experience and alternate ways of knowing; and images of the human being. In these pages we will explore some of the philosophical assumptions, claims, and implications of transpersonalism.

Despite the significant philosophical outline fashioned by Ken Wilber and others, transpersonalists as a group of like-minded thinkers and therapists have not taken up the responsibility of forming a transpersonal view of human nature, i.e., a distinctive transpersonal anthropology. They do, however, offer a shared conviction that the person (human being, individual) has experiences held to be illusory by the positivist/naturalist philosophies, which deny the spiritual, the inner depth dimension, the "trans" component.

In philosophical terms, the emphasis on the extraordinary indicates that transpersonalists tend to be closer to Plato than to Aristotle or the Sophists, closer to Hegel than to Hume, closer to James than to Dewey, closer to the Taoists than to the Confucians, closer to the Vedantists, Sufis, Buddhists, and mystics of all varieties than to traditional religious experience. While the transpersonal movement has been informed and inspired by peak experiences of virtually all religious traditions, it not surprisingly has drawn most comfortably from Buddhist theory and practice. With almost all forms of Buddhism, transpersonalism tends to value healing practices in response to *dukkha* (the pain of existence) without attachment to a particular ontology.

As a contemporary Western worldview and approach to healing with a significant, albeit implicit, philosophical attitude, transpersonalism stands against a cluster of philosophies variously identified as positivism and materialism, as well as scientific and naturalistic humanism. Hence, it stands in opposition to the philosophical materialism of Freud and the deterministic behaviorism of B. F. Skinner. The "trans" in transpersonal refers to a crossing over precisely to the kind of reality, to the kinds of experiences, which are ordinarily ruled to be philosophically inadmissible.

Modern Western scientism, or the kind of philosophical naturalism that explicitly excludes spiritual or transcendent experience, has generally not held an agnostic position with respect to the "trans" dimensions of the universe, but has rather insisted on an atheistic position, one that begins by rejecting all claims for knowledge derived from nonordinary states of consciousness; all forms of positivist thought insist that there are no possible sources of nonordinary states. Transpersonalism is of course emphatically opposed to this positivist worldview and image of the human being. With the humanism of a psychologist such as Carl Rogers, the transpersonalist shares an almost innate concern with the positive dimensions of human nature and human experience. But transpersonalism spans the range of interests from the safe perspectives of humanistic emphasis on the normal and ordinary to the transpersonal emphasis on the extraordinary, on the profoundly transformative and on alternate states of consciousness. With the exception of William James, whose philosophy was at once characteristically American and transpersonal, as well as radically empirical and pluralistic, philosophers have consistently ignored the experiential claims, and the range of experience, on which transpersonal psychology has focused.

In addition to the themes raised by William James's research into the varieties of religious experience and psychical phenomena, transpersonalism can also rightly claim as its forebear C. G. Jung's research and therapies concerning the pan-human expression of archetypal images. There is an important difference between these two paradigmatic transpersonal psychologists. James began his thought with his psychology (*Principles of Psychology*, 1890) and proceeded to develop its philosophical justification, as well as its ethical and religious applications. Jung attempted to isolate his psychology from philosophy—which throughout his career was dominated by positivism—and from the obligation to justify his philosophical assumptions. Jung's archetypal psychology is surely the richest store of multicultural and transpersonal images and interpretations, but like many other transpersonalist perspectives, it does not advance the necessary examination of psychological research in the light of philosophical foundations.

TRANSPERSONALISM AS AMERICAN ROMANTICISM

The philosophical mindset of transpersonalism is also continuous with the creative genius of the nineteenth-century artists and thinkers who celebrated the infinite, the interior, and the intriguing relationship between ancient and modern. The most well-established general term for this philosophical attitude is Romanticism, the worldview that emerged in the eighteenth century and flourished in the nineteenth as a reaction against scientific rationalism. Transpersonalism is not related to Romanticism as one school or movement to another, however, but rather as a variation on the theme of affirming and exploring individual experiences of inner and transcendent realities, or, in James's phrase, varied experiences of "Something More." The term "vision" in the title of this book is especially apt in this discussion of transpersonalism and Romanticism because both of these movements are characterized by a commitment to ever larger visions both in their own right and in reaction to the shrunken vision espoused by their predecessors and contemporaries.

There are other instructive similarities and differences between Romanticism and transpersonalism. Both are essentially a commitment to a larger, more interior and transformative view of human experience, and in this respect both are committed to a highly participatory rather than a spectator theory of knowledge. The transformative power of all forms of Romanticism—and the potential transformative power of its latest expression, turn-of-the-millennium transpersonalism—resides primarily in this commitment to the practice of thinking that is essentially artistic, and reality-shaping. The success of transpersonalism will depend on the extent to which its exponents exemplify a Romantic epistemology, a way of knowing that shows the knower to have penetrated to the inner life of the cosmos, including the farthest reaches and most intimate details of nature, the grand and pedestrian components of human experience, and the range of human inquiry, from sciences through philosophy and history to religion and art. In short, transpersonalist thinkers will have to take up the agendas and advance the creative contributions of the paradigmatic but largely ignored nineteenth-century Romantics—Goethe, Coleridge, and Emerson.

In his *Romanticism Comes of Age*, Owen Barfield summarizes the thought of Goethe and Coleridge in terms that suggest ways in which they would be helpful in clearly establishing the problem with which transpersonalism has been primarily concerned:

> Both of them overcame (and hence the degree of misunderstanding which they have encountered) the arch fallacy of their age and our own, the fallacy that mind is exclusively subjective or, to put it more crudely, that mind is something which is shut up in a box called the brain, the fallacy that the mind of man is a passive onlooker at the processes and phenomena of nature, in the creation of which it neither takes nor has taken any part, the fallacy that there are many separate minds, but no such thing as Mind.[1]

Ralph Waldo Emerson offers a similar critique of this fallacy of our age and in terms at once Romantic and transpersonalist offers a fully formed and inexhaustible account of extraordinary states of consciousness. While we do not find in Emerson reports on the practice of Vipassana meditation or holotropic breathing or psychedelics, we do find an epistemology and an ethics that are transpersonal in their affirmation of the infinite Mind or Spirit and powerfully affirmative of nature and the free creative human being. For Emerson, individuals, by virtue of their original imaginative thinking, are the source of their own true relation to the universe. The generation of transpersonalism, like every generation of Romanticists and transcendentalists, must learn for itself the truth of Emerson's characteristically American plea:

> Why should not we also enjoy an original relation to the universe? Why should not we have a poetry and philosophy of insight and not of tradition, and a religion by revelation to us, and not the history of theirs? Embosomed for a season in nature, whose floods of life stream around and through us, and invite us, by the powers they supply, to action proportioned to nature, why should we grope among the dry bones of the past.[2]

Any one of these thinkers—Goethe, Coleridge, or Emerson—each of whom expresses the Romantic vision, can well serve as a worthy source of philosophic grounding for a full range of transpersonalist offerings.

While it seems to be a demonstrably good idea for thinkers who share a transpersonalist worldview to build on the participatory epistemology of Romantic thinkers such as Goethe, Coleridge, or Emerson, there is more than one way to philosophical enlightenment. Scarcely any conclusion from transpersonalist research is so obvious as the pluralism of positive assumptions, methods, and conclusions. In this respect, William James serves our purpose as well or better than any other single source of philosophic methodology and vision. A fruitful next task, then, would seem to be to render systematic and critical the nascent philosophical insights of representative transpersonalist thinkers, including those who have been writing for a decade or more—particularly Ken Wilber,[3] Stanislav Grof,[4] Charles T. Tart,[5] and Roger Walsh and Frances Vaughan[6]—and two recent contributors, Donald Rothberg[7] and Richard Tarnas.[8]

In the enormously insightful and provocative "Epilogue" of his *Passion of the Western Mind*, Richard Tarnas briefly but decisively articulates the essential terms of the participatory epistemology rooted in the Romantic vision and required for contemporary thought and culture:

> The bold conjectures and myths that the human mind produces in its quest for knowledge ultimately come from something far deeper than a purely human source. They come from the wellspring of nature itself, from the universal unconscious that is bringing forth through the human mind and

human imagination its own gradually unfolding reality. In this view, the theory of a Copernicus, a Newton, or an Einstein is not simply due to the luck of a stranger; rather, it reflects the human mind's radical kinship with the cosmos. It reflects the human mind's pivotal role as a vehicle of the universe's unfolding meaning. In this view, neither the postmodern skeptic nor the perennialist philosopher is correct in their shared opinion that the modern scientific paradigm is ultimately without any cosmic foundation. For that paradigm is itself part of a larger evolutionary process.[9]

Tarnas's call for a participatory epistemology deserves to be taken up with a view to its Romantic roots as well as to its capacity to serve as the foundation for multidisciplinary, multicultural, multiconsciousness modes of knowing.

It would be particularly productive if, in addition to a full development of Tarnas's participatory epistemology, the transpersonalist community were to take up at least these three challenges:

1. A systematic and richly textured portrait of the human being in the light of nonordinary experiences.
2. A critical evaluation of nonordinary states in the light of the evolution of consciousness, particularly by the use of Wilber's pre/trans fallacy (with respect, for example, to shamanism).
3. A careful review of implications of nonordinary states for ethics, particularly for the morality of ecology, community life, and interpersonal relations.

❏

34

The Perennial Philosophy

Aldous Huxley

More than twenty-five centuries have passed since that which has been called the Perennial Philosophy was first committed to writing; and in the course of those centuries it has found expression, now partial, now complete, now in this form, now in that, again and again. The Perennial

Philosophy has spoken almost all the languages of Asia and Europe and has made use of the terminology and traditions of every one of the higher religions. But under all this confusion of tongues and myths, of local histories and particularist doctrines, there remains a Highest Common Factor, which is the Perennial Philosophy in what may be called its chemically pure state. This final purity can never, of course, be expressed by any verbal statement. It is only in the act of contemplation, when words and even personality are transcended, that the pure state of the Perennial Philosophy can actually be known.

At the core of the Perennial Philosophy we find four fundamental doctrines.

First: the phenomenal world of matter and of individualized consciousness—the world of things and animals and men and even gods—is the manifestation of a Divine Ground within which all partial realities have their being, and apart from which they would be nonexistent.

Second: human beings are capable not merely of knowing *about* the Divine Ground by inference; they can also realize its existence by a direct intuition, superior to discursive reasoning. This immediate knowledge unites the knower with that which is known.

Third: man possesses a double nature, a phenomenal ego and an eternal Self, which is the inner man, the spirit, the spark of divinity within the soul. It is possible for a man, if he so desires, to identify himself with the spirit and therefore with the Divine Ground, which is of the same or like nature with the spirit.

Fourth: man's life on earth has only one end and purpose: to identify himself with his eternal Self and so to come to unitive knowledge of the Divine Ground.

A philosopher who is content merely to know about the ultimate Reality—theoretically and by hearsay—is compared by Buddha to a herdsman of other men's cows. Mohammed uses an even homelier barnyard metaphor. For him the philosopher who has not realized his metaphysics is just an ass bearing a load of books. Christian, Hindu and Taoist teachers wrote no less emphatically about the absurd pretensions of mere learning and analytical reasoning.

The Perennial Philosophy and its ethical corollaries constitute a Highest Common Factor, present in all the major religions of the world. To affirm this truth has never been more imperatively necessary than at the present time.

❑
35

The Great Chain of Being

Ken Wilber

What is the worldview that, as Arthur Lovejoy pointed out, "has been the dominant official philosophy of the larger part of civilized humankind through most of its history"? And why is it of interest to psychology?

Known as the "perennial philosophy"—"perennial" precisely because it shows up across cultures and across the ages with essentially similar features—this worldview has, indeed, formed the core not only of the world's great wisdom traditions, from Christianity to Buddhism to Taoism, but also of the greatest philosophers, scientists, and psychologists. So overwhelmingly widespread is the perennial philosophy that it is either the single greatest intellectual error ever to appear in humankind's history or it is the single most accurate reflection of reality yet to appear.

Central to the perennial philosophy is the notion of "the great chain of being." The idea itself is fairly simple. Reality, according to the perennial philosophy, is not one-dimensional; it is not a flatland of uniform substance. Rather, reality is composed of several *different* but *continuous* dimensions. Manifest reality, that is, consists of different grades or levels, reaching from the lowest and most dense and least conscious to the highest and most subtle and most conscious. At one end of this continuum of being or spectrum of consciousness is what we in the West would call "matter" or the insentient and the nonconscious, and at the other end is "spirit" or "godhead" or the "superconscious" (which is also said to be the all-pervading ground of the entire sequence, as we will see). Arrayed in between are the other dimensions of being arranged according to their individual degrees of reality (Plato), actuality (Aristotle), inclusiveness (Hegel), consciousness (Aurobindo), clarity (Leibniz), value (Whitehead), or knowingness (Garab Dorje).

Sometimes the great chain is presented as having just three major levels: matter, mind, and spirit. Other versions give five levels: matter, body, mind, soul, and spirit. Some of the yogic systems give literally dozens of discrete yet continuous dimensions. For the time being, our simple hierarchy of matter to body to mind to soul to spirit will suffice.

The central claim of the perennial philosophy is that *men and women can grow and develop (or evolve) all the way up the hierarchy to Spirit itself*, therein to realize a "supreme identity" with Godhead—the *ens perfectissimum* toward which all growth and evolution yearns.

But notice that the great chain is indeed a "hierarchy"—a word that has fallen on very hard times. Originally introduced by the great Christian mystic St. Dionysius, it essentially meant "governing one's life by spiritual principles" (*hiero*- means sacred or holy, and -*arch* means governance or rule). But it soon became translated into a political/military power play, where "governance by spirit" came to mean "ruled by the Catholic Church"—a spiritual principle mistranslated into a despotism.

But as used by the perennial philosophy—and indeed, as used in modern psychology, evolutionary theory, and systems theory—hierarchy is simply a ranking of orders of events *according to their holistic capacity*. In any developmental sequence, what is whole at one stage becomes merely a part of a larger whole at the next stage. A letter is part of a whole word, which is part of a whole sentence, which is part of a whole paragraph, and so on. Arthur Koestler coined the term "holon" to refer to that which, being a whole at one stage, is a part of a wider whole at the next.

Hierarchy, then, is simply an order of increasing holons, representing an increase in wholeness and integrative capacity. This is why hierarchy is so central to systems theory, the theory of wholeness or holism ("wholism"). And it is absolutely central to the perennial philosophy. Each step up in the great chain of being is an increase in unity and wider identities, from the isolated identity of the body through the social and community identity of the mind to the supreme identity of spirit, an identity with literally all manifestation. This is why the great hierarchy of being is often drawn as a series of concentric circles or spheres or "nests within nests." Thus, the common charge that all hierarchies are "linear" completely misses the point. And so, as Coomarasamy remarked, we can use the metaphors of "levels" or "ladders" or "strata" only if we use a little imagination in understanding what is actually involved.

Developmental and evolutionary sequences proceed by hierarchization, or by orders of increasing holism—molecules to cells to organs to organisms to societies of organisms, for example. In cognitive development, we find awareness expanding from simple images, which represent only one thing or event, to symbols and concepts which represent whole groups or classes of things and events, to rules which organize and integrate numerous classes and groups into entire networks. In moral development (male or female), we find a reasoning that moves from the isolated subject to a group or tribe of related subjects, to an entire network of groups beyond any isolated element. The *more holistic* patterns appear *later* in development because they have to await the emergence of the parts that they will then integrate or unify, just as whole sentences emerge only *after* whole words.

And some hierarchies do involve a type of control network—the lower levels (which means, less holistic levels) can influence the upper (or more holistic) levels, through what is called "upward causation." But just as important, the higher levels can exert a powerful influence or control on the lower levels—so-called "downward causation." For example, when you decide to move your arm, all the atoms and molecules and cells in your arm move with it, an instance of downward causation.

In any developmental or growth sequence, as a more encompassing stage or holon emerges, it *includes* the capacities and patterns and functions of the previous stage (i.e., of the previous holons), and then adds its own unique (and more encompassing) capacities. In that sense, and in that sense only, can the new and more encompassing holon be said to be "higher" or "wider." Whatever the important value of the previous stage, the new stage has *all* of that plus something extra (more integrative capacity, for example), and that "something extra" means "extra value" *relative* to the previous (and less encompassing) stage. This crucial definition of a "higher stage" was first introduced in the West by Aristotle and in the East by Shankara and Lieh-Tzu; it has been central to the perennial philosophy ever since. As Hegel first put it, and as developmentalists have echoed ever since, each stage is adequate and valuable, but each higher stage is more adequate, and, in that sense only, more valuable (which always means, more holistic).

It is for all these reasons that Koestler, after noting that all hierarchies are composed of holons, or increasing orders of wholeness, pointed out that the correct word for "hierarchy" is actually "holoarchy." He is absolutely right, and so from now on I will refer to hierarchy in general, and the great chain in particular, as holoarchy.

A normal or natural holoarchy is the sequential or stagelike unfolding of larger networks of increasing wholeness, with the larger or wider wholes being able to exert influence over the lower-order wholes. And as natural, desirable, and unavoidable as that is, you can already start to see how holoarchies *can* go pathological. If the higher levels can exert control over the lower levels, they can also overdominate or even repress and alienate the lower levels. That leads to a whole host of pathological difficulties, in both the individual and society at large.

It is precisely *because* the world is arranged holoarchically, precisely because it contains fields within fields within fields, that things can go so profoundly wrong, that a disruption or pathology in one field can reverberate throughout an entire system. And the "cure" for this pathology, in all systems, is essentially the same: rooting out the pathological holons so the holoarchy itself can return to harmony. The cure does not consist, as the reductionists maintain, in getting rid of holoarchy per se. This is exactly the "cure" we see at work in psychoanalysis (shadow holons refuse integration), critical social theory (opaque ideology usurps open communication), democratic social revolutions (monarchical or fascist holons oppress the body politic), medical science interventions (cancerous holons invade a benign system), radical feminist critique (patriarchal holons dominate the public sphere), and so on. It is not getting rid of holoarchy per se, but arresting (and integrating) arrogant holons.

As I said, all of the world's great wisdom traditions are variations of the perennial philosophy, of the great holoarchy of being. In his book *Forgotten Truth* Huston Smith summarizes the world's major religions in one phrase: "a hierarchy of being and knowing." Chogyam Trungpa Rinpoche pointed out that *the* essential and background idea pervading all of the philosophies of the East, from India to Tibet to China, lying behind everything from Shintoism to Taoism, is "a hierarchy of earth, human, heaven," which he also pointed out is equivalent to "body, mind, spirit."

Which brings us to the most notorious paradox in the perennial philosophy. We have seen that the wisdom traditions subscribe to the notion that reality manifests in levels or dimensions, with each higher dimension being more inclusive and therefore "closer" to the absolute totality of Godhead or Spirit. In this sense, Spirit is the summit of being, the highest rung on the "ladder" of evolution (as long as we don't take that metaphor literally). But it is also true that Spirit is the wood out of which the entire ladder and all its rungs are made; spirit is the suchness, the isness, the essence of each and every thing that exists.

The first aspect, the highest-rung aspect, is the *transcendental* nature of Spirit—it far surpasses any "worldly" or creaturely or finite things. The entire earth (or even universe) could be destroyed, and Spirit would remain. The second aspect, the wood aspect, is the *immanent* nature of spirit—Spirit is equally and totally present in all manifest things and events, in nature, in culture, in heaven and on earth, with no partiality. From this angle, no phenomenon is closer to Spirit than another, for all are equally "made of" Spirit. Thus, Spirit is *both* the highest *goal* of all development and evolution, and the *ground* of the entire sequence, as present fully at the beginning as at the end. Spirit is prior to this world, but not other to this world.

Failure to take both of those paradoxical aspects of Spirit into account has historically led people to some very lopsided (and politically dangerous) views of Spirit. Traditionally, the patriarchal religions have tended to overemphasize the transcendental nature of Spirit, thus condemning earth, nature, body, and woman to an inferior status. Prior to that, the matriarchal religions tended to emphasize the immanent nature of Spirit alone, and the resultant pantheistic worldview equated the finite and created earth with the infinite and uncreated Spirit. You are free to identify with a finite and limited earth; you are not free to call it the infinite and unlimited.

Both matriarchal and patriarchal religions, both of these lopsided views of Spirit, have had rather horrible historical consequences, from brutal and large-scale human sacrifice for the fertility of the earth Goddess to whole-sale war for God the Father. But in the very midst of these outward distortions, the perennial philosophy, the esoteric or inner core of the wisdom religions, has always avoided any of those dualities—earth or heaven, masculine or feminine, finite or infinite, ascetic or revelatory—and centered instead on their union or integration ("nondualism"). And indeed, this union of heaven and earth, masculine and feminine, infinite and finite, was made explicit in the "tantric" teachings of the various wisdom traditions, from Gnosticism in the West to Vajrayana in the East. And it is this nondual core of the wisdom traditions to which the term "perennial philosophy" most applies.

The point, then, is that if we are to try to think of Spirit in mental terms (which necessarily involves some distortions, since lower holons cannot totally embrace higher holons), then at least we should remember this transcendent/immanent paradox. Paradox is simply the way nonduality looks to the mental level. Spirit itself is not paradoxical; strictly speaking, it is not characterizable at all.

This applies doubly to hierarchy (holoarchy). We have said that when transcendental Spirit manifests itself, it does so in stages or levels—the great chain of being. But I'm not saying Spirit or reality itself is hierarchical. Absolute Spirit or reality is not hierarchical. It is not qualifiable at all in mental terms (lower holon terms). It is *shunyata*, or *nirquna*, or *apopathic*—unqualifiable, without a trace of specific and limiting characteristics at all. But it manifests itself in steps, in layers, dimensions, sheaths, levels, or grades—whatever term one prefers—and that's holoarchy. In Vendanta these are the *koshas*, the sheaths or layers covering Brahman; in Buddhism, these are the eight *vijnanas*, the eight levels of awareness, each of which is a stepped-down or more restricted version of its senior dimension; in Kabbalah these are the *sefiroth*, and so on.

The whole point is that these are levels of the manifest world, of *maya*. When maya is not recognized as the play of the Divine, then it is nothing but illusion. Hierarchy is illusion. There are levels of illusion, not levels of reality. But according to the traditions, it is exactly (and only) by understanding the hierarchical nature of samsara that we can in fact climb out of it.

We can look now at some of the actual levels of the holoarchy, of the great chain of being, as it appears in the three most widely practiced wisdom traditions: Judaeo-Christian-Muslim, Buddhism, and Hinduism (although any mature tradition will do). The Christian terms are the easiest, because we already know them: matter, body, mind, soul, and spirit. "Matter" means the physical universe and our physical bodies (e.g., those aspects of existence covered by the laws of physics). "Body" in this case means the emotional body, the "animal" body, sex, hunger, vital life force, and so on (e.g., those aspects of existence studied by biology). "Mind" is the rational, reasoning, linguistic, and imaginative mind (studied by psychology). "Soul" is the higher or subtle mind, the archetypal mind, the intuitive mind, and the essence or the indestructibleness of our own being (studied by theology). And "Spirit" is the transcendental summit of our being, our Godhead (studied by contemplative mysticism).

According to Vedanta Hinduism, the individual person is composed of five "sheaths" or levels or dimensions of being (the koshas), often compared to an onion, so that as we peel away the outer layers we find more and more the essence. The lowest (or more outer) is called the *annamayakosha*, which means "the sheath made of food." This is the physical body. Next is the *pranamayokosha*, the sheath made of *prana*. *Prana* means vital force, bioenergy, elan vital, libido, emotional-sexual energy in general. This is the body (as we are using the term). Next is the *manomayakosha*, the sheath of *manas* or mind—rational, abstract, linguistic. Beyond this is the *vijnanamayakosha*, the sheath of intuition, the higher mind, the subtle mind. Finally there is the *anandamayokosha*, the sheath made of *ananda*, or spiritual and transcendental bliss.

Further—and this is important—Vendanta groups these five sheaths into three major states: gross, subtle, and causal. The gross dimension consists of the lowest level in the holoarchy, the physical body (annamayokosha). The subtle dimension consists of the three intermediate levels: the emotional-sexual body (pranamayokosha), the mind (manomayokosha), and the higher or subtle mind (vijnanamoyakosha). And the causal dimension consists of the highest level, the anandamayokosha, or archetypal spirit, which is also sometimes said to be largely (but not totally) unmanifest, or formless. Vedanta correlates these three major dimensions of being with the three major states of consciousness: waking, dreaming, and deep dreamless sleep. Beyond all three of these states is absolute Spirit, sometimes called *turiya*, "the fourth," because it is beyond (and includes) the three states of manifestation; it is beyond (and thus integrates) gross, subtle, and causal.★

The Vedanta version of five sheaths is almost identical to the Judaeo-Christian-Muslim version of matter, body, mind, soul, and Spirit, as long as we understand "soul" to mean not just a higher self or higher identity, but higher or subtler mind and cognition, intuition, and the like. And *soul* also has the meaning, in *all* the higher mystical traditions, of being a "knot" or "contraction" (what the Hindus and Buddhists call the *ahamkara*), which has to be untied and dissolved before it can transcend itself, die to itself, and find its supreme identity with and as absolute Spirit.

So "soul" is both the highest level of individual growth we can achieve, but also the final barrier, the final knot, to complete enlightenment or supreme identity, simply because as transcendental witness it stands back from everything it witnesses. Once we push through the witness position, then the soul or witness itself dissolves and there is only the play of nondual awareness, awareness that does not look at objects but is completely one with all objects (Zen says, "It is like tasting the sky"). The gap between subject and object collapses, the soul is transcended or dissolved, and pure spiritual or nondual awareness—which is very simple, very obvious, very clear—arises. You realize that your being is of all space, vast and open, and everything arising anywhere is arising in you, as spirit, spontaneously.

The central psychological model of Mahayana Buddhism is the eight vijnanas, the eight levels of consciousness. The first five are the five senses. The next is the *manovijnana*, the mind that operates on sensory experience. Then there is *manas*, which means both higher mind and the center of the illusion of the separate-self. It is the manas that looks at the *alayavijnana* (the next higher level, that of supraindividual consciousness) and mistakes it for a separate-self or substantial soul, as we have defined it. And beyond these eight levels, as both their source and ground, is the pure *alaya* or pure Spirit.

I don't mean to minimize some of the very real differences between these traditions. I'm simply pointing out that they share certain deep structural similarities, which testifies eloquently to the genuinely universal nature of their insights.

★ I said that this distinction made by Vedanta is important, because it gives us, I believe, the key to understanding the relationship between *states* of consciousness and *structures* of consciousness. The waking *state*, for example, can contain dozens of different structures of consciousness, and these structures, unlike the general states, emerge through a specific process of development. Not all structures are present in the infant (such as concrete or formal operational logic), but the general states are: the infant wakes, sleeps, and dreams. In other words, the infant is immersed in the gross, subtle, and causal states, but has not the structures to consciously manifest them, a manifestation that is known as development. I believe this key distinction solves numerous recalcitrant theoretical problems in spiritual psychology.

And so we can end on a happy note: After being temporarily derailed in the nineteenth century by a variety of materialistic reductionisms (from scientific materialism to behaviorism to Marxism), the great chain of being, the great holoarchy of being, is back. This temporary derailment—an attempt to reduce the holoarchy of being to its lowest level, matter—was particularly galling in psychology, which first lost its spirit, then its soul, then its mind, and was reduced to studying *only* empirical behavior or bodily drives.

But now evolutionary holoarchy—the holistic study of the development and self-organization of fields within fields within fields—is once again the dominant theme in virtually all scientific and behavioral disciplines (as we will see), though it goes by many names—Aristotle's "entelechy," to give only one example, is now known as "morphogenetic fields" and "self-organizing systems." This is not to say that the modern versions of the great holoarchy and its self-organizing principles offer no new insights, for they do, particularly when it comes to the actual evolutionary unfolding of the great chain itself. Each glimpse of the great holoarchy is adequate; each advancing glimpse is more adequate.

But the essentials are unmistakable. Ludwig von Bertalanffy, the founder of General Systems Theory, summarized it perfectly: "Reality, in the modern conception, appears as a tremendous hierarchical order of organized entities, leading, in a superposition of many levels, from physical and chemical to biological and sociological systems. Such hierarchical structure and combination into systems of even higher order *is characteristic of reality as a whole* and of fundamental importance especially in biology, psychology and sociology."

Thus, for example, in modern psychology holoarchy is the dominant *structural* and *process* paradigm, cutting across the actual and often quite different content of the various schools. Every school of developmental psychology believes in hierarchy, or a series of discrete (but continuous), irreversible stages of growth and unfolding.

From Rupert Sheldrake and his "nested hierarchy of morphogenetic fields" to Sir Karl Popper's "hierarchy of emergent qualities" to Birch and Cobb's "ecological model of reality" based on "hierarchical values"; from Francisco Varela's groundbreaking work on autopoietic systems ("it seems to be a general reflection of the richness of natural systems . . . to produce a hierarchy of levels") to the brain research of Roger Sperry and Sir John Eccles and Wilder Penfield ("a hierarchy of nonreducible emergents") to the social critical theory of Jurgen Habermas ("a hierarchy of communicative competence")—the great chain is back. And the only reason *everybody* doesn't realize this is that it is hiding out under a variety of different names.

The truly wonderful thing about this homecoming is that modern theory can now, and is now, reconnecting with its rich roots in the perennial philosophy, reconnecting with not only Plato and Aristotle and Plotinus and Maimonides and Spinoza and Hegel and Whitehead in the West, but also with Shankara and Padmasambhava and Chih-I and Fatsang and Abinavagupta in the East—all made possible by the fact that the perennial philosophy *is* perennial, cutting across times and cultures alike to point to the heart and soul and spirit of humankind.

There is, really, only one major thing left to be done, one fundamental item on the homecoming agenda. While it is true, as I said, that the unifying paradigm in modern thought, from physics to biology to psychology to sociology, is evolutionary holoarchy, nonetheless most orthodox schools of inquiry admit the existence only of matter, body, and mind. The higher dimensions of soul and Spirit are not yet accorded quite the same status. We might say that the modern West has still only acknowledged three-fifths of the great holoarchy of being. The agenda, very simply, is to reintroduce the other two-fifths (soul and spirit)

Once we recognize *all* the levels and dimensions of the great chain, we simultaneously acknowledge all the corresponding modes of knowing— not just the eye of flesh, which discloses the physical and sensory world, or just the eye of mind, which discloses the linguistic and logical world, but also the eye of contemplation, which discloses the soul and spirit. When one relies solely on the eye of flesh, the empirical eye, then in psychology one gets behaviorism and in philosophy, positivism (these were the two general movements most responsible for that nineteenth-century derailment). When we reintroduce the eye of mind we then get, in psychology, the introspective schools including psychoanalysis, gestalt, existential, and humanistic; and in philosophy, we get philosophy proper—phenomenology, hermeneutics, existentialism, critical theory.

And so there is the agenda: Let us take the last step and also reintroduce the eye of contemplation, which, as a scientific and repeatable methodology, discloses soul and spirit. The result is transpersonal psychology and philosophy. And that transpersonal vision is, I submit, the final homecoming, the reweaving of our modern soul with the soul of humanity itself— the true meaning of multiculturalism—so that, standing on the shoulders of giants, we transcend but include, which always means honor, their ever-recurring presence.

❏

36

Hidden Wisdom

Roger Walsh

Western philosophers usually assume that intellectual training and analysis alone provide the royal road to understanding. However, transpersonal philosophers—especially those of Asian traditions such as Vedanta, Sankhya, Buddhism, and Taoism—think differently. They emphasize that while intellectual training is necessary, by itself it is not sufficient for deep understanding. They claim that the mind must also be given a multidimensional contemplative or yogic training that refines ethics, emotions, motivation, and attention. [1,2]

This training is designed to develop "the eye of contemplation" by inducing specific states of consciousness in which one has "the keenness, subtlety and quickness of cognitive response" [3] that are required for penetrating insights into the nature of mind and reality. These insights collectively constitute the transcendental wisdom variously known as *prajna*, (Buddhism), *jnana* (Hinduism), *ma'rifah* (Islam), or *gnosis* (Christianity). This wisdom is the goal of contemplative training and is said to liberate those who acquire it from delusion and the suffering it produces.

This wisdom is described as a direct nonconceptual intuition that is beyond words, concepts, and dualities; hence it is described as transverbal, transrational, and nondual. "Not by reasoning is this apprehension attainable," say the Upanishads, and according to the Third Zen Patriarch "to seek Mind with the [discriminating or logical] mind is the greatest of all mistakes." It is a mistake because, in the words of the great Indian philosopher Radhakrishnan, "The real transcends, surrounds and overflows our miserable categories." [4]

Although intellectual analysis by itself is insufficient to acquire or comprehend this wisdom, one can subsequently derive intellectual ideas, psychologies and philosophies from this wisdom. Indeed, the perennial philosophy and the world's traditional transpersonal philosophies and psychologies probably were derived in just this way. Moreover, unless this wisdom is directly experienced in succeeding generations, traditions easily ossify into mere dogma.

So contemplatives first train the eye of contemplation in order to develop specific capacities and states of consciousness. Then they investigate, describe, and philosophize from the perspectives of both contemplative and ordinary states. This means that transpersonal philosophies and psychologies are multistate systems. Significant parts of their knowledge may therefore be state-specific and comprehensible only to those who have themselves adequately trained their eye of contemplation. The result is that their insights "cannot be judged by unenlightened people from the worm's eye view of book learning."[5]

For example, the idea that our sense of self, which we usually assume to be relatively stable and enduring, is actually constructed anew each moment out of a ceaseless flux of thoughts, images, and sensations may be an interesting concept when we read about it. But when seen directly in meditation it becomes undeniably clear, and by undercutting egocentricity it can be life-changing and helpful.

Aldous Huxley said, "Knowledge is a function of being."[6] Without contemplative training our being is not adequate for accessing such insights. According to the Buddhist economist E. F. Schumacher:

> If we do not have the requisite organ or instrument, or fail to use it, we are not *adequate* to this particular part or facet of the world with the result, as far as we are concerned, it simply does not exist.[7]

If it is true that without an open eye of contemplation, we are not fully adequate to the deeper profundities of transpersonal philosophies and psychologies, then what aspects of them are lost to us and how are we likely to respond to our truncated vision of them? One common response is simply to dismiss them as nonsensical. In such cases the entire wisdom of the traditions is lost to us.

In other cases the loss may be more insidious. For when we approach transpersonal disciplines without the requisite contemplative training, the more subtle, profound, state-specific depths tend to be overlooked. And what is crucial to understand is that we will not even recognize that we are overlooking these more profound depths of meaning.

This occurs because the higher "grades of significance" are lost. The easiest way of illuminating this term is by means of a classic example of the diverse responses and grades of significance that an object may elicit. For example, an animal may see an oddly shaped black and white object, a tribal person a rectangular flexible object with curious markings. To a Western child it is a book, while to an adult it may be a particular type of book, namely a book that makes incomprehensible, even ridiculous, claims about reality. Finally, to a physicist it may be a profound text on quantum physics.

What is important to see is that all the observers are partly correct in their characterization of the book, but all except the trained physicist are unaware how much more meaningful and significant the object is than they can recognize. And, most important, to the nonphysicist adult it is a book that seems incomprehensible, even ridiculous. What this example so nicely demonstrates is that when we cannot comprehend higher grades of significance, we can blithely believe that we have fully understood something whose true significance we have completely missed. As Schumacher pointed out:

> Facts do not carry labels indicating the appropriate level at which they ought to be considered. Nor does the choice of an inadequate level lead the intelligence into factual error or logical contradiction. All levels of significance up to the adequate level, i.e., up to the level of meaning in the example of the book, are equally factual, equally logical, equally objective, but not equally real. . . . When the level of the knower is not adequate to the level (or the grade of significance) of the object of knowledge, the result is not factual error but something much more serious: an inadequate and impoverished view of reality.[7]

This raises an arresting question: What higher grades of significance, what profound meanings and messages, does the world give us that we are overlooking? It is said that to a sage the leaves on the trees are like the pages of a sacred text, filled with transcendent meaning. We do not see things only as they are, but also as we are. Contemplative training changes the way we are and opens us to the hidden wisdom and higher grades of significance in transpersonal traditions, in the world, and in ourselves.

SECTION TEN

❑

MINDING OUR WORLD:
SERVICE AND SUSTAINABILITY

*The empirical fact is that self-actualizing people, our best
experiencers, are also our most compassionate, our great
improvers and reformers of society, our most effective
fighters against injustice, inequality, slavery, cruelty, ex-
ploitation (and also our best fighters for excellence, effectiveness, competence). And it also becomes clearer and
clearer that the best "helpers" are the most fully human
persons. What I may call the bodhisattvic path is an
integration of self-improvement and social zeal, i.e., the
best way to become a better "helper" is to become a better
person. But one necessary aspect of becoming a better
person is via helping other people. So one must and can do
both simultaneously.*

—ABRAHAM MASLOW[1]

IT IS no secret that we have reached a new and critical time in human
history: a time that may decide the fate of our planet, our species, and
countless other species. We possess unprecedented powers and possibilities, yet also face unprecedented dangers and suffering. How extraordinary that we should be the first generation that will decide whether we
make of earth a heaven or hell: whether we create a sustaining and
sustainable society or leave a plundered, polluted, radioactive planet. For
we have the power to produce both.

Everyone knows we face dangers, yet few appreciate just how awesome and urgent they are. The following summary therefore outlines some of the more pressing problems.

The population bomb is exploding at the staggering rate of 100 million people each year. It took humankind over a million years of evolution to reach a population of one billion in A.D. 1800. Yet now we add another billion each thirteen years and double our population every forty years. Obviously, this human explosion cannot continue and will end soon, either by our rapidly making birth control available worldwide, or by starvation, sickness and social disruption on a scale so incomprehensibly large as to dwarf all previous famines and epidemics.[2]

This population explosion is exaggerating the gaping disparities between the world's rich and poor. Income per person in the developed countries is some thirty times that in the poorest.[2,3] Perhaps poverty's most devastating toll is taken by malnutrition and starvation. Some fifteen to twenty million people die of malnutrition each year while another half billion people go malnourished.[4] Today starvation kills as many people every four months as did the entire Holocaust.

These are extraordinary, incomprehensible figures, yet they convey little of the suffering and desperation that lie behind them. They are a far cry from the United Nations declaration that "everyone has the right to a standard of living which is adequate to the health and well-being of himself and of his family, including food, clothing, housing and medical care."

The population explosion is of course gobbling up resources and destabilizing the environment. We have only a few decades of oil supplies left, the world's forests are shrinking, species are being extinguished at a rate unheard of since the dinosaurs died out, and much of the world's farmland is deteriorating. Meanwhile, above our heads, air pollution, acid rain, ozone depletion, and rising carbon dioxide concentrations are destroying the atmosphere.

Yet while the world's natural resources are depleted, huge amounts of human resources are sucked into massive military budgets and weapons of inconceivable destructive power. The total explosive power of the world's nuclear weapons is equivalent to billions of tons of TNT.

The world's military expenditures now exceed one trillion dollars each year. The president of the International Physicians for the Prevention of Nuclear War pointed out, "A small fraction of these expenditures could provide the world with adequate food and sanitary water supply, housing, education, and modern health care." Indeed, the Presidential Commission on World Hunger estimated that it would cost only six billion dollars per year to eradicate malnutrition, an amount less than one week's arms expenditure.[4] Pope Paul IV lamented that the arms race kills, whether the weapons are used or not.

What these and many other facts make clear is that we are in a phase of unprecedented ecological disruption and are consuming the planet's resources faster than they can be replaced. We are mortgaging our future and that of all future generations. Yet as Erik Dammann pointed out in his book *The Future in Our Hands*:

> The world is not threatened by catastrophe in the future. The greater part of mankind is already experiencing catastrophe today. None of us would talk in terms of future catastrophe if our present family income amounted to less than one dollar a day, if we lived with our family in a hut or shack without water or electricity, if we were starving and lost every second child which was born, if our surviving children were physically or mentally destroyed by deficiency diseases, if there were no doctors available. If we lived like this, it would be perfectly clear that catastrophe was already an accomplished fact. This is the way humanity lives today. Not distant, small groups. Mankind is living like this. The majority of us. [5]

The global crises we face today are unique in many ways, not only in their scope, complexity, and urgency, but also in that for the first time in human history each and every one of them is caused by humans. They are creations of our individual and collective behavior and can therefore be traced, in significant part, to psychological origins: to our individual and collective beliefs, greed, fear, fantasies, defenses, and misperceptions. Our global problems are global symptoms, and the state of the world reflects the state of our minds. [6]

Of course, this is not to deny the importance of social, political, and economic forces. It is to emphasize that political, economic, and military interventions alone are insufficient and that truly effective long-term cures require responses at all levels. In other words, we need not only to feed the starving and reduce nuclear stockpiles, but also to understand and correct the psychological and social forces that led to this situation in the first place. [7]

Unfortunately, while there is growing awareness of global crises, to date most responses have been only military, political, or economic. This is changing slowly, as more people emphasize the importance of both inner and outer work to change both the psyche and the world.

One of the most eminent advocates of this integrated approach is the Dalai Lama. In his Nobel Peace Prize acceptance speech, "A Call for Universal Responsibility," he emphasizes the increasing extent of interconnection and interdependence in the world. Environmental crises affect us all. The Dalai Lama therefore points out that our sense of responsibility and compassion must encompass our entire planet and all people. He argues that our current crises can be solved only by balanced development of outer scientific and inner psychological capacities. Two of the most valued inner capacities are transpersonal emotions: love and compassion. Ram Dass explores "Compassion: The Delicate Balance," while John Welwood explores the possibility of using romantic relationships to foster "Conscious Love."

Just as the transpersonal movement has been based on an expanded sense of identity, so too has the movement of "deep ecology." This important discipline takes its name from its commitment to asking ever deeper questions about humankind and nature and their optimal relationships. The conventional Western worldview perceives humans as superior, separate, and dominant over other creatures and nature. This anthropocentric view sees humans as the most important part of the universe. Deep ecology, on the other hand, argues for the importance of shifting our perception to recognize the intrinsic worth and interconnection of all creatues and nature. Moreover, it emphasizes that our true (transpersonal) identity encompasses all nature and the world. It therefore argues for a shift in identity from anthropocentric to biocentric, from egocentric to ecocentric, together with corresponding shifts in attitudes, values, and behavior. Deep ecology goes beyond environmental efforts such as resource conservation and wilderness preservation, which implicitly assume that the primary reason for preserving nature is for human benefit.

Since their worldviews have so much in common, the deep ecology and transpersonal movements obviously have much to offer each other. Deep ecologists could benefit from greater psychological sophistication, while transpersonal psychologists could develop greater ecological sensitivity and concern.

Transpersonal psychology also raises two central issues for deep ecology, the first ontological and the second practical. Deep ecologists call for a transpersonal expansion of identity beyond our skin-encapsulated ego to fulfill Albert Einstein's request that we "embrace all living creatures and all of nature in its beauty." However, some transpersonalists feel that the expansion of identity that deep ecologists propose may be partial because it is usually a horizontal extension encompassing the physical world, but not necessarily a vertical expansion that encompasses other realms of psyche and consciousness.

The second question is how this expansion of identity, be it horizontal, vertical, or both, is to be achieved. Most contemplatives believe that developing a stable transpersonal identity requires long-term inner work. However, deep ecologists do not usually address this issue, and some imply that inner work, particularly spiritual work, is a distraction from the desperately needed work in the world. Yet the Dalai Lama argues that balance between inner and outer work may be essential, and as Eric Dammann said, "Nothing can be changed until we change ourselves."[5]

The possibility of combining the wisdom of both deep ecology and transpersonal psychology in a mutually enriching synthesis to create a transpersonal ecology is obviously attractive. The Australian ecologist Warwick Fox began this synthesis in a thoughtful book appropriately called *Toward a Transpersonal Ecology*[8] and in the article printed here.

In "The Tao of Personal and Social Transformation," Duane Elgin suggests that expanded awareness is reflected in a quality of life that seeks harmony with nature, both inner and outer, rather than domination over it. For such people there is no question of their connection with, and responsibility for, the larger whole with which they feel intimately linked. Fewer egocentric desires mean less consumerism, greater voluntary simplicity, less wish to impose one's will on others, and more interest in harmonizing with nature in an ecological, Taoistic manner.

Some of the motives powering these changes are identified by Stanislav and Christina Grof in their paper "Transpersonal Experience and the Global Crisis." They point out that many people who have plumbed their inner depths and had powerful transpersonal experiences find that their values shift automatically toward service and a greater reverence for all life.

The task of forging a psychological understanding and response adequate to the enormity of our global crises is clearly the most urgent challenge facing our generation. Peter Russell suggests that we need no less than "An Inner Manhattan Project," devoting our best human and technical resources to the task.

Clearly, we are in a race between consciousness and catastrophe. There may be no more urgent task for each of us than to apply our transpersonal understanding to the preservation of our planet and nature. The aim is to illuminate the destructive psychological and social forces that have brought us to this turning point in history and transform them into constructive forces for our collective survival, well-being, and awakening.

◻
37

The Nobel Peace Prize Lecture: A Call for
Universal Responsibility

The Dalai Lama

Brothers and Sisters:

Thinking over what I might say today, I decided to share with you some of my thoughts concerning the common problems all of us face as members of the human family. Because we all share this small planet earth, we have to learn to live in harmony and peace with each other and with nature. That is not just a dream, but a necessity. We are dependent on each other in so many ways that we can no longer live in isolated communities and ignore what is happening outside those communities.

The realization that we are all basically the same human beings, who seek happiness and try to avoid suffering, is very helpful in developing a sense of brotherhood and sisterhood—a warm feeling of love and compassion for others. This, in turn, is essential if we are to survive in this ever-shrinking world we live in. For if we each selfishly pursue only what we believe to be in our own interest, without caring about the needs of others, we not only may end up harming others but also ourselves. This fact has become very clear during the course of this century. We know that to wage a nuclear war today, for example, would be a form of suicide; or that to pollute the air or the oceans, in order to achieve some short-term benefit, would be to destroy the very basis for our survival. As individuals and nations are becoming increasingly interdependent we have no other choice than to develop what I call a sense of universal responsibility.

Today, we are truly a global family. What happens in one part of the world may affect us all. This, of course, is not only true of the negative things that happen, but is equally valid for the positive developments. We not only know what happens elsewhere, thanks to the extraordinary modern communications technology, we are also directly affected by events that occur far away. We feel a sense of sadness when children are starving in Eastern Africa. Similarly, we feel a sense of joy when a family is reunited after decades of separation by the Berlin Wall. Our crops and livestock are contaminated and our health and livelihood threatened when a nuclear accident happens miles away in another country. Our own security is enhanced when peace breaks out between warring parties in other continents.

But war or peace; the destruction or the protection of nature; the violation or promotion of human rights and democratic freedoms; poverty or material well-being; the lack of moral and spiritual values or their existence and development; and the breakdown or development of human understanding, are not isolated phenomena that can be analyzed and tackled independently of one another. In fact, they are very much interrelated at all levels and need to be approached with that understanding.

Peace, in the sense of the absence of war, is of little value to someone who is dying of hunger or cold. It will not remove the pain of torture inflicted on a prisoner of conscience. It does not comfort those who have lost their loved ones in floods caused by senseless deforestation in a neighboring country. Peace can only last where human rights are respected, where the people are fed, and where individuals and nations are free. True peace with ourselves and with the world around us can only be achieved through the development of mental peace.

Material progress is of course important for human advancement. At the same time, material development without spiritual development can also cause serious problems. I believe both are important and must be developed side by side so as to achieve a good balance between them.

Inner peace is the key: if you have inner peace, the external problems do not affect your deep sense of peace and tranquillity. In that state of mind you can deal with situations with calmness and reason, while keeping your inner happiness. That is very important. Without this inner peace, no matter how comfortable your life is materially, you may still be worried, disturbed or unhappy because of circumstances.

Clearly, it is of great importance, therefore, to attempt to solve problems in a balanced way that takes these different aspects into consideration. Of course it is not easy. But it is of little benefit to try to solve one problem if doing so creates an equally serious new one. So really we have no alternative: we must develop a sense of universal responsibility not only in the geographic sense, but also in respect to the different issues that confront our planet.

Responsibility does not only lie with the leaders of our countries or with those who have been appointed or elected to do a particular job. It lies with each of us individually. Peace, for example, starts within each one of us. When we have inner peace, we can be at peace with those around us. When our community is in a state of peace, it can share that peace with neighboring communities, and so on. When we feel love and kindness towards others, it not only makes others feel loved and cared for, but it helps us also to develop inner happiness and peace. And there are ways in which we can consciously work to develop feelings of love and kindness. For some of us, the most effective way to do so is through religious practice. For others it may be nonreligious practices. What is important is that we each make a sincere effort to take seriously our responsibility for each other and for the natural environment.

❏

38

Compassion: The Delicate Balance

Ram Dass

When we look about at the vast suffering in the world, we often experience intense pain in our own hearts and a sense of despair. The suffering so often seems cruel, unnecessary, unjustified—reflecting a heartless universe. The human greed and fear which is causing so much of the suffering seems out of control.

When we are caught in such a worldview, any effort to change things seems trivial. In such a situation of impotence, we often defend ourselves against the pain by rationalization—by using our intellect to protect our hearts. In so doing, we stifle our hearts' innate generosity of spirit. Acting from this worldview often colors our acts with anger or self-righteousness, imbues them with sadness or a sense of futility. Our warmth becomes "professional warmth" instead of the real thing; we are not fed by our "helping" interactions with others because our hearts are closed. We may work harder and harder, but the result is ultimately fatigue and burnout.

At other times, however, in the silence of our deepest meditative moments, when we are removed from the immediacy of the marketplace of sorrow, we intuitively feel a unitive wisdom lying behind and inspiring the forms in the universe. We sense a spiritually guided evolution that gives all life experience a deeper meaning than the one which is superficially apparent. We are appreciative of things just as they are.

In such moments of luminous awareness, we sense a wisdom in suffering, a wisdom that our intellects cannot fathom. With our intuitive heart-mind, we seem to be privy to a view of the universe in which even suffering is not devoid of grace. The suffering itself is a part of the perfection of the evolving nature of spirit through matter. Everything is unfolding as it must. We experience only wonder and awe, and a joy that opens our hearts wide.

These two worldviews, seemingly antithetical, each have in the appropriate contexts the ring of truth. But how to reconcile them? They are two different planes of consciousness, two different domains of relative reality.

When the world and its suffering are very much with us, to consider that "it's all perfect" seems little short of profanity, a gross polyanna-ish rationalization. On the other hand, in our more transcendent moments, our fears and sense of urgency about the human condition seem poignant at best, reflecting only our lack of faith.

How can we find a place within ourselves to stand, from which we can integrate these disparate worldviews, so that we need not embrace one of these truths at the expense of the other? How do we develop both the quietness of mind that allows us to hear the deepest spiritual truths, and the openness of heart that engages us fully with our humanity? It is in living the answer to this question, day by day, that we discover the meaning of true compassion and recognize, from within, our own innate generosity that arises spontaneously out of equanimity.

When we rest in that point of tension or balance, we also find a new intensity and richness in each moment. For, to find that point, we must quiet our minds. The quieter our minds get, the more we seem to open our hearts in ever expanding circles to embrace all beings with love. When the heart is very open, we see all beings as our beloved family.

Now, as we love more people, their suffering hurts our hearts all the more, because the worst pain for our heart is to witness the suffering of those whom we love. But at the same moment, the quieter our minds, the deeper the spacious awareness that spawns our faith, and thus our equanimity. Both sides of the balance have been intensified. We find ourselves able to bear what previously was unbearable. We are able to keep our hearts open in hell.

From this point of balance, we recognize that the hurt that our human heart feels in the presence of others' suffering is a part of the perfection. And the yearning of that heart to do something about the suffering is also right. It is part of a larger web or network of compassion. But we find, often to our considerable surprise, that acting to alleviate the suffering of others need not upset our equanimity. It need not force us into a position of judgment of the universe, or God. We find ourselves acting, in the domain of good and evil, on the side of the angels; yet our awareness rests in the One.

Now we find ourselves ever more strongly drawn into service as an act of celebration; an act we perform with delight and equanimity. Such action heals our hearts. It does not lead to fatigue or burnout. Mahatma Gandhi spelled this out when he said: "God demands nothing less than complete self-surrender as the price for the only real freedom that is worth having. And when a person thus loses her/himself, (s)he immediately finds her/himself in the service of all that lives. It becomes her/his delight and recreation. (S)he is a new person never weary of spending her/himself in the service of God's creation."

Where do we begin this amazing journey to our center point of balance? We begin right where we are. We look around and find a way to engage our hearts and hands with the suffering in the world around us. And, at the same moment, we set about cultivating a more reflective state of mind through giving ourselves quiet moments for meditation, for study, for contemplation. These are the ingredients we put into the pot. And then we stir.

In the course of the journey, we can expect that many times we will lose that balance point and be pulled to one side or the other. But we will regain it, because there is a wisdom in our very bones that knows that the balance point between our humanity and our divinity is the seat of our compassion—the home of true happiness.

❏

39

Conscious Love

John Welwood

People generally consider an intimate relationship successful if it provides basic fulfillment in such areas as companionship, security, sex, and self-esteem. Yet in regarding relationship as path, especially as a sacred path, we hold a larger vision, one that includes these needs, but is not limited to them. Our central concern is with cultivating a conscious love, which can inspire the development of greater awareness and the evolution of two people's beings.

Yet we should not be too idealistic about this, for intimate relationships never function entirely on a conscious level. We live on many levels simultaneously, all with different needs.

LEVELS OF CONNECTION

The most primitive bond that may form between intimate partners is the urge for symbiotic *fusion*, born out of a desire to obtain emotional nurturance that was lacking in childhood. Of course, it is common for many couples, when they first get together, to go through a temporary symbiotic phase, when they cut out other activities or friends and spend most of their free time together. This stage in a relationship may help two people establish close emotional bonding. Yet if symbiosis becomes the primary dynamic in a relationship or goes on for too long, it will become increasingly confining. It sets up a parent-child dynamic that limits two people's range of expression and interaction, undermining the male-female charge between them and creating addictive patterns.

Beyond the primitive need for symbiotic fusion, the most basic desire in an intimate relationship is for *companionship*. This can take more or less sophisticated forms. Basic companionship plays a part in all relationships, although some people do not seem to want anything more than this from an intimate partner.

A further level of connectedness can happen when two people share not only activities and each other's company, but also common interests, goals, or values. We could call this level, where a couple begins to create a shared world, *community*. Like companionship, community is a concrete, earthy form of relatedness.

Beyond sharing values and interests lies *communication*. On this level, we share what is going on inside us—our thoughts, visions, experiences, and feelings. Establishing good communication is much more arduous than simply creating companionship and community. It requires that a couple be honest and courageous enough to expose what is going on inside them and be willing to work on the inevitable obstacles in the way of sharing their different truths with each other. Good communication is probably the most important ingredient in the everyday health of a relationship.

A further extension of communication is *communion*. Beyond just sharing thoughts and feelings, this is a deep recognition of another person's being. This often takes place in silence—perhaps while looking into our partner's eyes, making love, walking in the woods, or listening to music together. Suddenly we feel touched and seen, not as a personality, but in the depth of our being. We are fully ourselves and fully in touch with our partner at the same time. This kind of connection is so rare and striking that it is usually unmistakable when it comes along. While two people can work on communication, communion is more spontaneous, beyond the will. Communication and communion are deeper, more subtle forms of intimacy than companionship and community, taking place at the level of mind and heart.

The deeper intimacy of communion may stir up a longing to overcome our separateness altogether, a longing for total *union* with someone we love. Yet though this longing expresses a genuine human need, it is more appropriately directed to the divine, the absolute, the infinite. When attached to an intimate relationship, it often creates problems. Putting our whole longing for spiritual realization onto a finite relationship can lead to idealization, inflation, addiction, and death. The most appropriate way to address our longing for union is through a genuine spiritual practice, such as meditation, that teaches us how to go beyond oppositional mind altogether, in every area of our life. By pointing us in this direction, intimate relationship may inspire this kind of practice, but it can never be a complete substitute for it.

Every relationship will have different areas of strength along this continuum of connectedness. Couples who share a deep being-connection, good communication, common interests and values, and a simple enjoyment of each other's company will have an ideal balance of heaven and earth connectedness. (Sexuality can operate at any of these levels—as a form of symbiotic fusion, as a body-companionship, as a shared sport, as a form of communication, or as a deeper communion.)

Conscious love begins to develop in a relationship where two people share a being-to-being communion. This is because it is love of being rather than love of personality. In moments of communion, I am in touch with the depth of my own being and my partner's being at the same time. And yet, I *am* separate. No matter how close she and I are, we can never fully share our different worlds: She can never really know what it is like to be me and I can never really know what it is like to be her. Although we may share fleeting moments of oneness when our beings touch, complete union remains forever just out of reach.

Nor is there any way to hold on to each other or use our closeness to shield ourselves from the truth of our aloneness. We are on temporary loan to each other from the universe, and we never know when it will claim us back. At the core of devotion to another is a sweet, sad fullness of heart, which longs to overflow.

Since my aloneness is also what makes me want to overflow, it need not isolate me. As a simple presence to life, it is what I share with all the creatures of the earth. It is an inner depth from which many treasures arise: a passion to reach out, extend myself, write a poem or a song, give something of substance or beauty.

Thus when we appreciate our aloneness, we can be ourselves and give ourselves most fully, and we no longer need others to save us or make us feel good about ourselves. Instead, we want to help them become *them-*

selves more fully as well. In this way, conscious love is born as a gift from our broken heart.

All the great spiritual traditions teach that single-minded pursuit of one's own happiness cannot lead to true satisfaction, for personal desires multiply endlessly, forever creating new dissatisfaction. Real happiness, which no one can ever take away, comes from breaking our heart open, feeling it radiating toward the world around us, and rejoicing in the well-being of others. Cherishing the growth of those we love exercises the larger capacities of our being and helps us ripen. Since their unfolding calls on us to develop all our finest qualities, we know that we are being fully used. Thus all the current difficulties of relationships present us with a rare opportunity: to discover love as a sacred path, which calls on us to cultivate the fullness and depth of who we are.

THE FARTHER SHORE OF LOVE

In its final outreach, conscious love leads two lovers beyond themselves toward a greater connectedness with the whole of life. Indeed, two people's love will have no room to grow unless it develops this larger focus beyond themselves. The larger arc of a couple's love reaches out toward a feeling of kinship with all of life, what Teilhard de Chardin calls "a love of the universe." Only in this way can love, as he puts it, "develop in boundless light and power."

So, the path of love expands in ever-widening circles. It begins at home—by first finding our seat, making friends with ourselves, and discovering the intrinsic richness of our being, underneath all our ego-centered confusion and delusion. As we come to appreciate this basic wholesomeness within us, we find that we have more to give to an intimate partner.

Further, as a man and woman become devoted to the growth of awareness and spirit in each other, they will naturally want to share their love with others. The new qualities they give birth to—generosity, courage, compassion, wisdom—can extend beyond the circle of their own relationship. These qualities are a couple's "spiritual child"—what their coming together gives to the world. A couple will flourish when their vision and practice are not focused solely on each other, but also include this larger sense of community and what they can give to others.

From there, a couple's love can expand still further, as Teilhard suggests. The more deeply and passionately two people love each other, the more concern they will feel for the state of the world in which they live. They will feel their connection with the earth and a dedication to care for this world and all sentient beings who need their care. Radiating out to the whole of creation is the farthest reach of love and its fullest expression, which grounds and enriches the life of the couple. This is the great love and the great way, which leads to the heart of the universe.

◻

40

Transpersonal Ecology

Warwick Fox

Since the time of the classical Greeks, Western thinking has been overwhelmingly anthropocentric (i.e., human-centered). As Bertrand Russell (1979, 90) pointed out in his *History of Western Philosophy*, "What is amiss, even in the best philosophy after Democritus [i.e., after the pre-Socratics], is an undue emphasis on man as compared with the universe."

Karl Popper, the most influential philosopher of science of the twentieth century, expressed his view on the upshot of this philosophical tradition as follows:

> It is very necessary these days to apologize for being concerned with philosophy in any form whatever. . . . In my opinion, the greatest scandal of philosophy is that, while all around us the world of nature perishes—and not the world of nature alone—philosophers continue to talk, sometimes cleverly and sometimes not, about the question of whether this world exists. (1974, 32)

In recent years, the most concerted attempt to challenge this anthropocentric tradition has come from a loose grouping of philosophers writing under the banner of "deep ecology." Deep ecology is associated with three basic ideas. The first is the idea of ecocentrism, that is, the idea of adopting an ecology-centered (or an Earth-centered) approach in our interactions with the world around us, rather than an anthropocentric or human-centered approach. In this view, the nonhuman world is considered to be valuable *in and of itself* and not simply because of its obvious use-value to humans. The second basic idea is that of asking deeper questions about the ecological relationships of which we are a part, by addressing the root causes of our interlinked ecological crises rather than simply focusing on their symptoms. The third idea is that we are all capable of identifying far more widely and deeply with the world around us than is commonly recognized, and that this form of self-development, self-unfolding, or "Self-realization," as Naess would say, leads us sponta-neously to appreciate and defend the integrity of the world around us. I refer to this third sense of deep ecology as "transpersonal ecology" be-cause it clearly points to the realization of a sense of self that extends beyond (or that is *trans-*) any narrowly delimited biographical or egoic sense of self. Broadening and deepening our identification—or our sense of felt commonality—with the world around us leads us from a relatively narrow, atomistic, isolated, or particle-like sense of self to a wide, expan-sive, participatory, or field-like one.

It is, in my view, the last of these three themes that most distinguishes the work of deep ecological writers from that of other ecophilosophers. It is also this last theme that has been leading deep/transpersonal ecologists into a dialogue with transpersonal psychologists. This dialogue promises to be fruitful to both parties.

Potential sources of tension between these perspectives include (1) the question of the nature and purpose, if any, of evolution, and (2) the question of the adoption of a "this-worldly" or "consensus reality" focus of attention versus an "other-worldly" or "nonconsensus reality" focus. In regard to the first question, transpersonal ecologists follow evolutionary biologists in asking transpersonal psychology theorists: Is it at all legiti-mate to speak of an aim, or telos, of evolution? With respect to the second question, transpersonal ecologists ask transpersonal psychologists: Does a focus on consciousness per se put us in touch with genuinely "higher"—more real or more evolved—states of being and forms of reality or is consciousness more like a hall of mirrors in which we can "lose ourselves" in endless fascination but to no inherently "higher" end? This question is highly relevant to the question of whether we attempt to transcend our duly limited (and often painfully defensive) egoic sense of self by "verti-cal" means (i.e., by attempting to experience "higher" states of being and forms of reality) or by "horizontal" means (i.e., by attempting to experi-ence ourselves as intimately bound up with the world around us; as leaves, as it were, on a single evolutionary Tree of Life).

Notwithstanding these potential sources of tension, transpersonal ecol-ogy and transpersonal psychology can also be viewed as being highly complementary—perhaps even necessary—to each other's aims. Trans-personal ecology adds a needed ecological dimension to transpersonal psychology, just as transpersonal psychology adds a needed psychological dimension to transpersonal ecology. The interaction of these two perspec-tives may well constitute our strongest source of hope for the future.

❏
41

Deep Ecology: Living as If Nature Mattered

Bill Devall and George Sessions

The term *deep ecology* was coined by Arne Naess describing the deeper, more spiritual approach to Nature resulting from a more sensitive openness to ourselves and nonhuman life around us. The essence of deep ecology is to keep asking more searching questions about human life, society, and Nature.

Deep ecology goes beyond a limited piecemeal shallow approach to environmental problems and attempts to articulate a comprehensive religious and philosophical worldview. The foundations of deep ecology are the basic intuitions and experiencing of ourselves and Nature which comprise ecological consciousness. Certain outlooks on politics and public policy flow naturally from this consciousness.

Many of these questions are perennial philosophical and religious questions faced by humans in all cultures over the ages. What does it mean to be a unique human individual? How can the individual self maintain and increase its uniqueness while also being an inseparable aspect of the whole system wherein there are no sharp breaks between self and the *other*? An ecological perspective, in this deeper sense, results in what Theodore Roszak calls "an awakening of wholes greater than the sum of their parts. In spirit, the discipline is contemplative and therapeutic."[1]

Ecological consciousness and deep ecology are in sharp contrast with the dominant worldview of technocratic-industrial societies which regards humans as isolated and fundamentally separate from the rest of Nature, as superior to, and in charge of, the rest of creation. But the view of humans as separate and superior to the rest of Nature is only part of larger cultural patterns. For thousands of years, Western culture has become increasingly obsessed with the idea of *dominance*: with dominance of humans over nonhuman Nature, masculine over the feminine, wealthy and powerful over the poor, with the dominance of the West over non-Western cultures. Deep ecological consciousness allows us to see through these erroneous and dangerous illusions.

For deep ecology, the study of our place in the Earth household includes the study of ourselves as part of the organic whole. Going beyond a narrowly materialist scientific understanding of reality, the spiritual and the material aspects of reality fuse together. While the leading intellectuals of the dominant worldview have tended to view religion as "just superstition" and have looked upon ancient spiritual practice and enlightenment as essentially subjective, the search for deep ecological consciousness is the search for a more objective consciousness and state of being through an active deep questioning and meditative process and way of life.

Many people have asked these deeper questions and cultivated ecological consciousness within the context of different spiritual traditions—Christianity, Taoism, Buddhism, and Native American rituals, for example. While differing greatly in other regards, many in these traditions agree with the basic principles of deep ecology.

Warwick Fox, an Australian philosopher, has succinctly expressed the central intuition of deep ecology: "It is the idea that we can make no firm ontological divide in the field of existence: That there is no bifurcation in reality between the human and the non-human realms . . . to the extent that we perceive boundaries, we fall short of deep ecological consciousness."[2]

From this most basic insight or characteristic of deep ecological consciousness, Arne Naess has developed two *ultimate norms* or intuitions which are themselves not derivable from other principles or intuitions. They are arrived at by the deep questioning process and reveal the importance of moving to the philosophical and religious level of wisdom. They cannot be validated, of course, by the methodology of modern science based on its usual mechanistic assumptions and its very narrow definition of data. These ultimate norms are *self-realization* and *biocentric equality*.

SELF-REALIZATION

In keeping with the spiritual traditions of many of the world's religions, the deep ecology norm of self-realization goes beyond the modern Western *self* which is defined as an isolated ego striving primarily for hedonistic gratification or for a narrow sense of individual salvation in this life or the next. Spiritual growth, or unfolding, begins when we cease to understand or see ourselves as isolated and narrow competing egos and begin to identify with other humans, from our family and friends to, eventually, our species. But the deep ecology sense of self requires a further maturity and growth, an identification which goes beyond humanity to include the nonhuman world. We must see beyond our narrow contemporary cultural assumptions and values, and the conventional wisdom of our time and place, and this is best achieved by the meditative deep questioning process. Only in this way can we hope to attain full mature personhood and uniqueness.

A nurturing nondominating society can help in the "real work" of becoming a whole person. The "real work" can be summarized symbolically as the realization of "self-in-Self," where "Self" stands for organic wholeness. This process of the full unfolding of the self can also be summarized by the phrase, "No one is saved until we are all saved," where the phrase "one" includes not only me, an individual human, but all humans, whales, grizzly bears, whole rain forest ecosystems, mountains and rivers, the tiniest microbes in the soil, and so on.

BIOCENTRIC EQUALITY

The intuition of biocentric equality is that all things in the biosphere have an equal right to live and blossom and to reach their own individual forms of unfolding and self-realization within the larger Self-realization. This basic intuition is that all organisms and entities in the ecosphere, as parts of the interrelated whole, are equal in intrinsic worth.

Biocentric equality is intimately related to the all-inclusive Self-realization in the sense that if we harm the rest of Nature then we are harming ourselves. There are no boundaries and everything is interrelated. But insofar as we perceive things as individual organisms or entities, the insight draws us to respect all human and nonhuman individuals in their own right as parts of the whole without feeling the need to set up hierarchies of species with humans at the top.

The practical implications of this intuition or norm suggest that we should live with minimum rather than maximum impact on other species and on the Earth in general. Thus we see another aspect of our guiding principle: "Simple in means, rich in ends."

We, as individual humans, and as communities of humans, have vital needs which go beyond such basics as food, water, and shelter to include love, play, creative expression, intimate relationships with a particular landscape (or Nature taken in its entirety) as well as intimate relationships with other humans, and the vital need for spiritual growth, for becoming a mature human being.

Our vital material needs are probably more simple than many realize. In technocratic-industrial societies there is overwhelming propaganda and advertising which encourages false needs and destructive desires designed to foster increased production and consumption of goods. Most of this actually diverts us from facing reality in an objective way and from beginning the "real work" of spiritual growth and maturity.

Many people who do not see themselves as supporters of deep ecology nevertheless recognize an overriding vital human need for a healthy and high-quality natural environment for humans, if not for all life, with minimum toxic waste, nuclear radiation, acid rain and smog, and enough free-flowing wilderness so humans can get in touch with their sources, the natural rhythms and the flow of time and place.

The ultimate norms of deep ecology suggest a view of the nature of reality and our place as an individual (many in the one) in the larger scheme of things. They cannot be fully grasped intellectually but are ultimately experiential. The table below summarizes the contrast between the dominant worldview and deep ecology.

Dominant Worldview	Deep Ecology
Dominance over Nature	Harmony with Nature
Natural environment as resource for humans	All nature has intrinsic worth/biospecies equality
Material/economic growth for growing human population	Elegantly simple material needs (material goals serving the larger goal of self-realization)
Belief in ample resource reserves	Earth "supplies" limited
High technological progress and solutions	Appropriate technology; nondominating science
Consumerism	Doing with enough/recycling

❏
42

The Tao of Personal and Social Transformation

Duane Elgin

Many persons who have explored the further reaches of human awareness agree on an essential perception: Behind the apparent disarray of random events there is a deeper harmony, a moving point of equilibrium and balance, a patterned unfolding of reality as a symbolic whole. In China, this patterned flow of the universe is called the Tao.

Congruent with this view of reality, the essence of wisdom is to act in harmony with the Tao, or natural rhythm of the universe. Actions that abuse our conscious, co-creative role in the evolutionary flow will rebound and, directly or indirectly, obtain their ecological retribution from persons and societies that have disrupted the equilibrium. If this is true, then it is important to examine the flow of industrialization in the West and the extent to which this flow has been resonant or discordant with the Tao.

Judged on its own terms, the industrial transformation has been an enormous success in achieving what its internal dynamic premised as its major objective: the realization of an unparalleled level of material abundance for a majority of people. Nonetheless, it no longer seems proper to judge the industrial era on its own terms. Because we have acted with only partial awareness we have upset the equilibrium and have torn the fabric of the universe, which now returns to exact its ecological reparation. Environmental degradation, alienation, urban decay, and social unrest are mirrors of the shortness of our vision. Our outer world reflects our inner conditions. The arrogance of an anthropocentric perspective has brought us to the edge of disaster as we confront the possibilities of nuclear holocaust, world famine, population outstripping our resources, and global environmental poisoning.

RESTORING THE BALANCE (I)—THE TAO
OF SOCIAL TRANSFORMATION

The idealistic vision of Taoistic action has become a pressing and realistic need. We cannot afford a lesser vision as we cope with enormously difficult and complex problems that reach global proportions. Presented below are personal perceptions of the natural flows of social form that seem to be emerging. Three dominant flows are considered: the failing impetus of the industrial paradigm, the pushes by natural and political ecology, and voluntary simplification.

To say that the industrial paradigm is losing momentum is to say that the interdependent constellations of values, beliefs, and behaviors of the industrial era are collectively faltering. In short, the powerful engine of technological advance and economic growth now appears to be running out of steam. A number of factors may account for this.

We confront a massive tangle of complexity in our social, political, and economic systems. Our capacity to create powerful supersystems does not automatically confer a commensurate capacity to comprehend that which we have created. Consequently, we are increasingly dependent upon those supersystems but are incapable of understanding them, thus becoming the servants of a technological society that we created to serve us. We have extended a rational concern for material well-being into an obsessive concern for unconscionable levels of material consumption. We are possessed by our possessions, consumed by that which we consume.

In sum, we are compelled to rethink what life means and where we wish to go. We are obliged to sort out the trivial from the significant, the ephemeral from the durable, and to find an alternative image of human and social possibility that captures our collective imagination and provides a renewed sense of direction as we proceed into the future.

Even if the momentum of the industrial paradigm were not abating, there are strong forces that are deflecting our society from the historical trajectory of increasing material growth. The success of our industrial era has been predicated, to a substantial degree, on the existence of an inexpensive and abundant supply of energy and raw materials. Now, however, we confront a "new scarcity," which is inexorably invalidating the crucial premise of energy and material abundance.

As the pace and confidence of industrialism slows and as its direction is turned by the new scarcity, hard necessity dictates that we forge a new relationship with the material aspects of existence. Explored below is one emerging social flow that may give greater coherence and balance to social actions—namely, the movement towards voluntary simplicity.

Historically, in the West in general and in America in particular, consumption has been viewed as a primary end of human activity. This view is reflected in the customary measure of happiness—the "standard of living"—which is calculated almost exclusively in material terms. We have attempted to maximize consumption, implicitly assuming that the level of consumption is directly related to the level of human well-being and happiness. This seems an ill-founded and excessively limiting assumption for approaching the totality of human satisfactions. There is much evidence that, beyond the level of material "sufficiency," money does not buy happiness.

In visceral response to this knowledge, a growing number of people appear to be adopting an alternative life-style which, though materially more modest, is overall more satisfying and enriching. Voluntarily simplifying the external/material aspects of one's life may significantly contribute to the enrichment of internal/nonmaterial aspects. The late Richard Gregg eloquently states the rationale for voluntary simplicity.

> Voluntary simplicity involves both inner and outer condition. It means singleness of purpose, sincerity and honesty within, as well as avoidance of exterior clutter, of many possessions irrelevant to the chief purpose of life. It means an ordering and guiding of our energy and our desires, a partial restraint in some direction in order to secure greater abundance of life in other directions. It involves a deliberate organization of life for a purpose. . . .

Material necessity seems to coincide with evolutionary possibility, so that we might restrain the material aspect of life to explore more fully the nonmaterial dimensions of human existence. Rather than a passing fad or an escapist retreat from the real world, this seems a rational response to a pressing situation.

RESTORING THE BALANCE (II)—THE TAO OF PERSONAL TRANSFORMATION

Simone de Beauvoir has written, "Life is occupied both in perpetuating itself and in surpassing itself; if all it does is maintain itself, then living is only not dying." At present, it is not clear whether we can either maintain ourselves or surpass ourselves. There seem to be two fundamental reasons for this evolutionary crisis: first, a lack of "internal" evolution commensurate with our external/material evolution and, second, a failure to recognize that "internal" growth is central to human evolutionary processes.

Our present civilizational crisis emerges, in part, out of a gross disparity between the relatively underdeveloped internal faculties of man and the extremely powerful external technologies at our disposal. . . . We must right the imbalance of our present era by fostering a degree of interior human growth and maturation that is at least commensurate with the enormous exterior technological growth that has occurred in the last several hundred years. If we are to assume a co-creative role in evolution-ary processes then we must do, with consciousness, care, and intention, what nature does in nonconscious and instinctive ways. Aurobindo states: "Man occupies the crest of the evolutionary wave. With him occurs the passage from an unconscious to a conscious evolution." In Julian Huxley's phrase, man must assume the position of "a trustee of evolution on this earth." In assuming that role we are obliged to act with a level of aware-ness or consciousness that is equal to the power and responsibility inherent in that role. The evolution of our consciousness (and supportive social forms) is not a peripheral concern; rather, it is of central importance to our human agenda. Krippner and Meacham state:

> Throughout time, the whole universe has been moving toward greater intensity and range of consciousness. "Evolution is an ascent towards con-sciousness," wrote Teilhard de Chardin, and man is at the frontal edge of this process.

This persistent theme emerges from many cultural perspectives; Auro-bindo states:

> An evolution of consciousness is the central motive of terrestrial exis-tence. . . . A change of consciousness is the major fact of the next evolution-ary transformation.

Nonetheless, this is a purpose so far removed from the daily life-worlds of most people in the West that it is almost totally unacknowledged. Our cultural conditioning has rendered us perceptually deaf to our own higher human possibilities even though Western culture provides a more fertile ground for exploring these potentials than perhaps any in history.

An important dimension of the vast spectrum of consciousness into which we may evolve is revealed through mystical experiences. These expanded states of awareness appear to constitute the *highest* common denominator of human experience. This is a profoundly hopeful discov-ery in that, before the people of the world can cope with the problems of our global village, there must be some degree of shared agreement as to the nature of "reality" within which we collectively exist. Mystical expe-riences may provide an important element of that common agreement at a level that transcends cultural differences.

Our era of relative abundance contrasts sharply with the material poverty of the past. Today, with simplicity, equity, and wisdom we can have both substantial freedom *from* want and freedom to evolve our consciousness as individuals in community with others. The industrial revolution, then, may be viewed as a major evolutionary breakthrough that provides the material base to support that pervasive, intentional evolution to expand states/processes of individual and sociocultural awareness.

Economic necessity (which dictates either enforced or voluntarily assumed simplicity), Taoistic 'necessity' (which impels us to evolve our awareness to assume evolutionary trusteeship), and human possibility (to evolve to higher levels of awareness/consciousness) all combine to create what seems to be a gentle but increasingly insistent evolutionary imperative toward individual and societal transcendence.

If we are to realize this 'new frontier' of social and human possibility, it seems likely that something akin to the following 'ethics' must emerge. First is a Self-Realization Ethic, which asserts that each person's proper goal is the evolutionary development of human potential. Accordingly, this ethic insists that social institutions provide an environment supportive of self-realization. Second, we must develop an Ecological Ethic, which accepts our earth as limited and recognizes the underlying unity of the human race as an integral part of the natural environment.

Accepting the challenge of this new frontier neither denies nor turns away from our earlier, largely external/material frontier. Both necessity and opportunity require a change in proportion and balance—a shift in the center of social gravity—toward the nonmaterial dimension of an evolving human consciousness. This is not to deny our technological and economic achievements; rather, we must build on them if we are to progress into the next frontier.

In conclusion, hard material necessity and human evolutionary possibility now seem to converge to create a situation where, in the long run, we will be obliged to do no less than realize our greatest possibilities. We are engaged in a race between self-discovery and self-destruction. The forces that may converge to destroy us are the same forces that may foster societal and self-discovery. The path of discovery requires us to first learn the way of the universe—the gentle imperative of the way of the Tao.

◻

43

Transpersonal Experiences and the Global Crisis

Stanislav Grof and Christina Grof

Modern science has all the knowledge necessary to eliminate most diseases, combat poverty and starvation, and generate an abundance of safe and renewable energy. We have sufficient resources and manpower to realize the wildest dreams humanity has ever had. When we have the means and technological know-how for feeding the population of the planet, guaranteeing a reasonable standard of living for all, combating most diseases, reorienting industries to inexhaustible sources of energy, and preventing pollution, what prevents us from taking these positive steps?

The answer lies in the fact that all of the critical developments mentioned above are symptoms of one fundamental crisis. In the last analysis, the problems we are facing are not merely economic, political, or technological in nature. They are all reflections of the emotional, moral, and spiritual state of contemporary humanity. Among the most destructive aspects of the human psyche are malignant aggression and insatiable acquisitiveness. These are the forces that are responsible for the unimaginable waste of modern warfare. They also prevent a more appropriate division of resources among individuals, classes, and nations, as well as a reorientation toward ecological priorities essential for the continuation of life on this planet. These destructive and self-destructive elements in the present human condition directly reflect the alienation of modern humanity from itself and from spiritual life and values.

In view of these facts, one of the few hopeful and encouraging developments in the world today is the renaissance of interest in ancient spiritual traditions and the mystical quest. People who have had powerful transformative experiences and have succeeded in applying them to their everyday lives show very distinct changes in their values. This development holds great promise for the future of the world, since it represents a movement away from destructive and self-destructive personality characteristics and an emergence of those that foster individual and collective survival.

People who are involved in the process of spiritual emergence tend to develop a new appreciation and reverence for all forms of life and a new understanding of the unity of all things, which often results in strong ecological concerns and greater tolerance toward other human beings. Consideration of all humanity, compassion for all of life, and thinking in terms of the entire planet take priority over the narrow interests of individuals, families, political parties, classes, nations, and creeds. That which connects us all and that which we have in common become more important than our differences, which are seen as enhancing rather than threatening. In the attitudes characteristic of spiritual emergence, we can see the counterpoint to the intolerance, irreverence toward life, and moral bankruptcy that are the root causes of the global crisis. Thus we hope that the growing interest in spirituality and the high incidence of spontaneous mystical experiences herald a shift in the consciousness of humanity that will help to reverse our current self-destructive course.

❑

44

An Inner Manhattan Project

Peter Russell

Perhaps we need the psychological equivalent of the "Manhattan Project"—the code word for the development of the first atomic bomb. It had been realized that the newfound energies of the atomic nucleus could create a bomb a thousand times more powerful than the high explosives of the day. The development of such a bomb was seen to be of the highest importance for ending World War II, and hence for global security. Consequently scientific, technical and financial resources were pumped into a number of research and development institutions across the USA. The result was the detonation within less than three years of the first atomic bomb.

Now, nearly fifty years later, it is becoming clear that there are enormous untapped potentials within human consciousness, the nucleus of our being. If this power can be released, humanity could begin to tackle its problems much more wisely, ending the possibility of world war, and greatly increasing our chances of survival. If this need were recognized and resources put into projects to explore how to facilitate our awakening, then we could have an Inner Manhattan Project, and one of far greater value than the original project.

The wisdom of the human psyche already exists in many spiritual traditions, philosophies and psychologies. But it needs to be pulled together and researched. This is not to advocate a return to religions of the past, but to rediscover the sacred within us in the language and technologies of the twentieth century.

Any lasting remedy to our global problems must seek to find the underlying cause of the malady. Certainly we need to do everything we can to reduce the damage we are causing to the environment. But if this is all that we do, we shall find the same inner malady reappearing in other symptoms.

The root of our environmental crisis is an inner spiritual aridity. Any truly holistic environmental policy must include this in its approach. We need not only to conduct research in the physical and biological sciences; we also need to explore the psychological and more sacred sciences.

SECTION ELEVEN

□

ENVISIONING THE FUTURE

◻
45

Paths Beyond Ego in the Coming Decades

Ken Wilber

There are several exciting developments in transpersonal theory that I believe will be particularly important in the coming decade. They involve research into *states* of consciousness and *structures* of consciousness; cross-cultural investigations of contemplative paths and patterns; situating the transpersonal movement in the larger currents of the postmodern world; a rereading of world philosophies, religions, and psychologies from the vantage point of the transpersonal orientation; a continued study of the relation of the various "breaks from normality" (i.e., the relation of psychoses to mysticism); the excruciatingly difficult problem of the relation of mind and body (or brain); more precise mappings of the developmental spectrum of consciousness in its conventional, contemplative, and pathological dimensions; the relation of Jungian to general transpersonal psychology; a finer theoretical understanding of the relation of "marginal groups," such as the transpersonal to the "larger forces" of world development and technological advance; the relation of the transpersonal domain to the three great "Others," the neglected domains of the World Traditions, namely, body, nature, woman; the relation of nature and Spirit; the relation of general theory to individual practice; and, most importantly, continued work in the "grand theories" aiming at a coherent representation of the transpersonal in all the various "conventional" disciplines, including anthropology, medicine, ecology, economics, and the humanities. To take them in that order:

1. STATES AND STRUCTURES

Two dominant paradigms now govern transpersonal studies: altered states of consciousness and developmental structures of consciousness. Both of these two paradigms have their archetypal representation in Vedanta, where a distinction and correlation is made among the five major sheaths or structures (koshas) of consciousness (matter, body, mind, higher mind, collective mind) and the three major states or bodies of consciousness (gross, subtle, causal, experienced in waking, dreaming, and deep sleep states). Vedanta maintains that a given state of consciousness can support several different structures. Aurobindo added the insight that structures, but not states, develop (thus, the infant has access to all three major states of waking, dreaming, and sleeping, but it has access to only the *lowest* structures of the gross realm; the higher structures have not yet developed).

The research agenda: What is the relation of states (which can be prepersonal, personal, and transpersonal) to structures (which are also prepersonal, personal, and transpersonal)?

As yet little work has been done on how to integrate these two paradigms, and in many ways they appear incompatible: structures are cumulative and integrative; states are discrete and exclusionary. I suggest that the answer will involve the notion that developmental structures are the permanent unfolding or actualization, or coming into stable manifestation, of that which is only *temporarily* experienced in an altered state. To the extent that temporary and discrete states become actualized and are not just transitory, they must enter the stream of development and "obey" its patterns. Mapping and explaining these transformations will be one of the major breakthrough areas in transpersonal studies.

2. CROSS-CULTURAL STUDIES OF CONTEMPLATIVE DEVELOPMENT

Much pioneering work has been done in this area, but much more awaits the future researcher. Of particular importance are the careful phenomenological descriptions of contemplative states/structures (with all the difficulty involved in describing often trans-verbal realities). An extremely important question in this area is: Can the same developmental-logic governing the unfolding of conventional stages of cognition, conation, affect, and so forth be shown to apply to the higher states/structures as well? Is there a unity to evolution and development? I believe there is, but if not, then what does that say about the unity of Spirit and its unfolding (or lack thereof)?

3. SITUATING TRANSPERSONAL STUDIES IN THE LARGER CURRENTS OF POSTMODERNISM

There are now four main intellectual currents in the humanities of the postmodern world, all struggling for supremacy: the classical Enlightenment humanists, the deconstructionist "antithinkers" (Derrida), the "critical interpretives" (Foucault), and "communicative ethics" (Habermas).

Enlightenment humanism is marked by a belief in the power of instrumental rationality to discover any and all "truths" capable and worthy of being known, and a belief in the power of such rational truth to set men and women free, both personally and politically. However noble these aspirations, they have historically tended to degenerate into a "disenchanted" and fragmented worldview, with the domains of art, morality, and science radically divorced from one another and from individuals' lives, and with a rather blind faith that technological rationality can alone solve the resultant dilemmas.

In response to this fractured and rather limited rational worldview (traditional "modernism" and "humanism"), there have arisen three broad "postmodern" movements: the deconstruction of Jacques Derrida, the "neo-structuralism" of Michel Foucault, and the "universal pragmatics" of Jürgen Habermas. All of them are united by a critique of instrumental rationality and a critique of the isolated and autonomous ego (the foundation of humanism); they believe that truth is historically and linguistically situated (not eternally given); and they show a great concern with ethical action in a world that can no longer ground its truth claims in mechanistic rationality and positivism.

Deconstruction attempts to demonstrate that linguistic rationality ("logocentrism"), which has marked much of Western philosophy and civilization, is internally self-contradictory: it undermines its own position whenever it is applied to itself (e.g., the criterion for empirical truth is not itself empirical). This deconstruction of logocentrism is said to open up new pathways of moving beyond a rigidly dualistic rationality. Foucault's analysis of knowledge as structures of power, and his demonstration that various worldviews or "epistemes" have abruptly emerged throughout history both have an effect similar to deconstruction: they undermine thoroughly the traditional humanistic/rational assumptions about the world, truth, and ethics. Jürgen Habermas, whom many consider the world's greatest living philosopher, has attempted to move beyond instrumental rationality—and beyond the isolated and autonomous ego—by emphasizing "communicative ethics," or the ways in which human beings attempt to understand one another in a community of mutual exchange and mutual respect.

All of these postmodern movements are indeed post-ego movements. In fact, they often explicitly refer to their projects as the "death of the ego philosophies" or "the death of the subject philosophies." And while all of this is very encouraging from a transpersonal perspective, the "death of the ego" that they are referring to does not mean an opening to a genuine transpersonal dimension, but rather the transformation from a narrow, instrumental, rational egoic worldview to a multiperspective, systemic, organic, relational, and socially situated bodymind. (I have called this network-logic and the centaur, which is still a separate-self sense, but better than the previous "ego." Postmodernism is "moving in the right direction.")

But all of these postmodern movements contain explicit criticisms of any sort of mystical transcendentalism, of pure presence, of transhistorical realities. So a crucial topic for the coming decade will be: Where are transpersonal studies situated in these postmodern currents, and how can transpersonal studies answer their sharp criticisms? I would suggest that all of these postmodern theories *already* display hidden transcendentalism (the Divine slips into their theories whenever they aren't looking). This needs only to be pointed out so that they themselves can then be situated in the spectrum of transpersonal development. In other words, deconstruction can be deconstructed (à la Nagarjuna), Foucault can be situated in his own episteme, and even Habermas has held open the possibility that there are still higher stages of development yet to unfold, which is the precise province of transpersonal developmental studies. For conventional academic concerns in the humanities, *this* will be the hotbed of theoretical action.

4. RECONCEPTUALIZING WORLD PHILOSOPHIES FROM A TRANSPERSONAL PERSPECTIVE

The virtually uncontested assumption of modern Western intellectuals is that anything "transcendental" is simply a "narrative" or a mere "ideology," and thus history is to be read as a chronicle of shifting ideologies whose only grounding is the relative cultural legitimation given to them by particular (and equally shifting and relative) cultures. But what if *some* transcendentals are in fact direct experiences and direct disclosures that, although mediated by language, are in some important ways extralinguistic or cross-cultural? A diamond will cut a piece of glass, no matter what words we use for "diamond," "cut," and "glass"—and a soul can experience God, no matter what words we use for "soul," "experience," and "God."

History, then, would have to be entirely reread as a chronicle of the growth and accumulation of true transcendental experiences filtered through various ideologies, and not merely reduced to one ideology among others. This would completely revolutionize our concepts of human potentials and divine possibilities, and place the growth of spiritual knowledge correctly alongside any other scientific advances.

5. THE RELATION OF PSYCHOSIS TO MYSTICISM

This always fascinating topic is significant not just in itself, but for several vitally important and related topics: creativity and madness, normalization and marginalization, ordinary and extraordinary potentials, personal breakdown and personal breakthrough. The important field of *spiritual emergency* is also intimately connected with this topic. Too many people diagnosed with psychotic breaks are clearly undergoing a spiritual emergency, and the details of these crises desperately need further investigation (not to mention the relation of spirituality to addictions, depressions, anxieties, and so forth). This whole topic is also related directly to how we conceptualize "the unconscious" (as demons, gods, infrarational, superrational, all of the above?). The continued mapping and conceptualization of the unconscious will be one of the most important and fruitful areas of transpersonal research in the coming decade.

6. THE RELATION OF BRAIN STATES TO MIND STATES

This perennial question affects—and infects—transpersonal studies much more than most fields, simply because the "separation" or "gap" between brain states and mind states (exterior matter and interior awareness) is "greater" in the transpersonal field. After all, some transpersonal experiences carry the overwhelmingly convincing apprehension that consciousness is prior to any manifestation, that it is eternal and timeless. How does this "eternal consciousness" relate to a purely finite and temporal brain?

My feeling is that this issue cannot be sidestepped by materialist concessions, and that a thoroughgoing Idealism of a very postmodern variety will have to be carefully elaborated and defended. But this task is today made easier by the common acceptance of the Big Bang, which has made Idealists out of virtually everybody who thinks about it. After all, what was there before the Big Bang? Since the first microatomic particles seem to have been following mathematical laws, and since those laws did not "develop," weren't they somehow existent prior to the Big Bang? Aren't there some sort of Platonic archetypes prior to evolution, in addition to any "archetypes" that might themselves have simply evolved? And couldn't some transpersonal experiences be experiences of those objectively real entities, Whitehead's "eternal objects"? Isn't Zen's "Original Face"—your own True Self—the Face you had before the Big Bang?

Whatever we decide, this issue cannot be avoided. For the transpersonalist, the seemingly innocuous question of the relation of mind (consciousness) to body (matter) is, in fact, the ultimate question of the relation of Emptiness to Form, the unmanifest to the manifest.

7. HOW DO ANY "CONSCIOUSNESS STATES" RELATE TO MATERIAL-PHYSIOLOGICAL "BRAIN STATES"?

On a more specific level, how do actual states and structures of consciousness relate to specific brain-wave patterns? Initial studies in this field have centered on major *states* of consciousness and their correlation with gross brain-wave patterns, PET scans, and so forth, usually revealing that some meditative states show an increase in alpha/theta activity or deep delta patterns, and so on.

I believe that major breakthroughs will occur in electronically inducing brain-wave patterns that appear to mimic meditation (such as deep theta/delta), and that the machines to do this will become widely available commercially. I believe nobody will become "enlightened" from this, precisely because brain and mind are not *merely* identical, and enlightenment occurs in the mind (consciousness), not in the brain, although changes occur there also.

What this research will show us, I believe, is that brain states more easily "allow" certain mind states, but do not determine them. A person might even get a "taste" of the transpersonal through electronic induction, like getting a taste through psychedelics, but without interior cognitive transformation, the state will fade; it will not become a structure.

This relationship will be a major field of research and will join psychedelic research as a profound tool for exploring the mind/body problem. In the meantime, the electronic induction of brain states will very likely be one of the most widespread "modern" sources of "transpersonal" experiences for the average individual, and the transpersonal realm will enter the fields of medicine, nursing, and psychiatry through that electronic door, just as yoga was given legitimation by scientists only when it was clinically connected with biofeedback.

8. CONTINUED MAPPINGS OF THE DEVELOPMENTAL SPECTRUM, IN CONVENTIONAL, CONTEMPLATIVE, AND PATHOLOGICAL DIMENSIONS

This is a crucial endeavor, made all the more pressing by the urgent need to clarify the relation between structures and states. If the transpersonal or contemplative stages and structures of consciousness also have specifiable pathologies (which I believe is the case), continuing to map these pathologies will be extremely important. Also, an enormously rich field awaits in the mapping and the clarification of the transpersonal stages of moral development, cognition, motivation, worldviews, and affect.

Transpersonal developmental studies are still one of the most promising and important areas of research. Unlike states of consciousness, which are temporary and noninclusive, stages or structures of consciousness can be studied using a *reconstructive science* (precisely as used by Piaget, Gilligan, Kohlberg, Habermas, Chomsky, even Freud). A reconstructive science does not postulate the existence of structures in an a priori or merely theoretical fashion, but rather studies those individuals who have already demonstrated a competence in the particular task (whether linguistic, cognitive, moral, or contemplative). It then reconstructs, after the fact, the components and stages of development that lead up to the competence. Buddha, in a sense, simply reconstructed the steps he went through to gain his enlightenment and presented them as a reconstructive science that could be tried and verified—or rejected—by a community of experimenters. Since reconstructive sciences reconstruct after the fact, they are not open to charges of a priori metaphysics, and, further, their claims can be subjected to nonverification, the so-called "fallibist criterion."

That transpersonal developmental psychology is a reconstructive science also means that it is open to the fallibist criterion of any true science. This is by far the single strongest argument the transpersonalist can present to the conventional community.

9. THE RELATION OF JUNGIAN THEORY TO TRANSPERSONAL THEORY

This is an enormously complicated and delicate topic. For almost half a century, the Jungian paradigm has been the major—and only—viable theory of transpersonal psychology in the West. I personally believe that the Jungian model has many strong points—but even more weak points—and that this debate will in fact be the most heated area of discussion in the coming decade, simply because so many people are involved in its outcome. But in any event the dialogue between the Jungian model and the general transpersonal field will continue to be a source of rich mutual stimulation and challenge, and will go hand in hand with the extremely important and even larger dialogue of transpersonal psychology with the other three major forces of psychology.

10. THE RELATION OF "MARGINAL" TO "NORMAL" GROUPS IN SOCIAL EVOLUTION

A large number of transpersonalists believe that many of the world's critically pressing problems, from social fragmentation to environmental crisis, can only be "solved" by a transpersonal transformation. I personally do not believe that this is so, but in either case, a cogent theory of how marginal knowledge (such as that of the transpersonal) becomes normalized or conventionally accepted needs to be worked out and thoroughly checked by then rereading history using that model. Work in this area is virtually nonexistent, yet without it any claim to "world transformation," or even the claim that transpersonal theory can have a world influence, is simply more ideology.

My own feeling is that a theory of world transformation will in effect be a "mystical Marxism"—that is, it will cover the intricate relations between the "material-technological-economic" base of any society and its worldviews, legitimation strategies, and consciousness states/structures. This field is virtually wide open.

11. THE RELATION OF THE THREE "OTHERS" (BODY, NATURE, WOMAN) TO THE GREAT TRADITIONS

The fully developed World Traditions (such as Judaism, Christianity, Hinduism, Buddhism, Islam, even aspects of Taoism) all arose in a climate of discourse that devalued the body, nature, and women. All three of these "Others" were, in fact, equated with evil, temptation, or illusion. How can women today develop any faith in the Great Traditions when every single aspect of those Traditions were developed exclusively by men?

And is not the alienation of women precisely parallel to the alienation of the body (asceticism) and nature (samsara)? And is not global alienation what we now see in the environmental crisis? Far from "saving" us, aren't the Great Traditions the root of a crisis that very well might kill us all? These are absolutely crucial questions for any contemplative/transpersonal discipline, and they need to be faced squarely.

The Great Traditions do indeed emphasize an Ascending and Transcendental current; but many of them also contain an equal emphasis on the Descending and Immanent nature of Spirit. The Tantric traditions, for example, emphasize a union of the Transcendental and Ascending God (Shiva) with the Immanent and Descending Goddess (Shakti), a union that is found in the nondual Heart and a union that emphasizes equally the masculine and feminine faces of Spirit.

Nonetheless, I believe that the entire pantheon of the Great Traditions will, in the coming years, have to be scrutinized thoroughly and "scrubbed clean" of the universal alienation of the three "Others"—nature, body, woman—but in a way that does not throw out the baby with the bathwater. To simply reject everything the Traditions have to tell us would be catastrophic; we might as well refuse to use the wheel just because a man may have invented it. But this field, too, is virtually wide open, and will yield an enormous number of insights in the coming decade. The next point is related to this one.

12. THE "OTHER" OF NATURE IN RELATION TO SPIRIT

I mention this as a separate issue simply because of the pressing nature of the global environmental crisis. There is no doubt in my mind that the purely Ascending (or Gnostic) Traditions, which see the manifest world merely and only as illusion, have indeed contributed to a set of cultural prejudices that have allowed a despoliation of the Earth.

And once again I believe that we will have to turn to the Tantric traditions (East and West, North and South). These Traditions universally see the finite realm (Earth and all) as a perfect manifestation of Spirit, not as a detraction from Spirit, and thus they celebrate and honor embodiment, descent, immanence, the feminine, the Earthbody values.

The "secret" relation of the Ascending (transcendent) and Descending (immanent) aspects of Spirit was given by Sri Ramana Maharshi, among many others:

> The world is illusory
> Brahman alone is real
> Brahman is the world.

A comprehensive Spirituality thus includes both of these two great currents (Ascending and Descending, "masculine" and "feminine"). Seeing that the world is illusory is the Transcendental or Ascending current, which is overemphasized by the Gnostic/Theravadin traditions wherever they appear. Seeing that Brahman is the world is the Immanent or Descending current, which embraces all manifestations as a Perfect Gesture of the Divine.

Either one of those currents taken in and by itself is catastrophic. We have seen the disasters of overemphasizing the masculine Ascending current. We are now privileged to watch the disasters of those movements' trying to equate the finite world with the Infinite. We are now in a flurry of Descending theories, from deep ecology to ecofeminism to Earthbound and geocentric revivals, all of which happily confuse shadows with Source. These Descending endeavors, as crucially important as they are, are nonetheless in their own ways just as lopsided, dualistic, and fragmented as their merely Ascending counterparts.

The work for the coming decade is to find a way to unite and honor both of these currents—the Finite and the Infinite, the Manifest and the Unmanifest, the Descending and the Ascending—without reducing one to the other or privileging one over the other.

13. THE RELATION OF THEORY AND PRACTICE

Transpersonal studies in themselves are not necessarily a spiritual practice, although, of course, the two are intimately connected. The nature of this connection will be a crucial topic in the coming decade.

There are any number of practices that induce or open one to the transpersonal dimension—meditation, shamanic techniques, Goddess rituals, kundalini exercises, holotropic breathwork, psychedelics, deep psychotherapy, biofeedback and electronic induction, the various yogas, life itself. It is from the community of those who have displayed a *competence* in any of these fields that the reconstructive science of transpersonal psychology draws its subjects. The *theory* of transpersonal psychology depends upon those who have *practiced* and achieved competence in a transpersonal/spiritual discipline.

Ideally, then, a transpersonal researcher also will have some sort of personal spiritual practice, be a "participant observer." How to separate—and relate—the theory and the practice will thus remain a pressing issue. This is complicated by the fact that transpersonal theory attempts to abstract from the various disciplines those universal factors that seem to be the common or key ingredients in each, but one still has to practice a *particular* discipline to attain competence.

Further, the various disciplines are themselves evolving in today's global village and postmodern world, as Buddhism meets science and Yoga meets the computer. This has rendered problematic many aspects of the traditional disciplines, such as the role of the guru, specific cultural artifacts such as life-style prescriptions or sexism.

I believe it is crucial for a transpersonal researcher to have a personal spiritual discipline. But the exact relation of theory and practice will remain an extremely important topic for discussion and shared insights, as the transpersonal field finds its way into the twenty-first century.

14. THE GRAND THEORIES

The transpersonal field is uniquely situated to synthesize and integrate various fields in humanity's knowledge quest, simply because it is the one field that is uniquely dedicated to exploring, honoring, and acknowledging all the dimensions of men and women's experience—sensory, emotional, mental, social, spiritual.

Transpersonal studies are the only truly global studies now in existence, studies that span the entire spectrum of human growth and aspiration. The coming decade, I have no doubt, will witness the emergence of transpersonal studies as the only comprehensive field of human endeavor.

And although I do not think that the world is entering anything resembling a "new age" or "transpersonal transformation," I do believe that transpersonal studies always will be that one beacon to men and women who see Spirit in the world and the world in Spirit.

❏

46

The Adventure of Consciousness

Roger Walsh and Frances Vaughan

A human being is a part of the whole called by us universe, a part limited in time and space. He experiences himself, his thoughts and feelings as something separated from the rest, a kind of optical delusion of his consciousness. This delusion is a kind of prison for us, restricting us to our personal desires and to affection for a few persons nearest to us. Our task must be to free ourselves from this prison by widening our circle of compassion to embrace all living creatures and the whole of nature in its beauty.
　　　　　　　　　　　　　　　　　　—ALBERT EINSTEIN

We have entered a new phase of the adventure of consciousness. Born humbly as an attempt to understand the peak experiences of exceptionally healthy people, transpersonal psychology has blossomed into an international, interdisciplinary movement. Transpersonal experiences, potentials, and traditions, long dismissed as fantasies, pathologies, or fictions, are at last being explored and appreciated. Each discovery unveils further possibilities.

This new appreciation is allowing us to draw upon the great reservoirs of transpersonal wisdom accumulated across centuries in many cultures. Viewing this wisdom in the light of modern research makes it understandable in contemporary terms and allows its true significance to be recognized.

Carl Jung spoke of the importance of gnostic intermediaries, those people who transmit a wisdom tradition by imbibing it themselves and then translating it into the language and concepts of another culture. Perhaps the transpersonal movement can function as a collective gnostic intermediary, whereby the timeless wisdom of traditional transpersonal disciplines can be translated, tested, and winnowed, and then can inspire and transform contemporary culture.

Yet the transpersonal movement is more than a gnostic intermediary. For in addition to translating knowledge it is actively involved in creating knowledge. New techniques are being devised, new data generated, and both ancient and contemporary claims are being tested scientifically, philosophically, clinically, and experientially.

The long-term effects of this enterprise may be far more than we can imagine. Already we have seen a shift to a more generous view of human nature and possibilities. We have moved from a perspective that encompassed only a single, healthy waking state of consciousness to a recognition of multiple states; from viewing normal development as our ceiling to seeing it as a culturally determined limit; from denying the possibility of lucid dreaming to exploring it in the laboratory; from regarding meditation as a regressive escape to appreciating it as a developmental catalyst; from dismissing mystical experiences as pathological to recognizing them as beneficial; and from devaluing non-Western psychologies and philosophies to appreciating that some of them are, in their own unique ways, highly sophisticated. These shifts and more may make transpersonal studies an essential cornerstone in the emerging paradigm.

These shifts also may change each of us, for what we do reflects our beliefs about who and what we are. The transpersonal vision of our possibilities may therefore call forth our individual and collective efforts to actualize them.

This actualization may be crucial for the survival of our planet and our species, for we have created a global situation that demands unprecedented psychological and social maturation. In the past we could consume without depletion, discard without pollution, multiply without overpopulation, and fight without fear of extinction. In other words, we could act out our immaturities whereas now we need to outgrow them. Our global crisis, like the transpersonal vision, calls us to grow up and wake up.

The need is great, but so too are the opportunities. For the first time in human history we have a transpersonal vision and all the world's paths beyond ego to help us awaken. This collective waking up is the adventure of consciousness, paths beyond ego are the means for the adventure, and the transpersonal vision is its guiding light.

□

Notes and References

Introduction, p. 1

1. Needleman, J. *Lost Christianity*. Garden City, N.Y.: Doubleday, 1980, p. 60.
2. Maslow, A. *Toward a psychology of being*, 2nd ed. Princeton: Van Nostrand, 1968, p. 5.
3. A fuller definition of transpersonal disciplines, which also applies in large part to individual disciplines and is therefore very similar to the definition of transpersonal psychology, is as follows: Transpersonal disciplines study transpersonal experiences and their correlates. These correlates include the nature, varieties, causes, and effects of transpersonal experiences and development, as well as the psychologies, philosophies, disciplines, arts, cultures, life-styles, reactions, and religions inspired by them, or that seek to induce, express, apply, or understand them.
4. Wilber, K. *A sociable god*. New York: McGraw-Hill, 1983, p. 55.
5. Satprem. *Sri Aurobindo or the adventure of consciousness*. New York: Harper & Row, 1968, p. 84.
6. Wilber, K. *The Atman project*. Wheaton, Ill.: Quest, 1980, p. 159.
7. Alexander, F., and Selesnich, S. *The history of psychiatry*. New York: New American Library, 1966, p. 372.

Introduction to Section One, "The Riddle of Consciousness," p. 3

1. Jung, C. *The collected works of C. G. Jung*. (Vol. 9, Part I) *Four Archetypes*. Princeton: Princeton University Press, 1969.
2. Baruss, I. *The personal nature of notions of consciousness*. New York: University Press of America, 1990.
3. Hofstadter, D., and Dennett, D. *The mind's I*. New York: Basic Books, 1981, p. 8.
4. Shearer, P., trans. *Effortless being: The yoga sutras of Patanjali*. London: Unwin, 1989, pp. 119, 78–79, 72.
5. Wilber, K. *Eye to eye: The quest for the new paradigm*. Garden City, N.Y.: Anchor/Doubleday, 1982, p. 18.
6. Sengstan, Third Zen Patriarch. *Verses on the faith mind*. Trans. R. Clarke. Sharon Springs, N.Y.: Zen Center, 1975.
7. Bourguignon, E., ed. *Religion, altered states of consciousness, and social change*. Columbus, Ohio: Ohio State University, 1973, p. 11.
8. Weil, A. *The natural mind*. Boston: Houghton Mifflin, 1972, p. 17.
9. Da Avabhasa, *The dawn horse testament: New standard edition*. Clearlake, Calif.: The Dawn Horse Press, 1991.

10. Goleman, D. *The meditative mind.* Los Angeles: Tarcher, 1988.
11. Tart, C. *Waking up: Overcoming the obstacles to human potential.* Boston: New Science Library/Shambhala, 1986, p. 80.
12. Harner, M. *The way of the shaman.* New York: Bantam, 1982.

Chapter 1, "Psychology, Reality, and Consciousness," p. 8.

1. Maslow's (1970) "plateau experience" is one near approximation in contemporary psychology; Sutich's (1973) concept of "ultimate states" may also subsume this category.

References

Berger, P. L., and Luckmann, T. *The social construction of reality.* New York: Anchor, 1967.
Goleman, D. The Buddha on meditation and consciousness. Part I: The teachings, *Journal of Transpersonal Psychology* 4, 1 (1972): 1–44.
James, W. *Psychology: Briefer course.* New York: Holt and Co., 1910.
Katz, R. Education for transcendence: Lessons from the !Kung Zhū/twāsi, *Journal of Transpersonal Psychology* 5, 2 (1973): 136–55.
LaBarre, W. The cultural basis of emotions and gestures, *J. Pers.* 16 (1947): 49–68.
Lee, D. Codification of reality: Lineal and nonlineal, *Psychosom. Med.* 12, 2 (1950): 89–97.
Mannheim, K. *Ideology and utopia.* London: Routledge & Kegan Paul, 1936.
Maslow, A. Theory Z, *Journal of Transpersonal Psychology* 2, 1 (1970): 31–47.
Sutich, A. J. Transpersonal therapy, *J. Transpersonal Psychol.* 5, 1 (1973): 1–6.
Whorf, B. L. *Language, thought, and reality.* Cambridge: M.I.T. Press, 1964.

Chapter 2, "Psychologia Perennis," p. 21.

Brown, N. O. *Life against death: The psychoanalytical meaning of history.* Middleton, Ohio: Wesleyan University Press, 1959.
Deutsch, E. *Advaita Vedanta.* Honolulu: East-West Center Press, 1969.
Fromm, E. Suzuki, D. T., and DeMartino, R. *Zen Buddhism and psychoanalysis.* New York: Harper & Row, 1970.
Huxley, A. *The perennial philosophy.* New York: Harper & Row, 1970.
Jung, C. *Analytical psychology: Its theory and practice.* New York: Vintage, 1968.
Maslow, A. H. *Towards a psychology of being.* New York: Van Nostrand Reinhold, 1968.
Maslow, A. H. *The farther reaches of human nature.* New York: Viking, 1971.
Mead, G. H. *George Herbert Mead on social psychology.* Ed. Anselm Strauss. Chicago: University of Chicago Press, 1964.
Perls, F., Hefferline, R., and Goodman, P. *Gestalt therapy.* New York: Delta, 1951.
Suzuki, D. T. *Studies in the Lankavatara Sutra.* London: Routledge & Kegan Paul, 1968.
White, J., ed. *The highest state of consciousness.* New York: Anchor, 1972.
Whorf, B. L. *Language, thought, and reality.* Cambridge: M.I.T. Press, 1956.

Chapter 4, "Mapping and Comparing States," p. 38.

1. Doore, G. *Shaman's path.* Boston: Shambhala, 1988, p. 223.
2. Kalweit, H. *Dreamtime and inner space.* Boston: Shambhala, 1988, p. 236.
3. Walsh, R. *The spirit of shamanism.* Los Angeles: Tarcher, 1990.
4. Harner, M. *The way of the shaman.* New York: Bantam, 1982.
5. Eliade, M. *Shamanism: Archaic techniques of ecstasy.* Princeton: Princeton University Press, 1964.
6. Goleman, D. *The meditative mind.* Los Angeles: Tarcher, 1988.
7. Eliade, M. *Yoga: Immortality and freedom.* Princeton: Princeton University Press, 1958.
8. Prabhavananda, S. and Isherwood, C. (Trans.). *How to know God: The yoga aphorisms of Patanjali.* Hollywood: Vedanta, 1953.
9. Brown, D., Forte, M., and Dysart, M. Differences in visual sensitivity among mindfulness meditators and non-meditators. *Perceptual and Motor Skills* 58 (1984): 727–33.
10. Eliade, M. *Yoga: Immortality and freedom.* 2nd ed. Princeton: Princeton University Press, 1969, p. 339.
11. Sengstan, Third Zen Patriarch. *Verses on the faith mind.* (Trans. R. Clarke) Sharon Springs, N.Y.: Zen Center.
12. Hultkrantz, A. Ecological and phenomenological aspects of shamanism. In *Shamanism in Siberia,* ed. V. Dioszegi and M. Hoppal. Budapest: Akadamiai Kiado, 1978, pp. 27–58.

Introduction to Section Two, "Meditation: Royal Road to the Transpersonal," p. 47.

1. Plotinus. *The essential Plotinus.* Trans. E. O'Brien. Hackett, Indianapolis, 1964, p. 42.
2. Freud, S. *A general introduction to psychoanalysis.* Garden City, N.Y.: Garden City Publishers, 1917, p. 252.
3. Prabhavananda, S. and Isherwood, C. (Trans.). *The song of God: Bhagavad Gita.* Hollywood: Vedanta Press, 1944, p. 85.
4. Ram Dass. *Association for Transpersonal Psychology Newsletter,* 1975, p. 9.
5. Plato. *The republic.* Trans. F. Cornford. Oxford: Oxford University Press, 1945, p. 516.
6. Ramana Maharshi. *Who am I?* (Trans. T. Venkataran.) 8th ed. India, 1955.
7. Gampopa. *The jewel ornament of liberation.* Trans. H. Guenther, Boston: Shambhala, 1971, p. 271.
8. Schumacher, E. *Small is beautiful: Economics as if people mattered.* New York: Harper & Row, 1973, p. 67.
9. James, W. *Talks to teachers on psychology and to students on some of life's ideals.* 1899. New York: Dover, 1962, p. 51.
10. James, W. *Principles of psychology.* 1910. New York: Dover, 1950, p. 424.
11. Ram Dass. *Journey of awakening.* New York: Doubleday, 1978.
12. Walsh, R. Meditation Research. This volume.

13. Schindler, C., and Lapid, G. *The great turning: Personal peace and global victory.* Santa Fe: Bear and Company, 1989.
14. Blake, W. The marriage of heaven and hell. In *Blake: Complete writings,* ed. G. Keynes. London: Oxford University Press, 1966.
15. Ellenberger, H. *The discovery of the unconscious.* New York: Basic Books, 1970, p. 376.
16. Perls, F. *Gestalt therapy verbatim.* Lafayette, Calif.: Real People Press, 1969, p. 16.
17. Hardy, T. *Collected poems of Thomas Hardy.* New York: Macmillan, 1926, p. 154.
18. Wilber, K. *A sociable god.* New York: McGraw-Hill, 1983.
19. Alexander, F. Buddhist training as an artificial catatonia (the biological meaning of psychic occurrences). *Psychoanalytic Review* 18 (1931): 129–45.
20. Wilber, K. *The Atman project.* Wheaton, Ill.: Quest, 1980, p. 155.
21. Novak, P. Buddhist meditation and the Great Chain of Being: Some misgivings. *Listening* 24 (1989): 67–78.

Chapter 6, "Meditation Research: The State of the Art," p. 60.

1. Alexander, C., et al. Growth of higher stages of consciousness. In *Higher stages of human development,* ed. C. Alexander and E. Langer. New York: Oxford University Press, 1991.
2. Shapiro, D. & Walsh, R, eds. *Meditation: Classic and contemporary perspectives.* New York: Aldine, 1984.
3. Kwee, M., ed. *Psychotherapy, meditation and health.* London: East-West, 1990.
4. Murphy, M., and Donovan, S. *The physical and psychological effects of meditation.* San Rafael, Calif.: Esalen Institute, 1988.
5. Alexander, C., Rainforth, M., and Gelderloos, P. Transcendental meditation, self-actualization and psychological health: A conceptual overview and statistical meta-analysis. *Journal of Social Behavior and Personality* 6 (1992): 189–247.
6. Wilber, K., Engler, J., and Brown, D., eds. *Transformations of consciousness: Conventional and contemplative perspectives on development.* Boston: New Science Library/Shambhala, 1986.
7. Shapiro, D. Comparison of meditation with other self-control strategies: Biofeedback, hypnosis, progressive relaxation. *American Journal of Psychiatry* 139 (1982): 267–74.
8. West, M., ed. *The psychology of meditation.* Oxford: Clarenden Press, 1987.
9. Earle, J. Cerebral laterality and meditation. *Journal of Transpersonal Psychology* 13 (1981): 155–73.
10. Kabat-Zinn, J. *Full catastrophe living.* New York: Delcorte, 1990.
11. Orme-Johnson, D., & Alexander, C. *Critique of the National Research Council's report on meditation.* Fairfield, Iowa: Maharishi International University, 1988.
12. Orme-Johnson, D., et al. International peace project in the Middle East: The effects of the Maharishi technology of the unified field. *Journal of Conflict Resolution* 32 (1988): 776–812.
13. Epstein, M., and Lieff, J. Psychiatric complications of meditation practice. *Journal of Transpersonal Psychology* 13 (1981): 57.
14. Wilber, K. The spectrum of pathologies. This volume.
15. Shapiro, D. Meditation, self-control, and control by a benevolent other. In *Psychotherapy, meditation and health,* ed. M. Kwee. London: East-West, 1990, pp. 65–123.

Introduction to Section Three, "Lucid Dreaming," p. 71.

1. Bible. Revised Standard Version, Numbers 12:6.
2. LaBerge, S. *Lucid dreaming*. Los Angeles: Tarcher, 1985, pp. 30–31.
3. Shearer, P., Trans. *Effortless being: The yoga sutras of Patanjali*. London: Unwin, 1989, p. 64.
4. Shah, I. *The sufis*. New York: Anchor/Doubleday, 1971, pp. 155–56.
5. Gyamtso, K. T. S. H. *Progressive stages of meditation on emptiness*. Oxford: Longchen, 1986, p. 42.
6. Schopenhauer, A. Transcendente Spekulation "über die anscheinende Absichtlichkeit im Schicksale des einzelnen." Vol. 8, *Sämtliche Werke*, Cottasche Bibliothek der Weltlitteratur, Stuttgart, 1911–1942, pp. 220–25.
7. Suzuki, D. T. *Studies in the Lankavatara Sutra*. London: Routledge & Kegan Paul, 1930, p. 267.
8. Anonymous. *A course in miracles*. Glen Ellen, Calif.: Foundation for Inner Peace, 1975.
9. Hegel, G. *The phenomenology of mind*. Trans. J. Baillie. London: Unwin, 1949, p. 85–86.
10. Jones, W. *A history of Western philosophy*. 2nd ed. 5 vols. New York: Harcourt Brace Jovanovich, 1975.
11. Nietzsche, F. *The portable Nietzsche*. Trans. W. Kaufman. New York: Viking, 1955, p. 101.
12. Dalai Lama. Talk given at the International Transpersonal Association, Davos, Switzerland, 1983.
13. Evans-Wentz, W., trans. *Tibetan yoga and secret doctrines*. 2nd ed. Oxford: Oxford University Press, 1958, p. 222.

Introduction to Section Four, "The Mind Manifesters: Implications of Psychedelics," p. 87.

1. Grinspoon, L., and Bakalar, J. *Psychedelic drugs reconsidered*. New York: Basic Books, 1979.
2. Dobkin de Rios, M. *Hallucinogens: Cross-cultural perspectives*. Albuquerque: University of New Mexico, 1984.
3. Jaffe, J. Drug dependence: Opioids, nonnarcotics, nicotine (tobacco) and caffeine. In *Comprehensive textbook of psychiatry*. 5th ed., vol 1, ed. H. Kaplan and B. Sadock. Baltimore: Williams & Wilkins, 1989, p. 677.
4. Grof, S. *LSD psychotherapy*. Pomona, Calif.: Hunter House, 1980.
5. Strassman, R. Adverse reactions to psychedelic drugs: A review of the literature. *Journal of Nervous and Mental Disease* 172 (1984): 577–95.
6. Grof, S. *The adventure of self-discovery*. Albany: State University of New York Press, 1988.

Chapter 13, "Do Drugs Have Religious Import?" p. 91.

1. Mylonas, G. *Eleusis and the Eleusinian Mysteries*. Princeton: Princeton University Press, 1961.
2. Bergson, H. *Two Sources of Morality and Religion*. New York: Holt, 1935.

3. Pahnke, W. *Drugs and mysticism: An analysis of the relationship between psychedelic drugs and the mystical consciousness.* A thesis presented to the Committee for Higher Degrees in History and Philosophy of Religion; Harvard University, 1963.

Chapter 15, "Realms of the Human Unconscious: Observations from LSD Research," p. 95.

1. The Viennese psychiatrist Otto Rank, a renegade from the mainstream of orthodox psychoanalysis, emphasized in his book *The trauma of birth* (1927) the paramount significance of perinatal experiences.

Introduction to Section Five, "Transpersonal Dimensions of Development," p. 109.

1. Maslow, A. H. *Toward a psychology of being,* 2nd ed. Princeton: Van Nostrand, 1968, pp. 71–72, 16.
2. Mumford, L. *The transformations of man.* New York: Harper & Row, 1956, p. 241.
3. Kapleau, P. *The three pillars of Zen.* Garden City, N.Y.: Anchor/Doubleday, 1980, p. 155.
4. Radhakrishnan, *Indian philosophy.* 2nd ed., vol. 1. Bombay: Blackie & Sons, 1929, p. 43.
5. Stace, W. *Mysticism and philosophy.* Los Angeles: Tarcher, 1987, p. 338.

Introduction to Section Six, "Problems on the Path: Clinical Concerns," p. 131.

1. Maslow, A. *Toward a psychology of being.* 2nd ed. Princeton, N.J.: Van Nostrand Reinhold, 1968, p. iv.
2. Lukoff, D. The diagnosis of mystical experiences with psychotic features. *Journal of Transpersonal Psychology* 17 (1985): 155–82, p. 157.
3. Walsh, R. *The spirit of shamanism.* Los Angeles: Tarcher, 1990.
4. Perry, J. Spiritual emergence and renewal. *ReVision* 8, 2 (1986): 33–340.
5. Maslow, A. *The farther reaches of human nature.* New York: Viking, 1971, p. 36.
6. The Bill W.–Carl Jung Letters. *ReVision* 10, 2 (1987): 19–21, 1987.
7. Wilber, K. *The Atman project.* Wheaton, Ill.: Quest, 1980, p. 106.
8. Shapiro, D., and Walsh, R., eds. *Meditation: Classic and contemporary perspectives.* New York: Aldine, 1984.
9. Peele, S. *Diseasing of America: Addiction treatment out of control.* Lexington, Mass.: Lexington Books, 1989.
10. Deikman, A. *The observing self.* Boston, Mass.: Beacon, 1982, p. 80.
11. Klong-Chen Rab-'Byams-Pa. *Kindly bent to ease us.* Trans. H. Guenther. Emeryville, Calif.: Dharma, 1975, p. 29.

Introduction to Section Seven, "The Quest for Wholeness: Transpersonal Therapies," p. 153.

1. Bugental, J. *Psychotherapy and process.* Reading, Mass.: Addison-Wesley, 1978.
2. Turner, R., Lu, F., and Lukoff, D. Proposal for a new Z code: Psychoreligious or psychospiritual problem. *Journal of Nervous and Mental Disease* (1992) 180, 673–82.

3. Byrom, T. (Trans.). *The Dhammapada: The sayings of the Buddha.* New York: Vintage, 1976.
4. Ram Dass. *Love, serve, remember* (audiotape). Santa Cruz, Calif.: Hanuman Foundation, 1973.

Chapter 25, "Healing and Wholeness: Transpersonal Psychotherapy," p. 160.

1. Grof, S. *The adventure of self-discovery.* Albany: State University of New York Press, 1988.
2. Jung, C. G. *Letters.* Ed. G. Adler. Princeton: Princeton University Press, 1973.
3. The Bill W.–Carl Jung letters. *Re-Vision* 10, 2 (1987): 21.
4. Fadiman, J., and Frager, R. *Personality and personal growth,* 2nd ed. New York: Harper & Row, 1984.
5. Boorstein, S., and Vaughan, F. Transpersonal psychotherapy. In *The newer therapies,* ed. L. Abt and I. Stewart. New York: Van Nostrand Reinhold, 1982. pp. 118–35.
6. Boorstein, S., ed. *Transpersonal psychotherapy.* Palo Alto, Calif.: Science and Behavior Books, 1980.

Chapter 26, "Assumptions of Transpersonal Psychotherapy," p. 165.

Anonymous. *A course in miracles.* Vol. I. *Text.* Tiburon, CA: Foundation for Inner Peace, 1975.
Perls, F. *Gestalt therapy verbatim.* Lafayette, Calif.: Real People Press, 1969.

Introduction to Section Eight, "Science, Technology, and Transcendence," p. 177.

1. Smith, H. *Forgotten truth.* New York: Harper & Row, 1976, p. 1, 16.
2. Whitehead, A. *Science and the modern world.* New York: Macmillan, 1967.
3. Flanagan, O. *The science of the mind.* Cambridge, Mass.: M.I.T. Press, 1984, pp. 273–74.
4. James, W. *The varieties of religious experience.* 1902. Reprint. New York: New American Library, 1958, p. 29.
5. Griffin, D., ed. *The reenchantment of science.* Albany: State University of New York Press, 1988.
6. Makarov, O. Preface, *The home planet,* ed. K. Kelly. New York: Addison-Wesley, 1988.
7. White, F. *The overview effect: Space exploration and human evolution.* Boston: Houghton Mifflin, 1987.

Chapter 29, "Eye to Eye: Science and Transpersonal Psychology," p. 184.

1. Wilber, K. *The Atman project.* Wheaton, Ill.: Quest, 1980.
2. Smith, H. *Forgotten truth.* New York: Harper & Row, 1976.
3. Schuon, F. *The transcendent unity of religions.* New York: Harper & Row, 1976.
4. Whitehead, A. N. *Science and the modern world.* New York: Macmillan, 1967.
5. Tart, C. *States of consciousness.* New York: E. P. Dutton, 1975.

Chapter 32, "The Near-Death Experience," p. 195.

Gallup, G., *Adventures in immortality*. New York: McGraw-Hill, 1982.

Greyson, B. Increase in psychic phenomena following near-death experiences. *Theta* 2 (1983): 1016.

Kohr, R. Near-death experiences, altered states and psi sensitivity. *Anabiosis* 3 (1983): 157–74.

Ring, K. *Life at death*. New York: Coward McCann & Geoghegan, 1980.

Ring, K. *Heading toward omega*. New York: William Morrow, 1984.

Sabom, M. *Recollections at death*. New York: Harper & Row, 1982.

Introduction to Section Nine, "The Philosophy of Transcendence," p. 203.

1. Russell, B. *The problems of philosophy*. New York: Oxford University Press, 1959, p. 12.
2. Wilber, K. Odyssey: A personal inquiry into humanistic and transpersonal psychology. *Journal of Humanistic Psychology* 22 (1982): 75.
3. Huxley, A. *The perennial philosophy*. New York: Harper & Row, 1945, p. vii.
4. Lovejoy, A. *The great chain of being*. Cambridge: Harvard University Press, p. 26.
5. Rothberg, D. Philosophical foundations of transpersonal psychology: An introduction to some basic issues. *Journal of Transpersonal Psychology* 18 (1986): 1–34.

Chapter 33, "Transpersonal Worldviews: Historical and Philosophical Reflections," p. 206.

1. Barfield, O. *Romanticism comes of age*. London: Rudolf Steiner Press, 1966, pp. 147–48.
2. Whicher, S. E., ed. *Selections from Ralph Waldo Emerson*, Boston: Houghton Mifflin, 1957, pp. 21–22.
3. Wilber, K. *Eye to eye*. Boston: Shambala, 1990; and *The Spectrum of Consciousness*, 3rd Ed. Wheaton, Ill.: Theosophical Publishing House, 1982.
4. Grof, S. *Beyond the brain: Birth, death, and transcendence in psychotherapy*. New York: State University of New York Press, 1985.
5. Tart, C. *Open mind, discriminating mind*. San Francisco: Harper, 1989.
6. See essays in this volume.
7. Rothberg, D. Philosophical foundations of transpersonal psychology: An introduction to some basic issues. *Journal of Transpersonal Psychology* 18 (1986): 1–34.
8. Tarnas, R. *The passion of the Western mind*. New York: Harmony Books, 1991.
9. *Ibid*., pp. 436–37.

Chapter 35, "The Great Chain of Being," p. 214.

References

Lovejoy, A. *The great chain of being*. 1936. Reprint. Cambridge: Harvard University Press, 1964, p. 26.

Smith, H. *Forgotten truth*. New York: Harper & Row, 1976.

Trungpa, C. *Shambhala: Sacred path of the warrior*. Boston: Shambhala, 1988.

Varela, F. *Principles of biological autonomy*. New York: North Holland, 1979, p. 86.

Von Bertalanffy, L. *General system theory*. New York: Braziller, 1968, pp. 74, 87.

Chapter 36, "Hidden Wisdom," p. 223.

1. Zimmer, H. *Philosophies of India*. Princeton: Princeton University Press, 1969.
2. Walsh, R. Can Western philosophers understand Asian philosophies? *Crosscurrents* 34 (1989): 281–99, 1989.
3. Nyanaponika Thera. *Abhidharma studies*. Kandi, Sri Lanka: Buddhist Publication Society, 1976, p. 7.
4. Radhakrishnan. *Indian philosophy*. Vol. 1. 1929. Reprint. Bombay: Blackie & Sons, 1940, p. 43.
5. Vimilo, B. *Awakening to the truth*. Visaka Puja, Thailand: Buddhist Assoc., 1974, p. 73.
6. Huxley, A. *The perennial philosophy*. New York: Harper & Row, 1945, p. vii.
7. Schumacher, E. F. *A guide for the perplexed*. New York: Harper & Row, 1977, pp. 61, 42, 43.

Introduction to Section Ten, "Minding Our World: Service and Sustainability," p. 227.

1. Maslow, A. *Religions, values, and peak experiences*. New York: Viking, 1970, pp. xii.
2. Ehrlich, P., and Ehrlich, A. *The population explosion*. New York: Simon & Schuster, 1990.
3. Porrit, J. *Save the earth*. Atlanta: Turner Publishing, 1991.
4. Presidential Commission on World Hunger. *Preliminary report of the Presidential Commission on World Hunger*. Washington, D.C.: U.S. Government Printing Office, 1979.
5. Dammann, E. *The future in our hands*. New York: Pergamon, 1979, pp. 46, 136.
6. Walsh, R. *Staying alive: The psychology of human survival*. Boston: New Science Library/Shambhala, 1984.
7. Gore, A. *Earth in the balance: Ecology and the human spirit*. New York: Houghton Mifflin, 1992.
8. Fox, W. *Toward a transpersonal ecology: developing new foundations for environmentalism*. Boston: Shambhala, 1990.

Chapter 40, "Transpersonal Ecology," p. 240.

Fox, W. *Toward a transpersonal ecology: developing new foundations for environmentalism*. Boston: Shambhala, 1990.

Popper, K. *Objective knowledge: An evolutionary approach*. Oxford: Clarenden Press, 1974.

Russell, B. *History of Western philosophy*. London: Unwin, 1979.

Chapter 41, "Deep Ecology: Living as If Nature Mattered," p. 232.

1. Roszak, T. *Where the wasteland ends*. New York: Anchor/Doubleday, 1972.
2. Fox, W. Deep ecology: A new philosophy of our time? *The Ecologist* 14 (1984): 5–6.

Further Reading

Clinical Issues

Grof, C. *The thirst for wholeness: Addiction, attachment and the spiritual path.* New York, HarperCollins, 1993. A transpersonal exploration of addiction.

Grof, S., and Grof, C., eds. *Spiritual emergency.* Los Angeles: Tarcher, 1989.

Grof, C., and Grof, S. *The stormy search for the Self.* Los Angeles: Tarcher, 1990. These two books are the major texts on transpersonal developmental crises or "spiritual emergencies."

Kabat-Zinn, J. *Full catastrophe-living: Using the wisdom of your body and mind to face stress, pain, and illness.* New York: Delacourte, 1990. A careful, well-documented guide to using meditative awareness for healing.

Lukoff, D., Lu, F., and Turner, R. Toward a more culturally sensitive DSM-IV: Psychoreligious and psychospiritual problems. *Journal of Nervous & Mental Diseases* 80 (1992): 673–82. A well-documented study of the need for training in religious and spiritual issues for mental health practitioners. It provides a valuable diagnostic framework for assessing religious and spiritual difficulties.

Consciousness

Tart, C. *States of consciousness.* El Cerrito, Calif.: Psychological Processes, 1983. This book describes one of the most comprehensive theories of states of consciousness.

Wilber, K. *No Boundary.* Boston: New Science Library/Shambhala, 1981. A simplified version of *The spectrum of consciousness* and a good introduction to Wilber's work.

Wilber, K. *The spectrum of consciousness.* Wheaton, Ill.: Quest, 1977. Wilber's first, and foundational book. It lays out in detail the basic idea underlying much of his work: Consciousness and its attributes, and the psychologies, philosophies, and religions that explore them, can be ordered along a spectrum. This book presents a broad-ranging synthesis of diverse disciplines.

Development

Maslow, A. *The farther reaches of human nature.* New York: Viking, 1971. A classic book on the farther reaches of psychological development by one of transpersonal psychology's founding fathers.

Metzner, R. *Opening to inner light.* Los Angeles: Tarcher, 1986. A well-researched account of ten classic metaphors of transformation used to describe spiritual development.

————. *The unfolding self: Varieties of transformative experience*. Novato, Calif.: Origin Press, 1998. Outlines the classic metaphors that guide and describe transpersonal development.

Vaughan, F. *Awakening intuition*. New York: Doubleday, 1979. One of the first books on intuition that addresses both personal and transpersonal levels.

Vaughan, F. *The inward arc: Healing in psychotherapy and spirituality*, 2nd ed. Nevada City, California: Blue Dolphin. An overview of transpersonal development and its facilitation that draws on both psychological and spiritual perspectives.

Wilber, K. *The Atman project*. Wheaton, Ill.: Quest, 1980. An interdisciplinary synthesis that traces development from infancy through adulthood into transpersonal stages.

Wilber, K., Engler, J., and Brown, D., eds. *Transformations of consciousness: Conventional and contemplative perspectives on development*. Boston: New Science Library/ Shambhala, 1986. A collection of theoretical and research papers on transpersonal development and its stages, pathologies, and therapies.

Wilber, K. *Up from Eden*. New York: Doubleday, 1981. Here Wilber attempts to apply his theory of human development to map the evolution of human consciousness across the ages. A brilliant though controversial book.

Ecology and Global Issues

Devall, B., and Sessions, G. *Deep ecology: Living as if nature mattered*. Layton, Utah: Gibbs Smith, 1985. One of the classic books on deep ecology.

Elgin, D. *Voluntary simplicity*. New York: William Morrow, 1981. A thoughtful exploration of a life-style that may be inherently satisfying, supportive of transpersonal growth, and essential for human survival.

Fox, W. *Toward a transpersonal ecology*. Boston: New Science Library Shambhala, 1990. A thoughtful academic effort to create a transpersonal ecology by wedding deep ecology and transpersonal psychology.

Gore, A. *Earth in the balance: Ecology and the human spirit*. New York: Houghton Mifflin, 1992. A sophisticated discussion of our global crises with courageous suggestions for far-reaching political and social responses, written by the vice president of the United States.

Ram Dass and Gorman, P. *How can I help?* New York: Knopf, 1985. A beautiful exploration of service as a spiritual practice.

History

Tarnas, R. *The passion of the Western mind*. New York: Harmony Books, 1991. This highly praised transpersonally sympathetic book has been described as the best single-volume survey of the history of Western thought.

Lucid Dreaming

Gackenbach, J., and Bosveld, J. *Control your dreams*. New York: HarperCollins, 1989.

LaBerge, S. *Lucid dreaming*. Los Angeles: Tarcher, 1985. These are two readable overviews of lucid-dreaming research and practice by leading authorities.

Meditation

Goldstein, J. *The experience of insight*. Boston: New Science Library/Shambhala, 1983. A clear introduction to the basic Buddhist meditation: insight (Vipassana) meditation.

Murphy, M., and Donovan, S. *The physical and psychological effects of meditation*. San Rafael, Calif.: Esalen Institute, 1989. A review of over one thousand studies of the effects of meditation.

Ram Dass. *Journey of awakening: A meditator's guidebook*. 2nd ed. New York: Bantam, 1990. A clear introduction to meditation practice and a list of meditation centers and teachers.

Shapiro, D., and Walsh, R., eds. *Meditation: Classic and contemporary perspectives*. New York: Aldine, 1984. A collection of outstanding papers on meditation theory and research.

West, M., ed. *The psychology of meditation*. Oxford: Clarenden Press, 1987. An anthology of research reviews.

Philosophy

Koller, J. *Oriental philosophies*. 2nd ed. New York: Charles Scribner's Sons, 1985. An introduction to the major Oriental philosophies.

Smith, H. *Beyond the postmodern mind*. 2nd ed. Wheaton, Ill.: Quest, 1989. This book lucidly describes the current impasse of contemporary postmodern philosophy, in which so many philosophies and truth claims have been invalidated, and suggests that a transpersonal perspective may offer a way to go beyond the postmodern mind.

Stace, W. *Mysticism and philosophy*. Los Angeles: Tarcher, 1987. A clearly written classic on the philosophy of mysticism that argues for the similarity or even identity of mystical experiences across cultures.

Wilber, K. *Eye to eye: The quest for the new paradigm*. Garden City, N.Y.: Anchor/Doubleday, 1983. Contains an important discussion of the epistemological foundation of transpersonal disciplines as well as essays on a variety of other topics.

————. *The eye of spirit*. Boston: Shambhala, 1997. A broad-ranging collection of essays.

Zimmer, H. *Philosophies of India*. Princeton: Princeton University Press, 1969. One of the more readable introductions to Indian philosophies.

Psychedelics

Grinspoon L., and Bakalar, J. *Psychedelic drugs reconsidered*. New York: Basic Books, 1979. A careful, comprehensive, open-minded overview by two major authorities.

Grof, S. *The adventure of self-discovery*. Albany: State University of New York Press, 1988. A far-reaching account and theoretical exploration of transpersonal experiences, especially, but not exclusively, those induced by psychedelics. From these experiences Grof deduces one of the most comprehensive contemporary maps of consciousness available today.

————. *The cosmic game*. Albany, N.Y.: SUNY Press. A vast map of reality.

Lee, M., and Shlain, B. *Acid dreams: The CIA, LSD, and the sixties rebellion*. New York: Grove Weidenfeld, 1985. A well-documented, disturbing account of the use, misuse, and abuse of psychedelics by the public and the CIA during the sixties.

Lukoff, D., Zanger, R., and Lu, F. Psychoactive substances and transpersonal states.

Journal of Transpersonal Psychology 22, 22 (1990): 107–48. A transpersonally oriented review of recent psychedelic research.

Stafford, P. *Psychedelics encyclopedia.* 3rd ed. Berkeley: Rowin Publishers, 1992. A comprehensive, well-documented, yet readable encyclopedia.

Psychology, Transpersonally Oriented Schools

Ferrucci, P. *What we may be.* Los Angeles: Tarcher, 1982. A practical introduction to the use of psychosynthesis for personal and transpersonal growth.

Frager, R., and Fadiman, J. *Personality and personal growth.* 2nd ed. New York: Harper & Row, 1984 (3rd edition forthcoming). The first transpersonally oriented exploration of personality theories of both East and West.

Jung, C. *Memories, dreams, reflections.* Trans. R. Winston and C. Winston. New York: Vintage Books, 1961. Jung's autobiography chronicles his courageous and pioneering explorations of depths of the psyche that had previously been ignored in the West.

Singer, J. *Boundaries of the soul.* Garden City, N.Y.: Doubleday, 1972. A clear overview of Jungian psychology by an author who is also at home in transpersonal psychology.

Relationship

Welwood, J. *Journey of the heart.* New York: HarperCollins, 1990. An exploration of relationships as a spiritual practice.

Near-Death Experiences

Moody, R. *The light beyond.* New York: Bantam, 1988. A readable overview of the advances in understanding since the author's original groundbreaking publications.

Ring, K. *Life at death.* New York: Coward, McCann & Geoghegan, 1980. A review by one of the leading researchers.

Religion

Anthony, D., Ecker, B., and Wilber, K., eds. *Spiritual choices: The problem of recognizing authentic paths to inner transformation.* New York: Paragon, 1987. Provides theory and research on differentiating helpful paths from problematic ones.

Hixon, L. *Coming home: The experience of enlightenment in sacred tradition.* Los Angeles: Tarcher, 1989. An excellent introduction to different spiritual paths.

James, W. *The varieties of religious experience.* 1902. Reprint. New York: New American Library, 1958. The classic study that laid the foundations for a psychology of religion.

Smith, H. *The world's religions.* San Francisco: Harper, 1991. This book provides clear, sympathetic introductions to major religious traditions. Together with its original edition titled *The religions of man*, it has sold some two million copies.

Tart, C., ed. *Transpersonal psychologies.* 3rd ed. New York: HarperCollins, 1992. An examination of spiritual traditions as applied transpersonal psychologies.

Underhill, E. *Mysticism*. New York: New American Library, 1974. The classic work on Christian mysticism.

Walsh, R. *The spirit of shamanism*. Los Angeles: Tarcher, 1990. A transpersonal exploration of shamanism.

Wulff, D. *Psychology of religion: Classic and contemporary views*. New York: John Wiley, 1991. A comprehensive, scholarly, yet readable text. The author comes closer to mastery of this enormous literature than anyone else in many years.

Science

Griffin, D., ed. *The reenchantment of science: Postmodern proposals*. Albany: State University of New York Press, 1988. Describes how modern science and scientism have resulted in what Mumford called "a disqualified universe": a world stripped of meaning, purpose, or higher value. It summarizes recent developments that call this view into question.

Laughlin, C., McManus, J., and d'Aquili, E. *Brain, symbol and experience*. New York: Columbia University Press, 1992. This transpersonal anthropology text integrates cross-cultural studies, neuroscience, and contemplative disciplines.

Wilber, K. *A sociable god*. New York: McGraw-Hill, 1983. In this short, compact book Wilber outlines a new field of transpersonal sociology.

Somatics

Murphy, M. *The future of the body*. Los Angeles: Tarcher, 1992. A comprehensive work that reviews and synthesizes data on exceptional functioning and potentials.

Psychotherapy

Mahoney, M. *Human change processes: The scientific foundations of psychotherapy*. New York: Basic Books, 1991. This massive (590 page) work is remarkable for its scope, scholarship, and combination of scientific rigor, clinical skill and spiritual sensitivity.

Vaughan, F. *Shadows of the sacred: Seeing through spiritual illusions*. Wheaton, Illinois: Quest Books, 1995. An integration of psychological and spiritual approaches to growth and to working with traps on the path.

Psychiatry

Scotton, B., Chinen, A. and Battista, J., eds. *Textbook of transpersonal psychiatry and psychology*. New York: Basic Books, 1996. This large and carefully prepared volume provides an overview of the field.

□

Resources

Associations

Association for Transpersonal Psychology
345 California Street
Palo Alto, California 94306
(415) 327-2066

A membership organization that holds an annual meeting in California and
publishes a newsletter and journal.

Common Boundary
4304 East-West Hwy.
Bethesda, Maryland 20814
(301) 652-9495

Holds an annual meeting near Washington, D.C., and publishes a magazine.

International Transpersonal Association
20 Sunnyside Avenue, A-257
Mill Valley, California 94941
(415) 389-6912

Holds biannual meetings at various places around the world.

European Transpersonal Association
% Associazione Italiana di Psicologia Transpersonale
Via Collato Sabino 21, 1-00199 Rome, Italy
39.6.3621-8495 phone and fax

Training Programs

For a description of transpersonally oriented colleges and training programs see *The Common Boundary Education Guide* (1991; P. Demetrios, C.
Simpkinson, and C. Bennett, eds. Bethesda, MD: Common Boundary).

Journals

The Anthropology of Consciousness
American Anthropological Association
1703 New Hampshire Avenue, N.W.
Washington, D.C. 20009

Common Boundary
4204 East-West Hwy.
Bethesda, Maryland 20814
(301) 652-9495

Common Boundary is a readable, nontechnical bimonthly focusing on current
issues and interviews related to the interface between spirituality and
psychotherapy. Less technical than other journals.

Journal of Humanistic Psychology
1172 Vallejo Street, #3
San Francisco, California 94123
(415) 346-7929

Journal of Transpersonal Psychology
P.O. Box 4437
Stanford, California 94309
(415) 327-2066

ReVision: A Journal of Consciousness and Transformation
Heldref Publications
1319 Eighteenth Street, N.W.
Washington, D.C. 20036-1802
(202) 296-6267

Journal of Consciousness Studies

for orders in USA		for orders outside USA
Department of Philosophy	OR	Imprint Academic
Virginia Commonwealth University		P.O. Box 1
Richmond, Virginia 23284-2025		Thorverton
		Exeter EX5 5YX
		44 (0) 392-841600 phone & fax

Contributors

Sri Aurobindo was an Indian intellectual and religious genius who is widely regarded as one of the greatest philosopher-sages of all time.

Jane Bosveld is a writer and coauthor of *Control Your Dreams*.

Fritjof Capra, Ph.D, physicist and systems theorist, is the founder and president of the Elmwood Institute, an ecological think tank, and the author of *The Tao of Physics* and *The Turning Point*. The film *Mindwalk* is based on his books.

His Holiness the Dalai Lama is a Buddhist monk as well as the spiritual and political leader of the Tibetan people and of the Tibetan government in exile. His tireless work for world peace and for a nonviolent end to the Chinese occupation of his country earned him the 1989 Nobel Peace Prize.

Ram Dass is one of today's most influential spiritual teachers. Initially known as Richard Alpert, he was a psychologist at Harvard and performed some of the earliest research on LSD. He is cofounder of Seva, an organization committed to serving the poor and blind, and author of *Journey of Awakening*, and *How Can I Help?*

Bill Devall, Ph.D, is one of the foremost writers on deep ecology and coauthor of the classic book *Deep Ecology: Living as If Nature Mattered*.

Duane Elgin is a futures researcher who has done extensive work on the conscious use of mass media. He is the author of *Voluntary Simplicity* and *Awakening Earth*.

John Engler, Ph.D, is a psychologist and Buddhist meditation teacher who has pioneered the integration of Buddhist and psychoanalytic ideas.

Mark Epstein, M.D., is an author, a longtime student of Buddhism, and a psychiatrist with a private psychotherapy practice in New York City.

Georg Feuerstein, Ph.D., is internationally known for his interpretative work on Hindu esotericism. He is the author of over twenty books, including *Holy Madness* and *Structures of Consciousness*.

Warwick Fox, Ph.D., is an Australian Research Fellow at the Centre for Environmental Studies, at the University of Tasmania, a leading ecologist, and the author of *Toward a Transpersonal Ecology*.

Jayne Gackenbach, Ph.D., one of the foremost researchers of lucid dreaming, is the founding editor of the journal *Lucidity* and coauthor of *Control Your Dreams*.

Gordon Globus, M.D., is professor of both psychiatry and philosophy at the University of California at Irvine. His most recent book is *Dream Life, Wake Life: The Human Condition through Dreams*.

Daniel Goleman, Ph.D., covers psychology for the *New York Times*. His many publications include *Mind/Body Medicine* and *Mind Science*.

Christina Grof is the founder of the Spiritual Emergence Network. Her particular area of interest is the spiritual aspects of addiction and recovery. She is the author of *The Thirst for Wholeness: Addiction, Attachment, and the Spiritual Path* and coauthor of *The Stormy Search for the Self*.

Stanislav Grof, M.D., a psychiatrist, is former president of the International Transpersonal Association; he has published over a hundred articles and many books, including *Beyond the Brain* and *The Adventure of Self-Discovery*.

Aldous Huxley was a polymath and influential social critic who popularized the idea of the perennial philosophy. His many books include *The Perennial Philosophy* and *Island*.

William James was one of America's most influential philosophers and psychologists. His many books include *Varieties of Religious Experience* and *Principles of Psychology*.

Jack Kornfield, Ph.D., was trained as a Buddhist monk and clinical psychologist and is a founder of the Insight Meditation Society and the Spirit Rock Center. His books include *Seeking the Heart of Wisdom* and *Stories of the Spirit, Stories of the Heart*.

Stephen LaBerge, Ph.D., was one of the first people to scientifically demonstrate the existence of lucid dreams. He remains one of the field's foremost researchers and is author of *Lucid Dreaming* and *Exploring the World of Lucid Dreaming*.

Charles Laughlin, Ph.D., is professor of anthropology at Carleton University, Ottawa, Canada. He has done ethnographic fieldwork with Tibetan lamas in Nepal and is editor of the journal *Anthropology of Consciousness* and coauthor of *Brain, Symbol and Experience*.

John Mack, M.D., is professor of psychiatry at Cambridge Hospital and Harvard University, founder of the Harvard Center for Psychology and Social Change, former president of the International Society of Political Psychology, and recipient of a Pulitzer Prize in biography for his book *A Prince of Our Disorder: The Life of T. E. Laurence*. He has been a leader in applying psychological understanding to contemporary nuclear and ecological concerns.

Judith Malamud, Ph.D., has written extensively on lucid dreaming.

Abraham Maslow, Ph.D., was one of the twentieth century's most influential psychologists and has been described as a founding father of both humanistic and transpersonal psychologies. His books include *Toward a Psychology of Being* and *The Farther Reaches of Human Nature*.

Robert A. McDermott, Ph.D., is president of the California Institute of Integral Studies and professor emeritus of philosophy at Baruch College. His publications include *The Essential Steiner* and *The Essential Aurobindo*.

John McManus, Ph.D., is a researcher who has made major contributions to psychology and cognitive science.

Michael Murphy cofounded Esalen Institute and helped initiate Esalen's Soviet-American Exchange Program. He is the author of three novels, as well as *The Future of the Body*.

Kenneth Ring, Ph.D., is professor of psychology at the University of Connecticut and past president of the International Association for Near Death Studies. He is the author of *Life at Death* and *The Omega Project*.

Peter Russell holds degrees in physics, psychology, and computer science, published *The Upanishads* and *The White Hole in Time*, and produced the award-winning video *The Global Brain*.

George Sessions, Ph.D., is one of the foremost writers on deep ecology and coauthor of the classic book *Deep Ecology: Living as If Nature Mattered*.

Jon Shearer, Ph.D., is one of the earliest contributors to the field of transpersonal anthropology.

Huston Smith, Ph.D., is visiting Professor of Religious Studies at the University of California, Berkeley. His seven books include *The World's Religions* (formerly *The Religions of Man*) and *Essays on World Religion*. His documentary films on Hinduism, Tibetan Buddhism, and Sufism have all won international awards.

Charles Tart, Ph.D., is emeritus professor of psychology at the University of California and professor at California Institute of Integral Studies. He is one of the foremost researchers on states of consciousness and transpersonal theory; his books include *Waking Up* and *Transpersonal Psychologies*.

Frances Vaughan, Ph.D., is a psychotherapist in private practice in Mill Valley, California, and is past president of the Association for Transpersonal Psychology.

Roger Walsh, MB.BS., Ph.D., is a professor at the University of California at Irvine.

John Welwood, Ph.D., is a psychologist and professor at the California Institute of Integral Studies. He has written on East-West psychology, meditation, and relationships. His books include *Challenge of the Heart* and *Journey of the Heart*.

Ken Wilber is one of the leading transpersonal theorists. His cross-disciplinary syntheses encompass the psychologies, philosophies, and religions of both East and West, as well as sociology, anthropology and postmodern thought.

Bryan Wittine, Ph.D., is a psychotherapist in private practice in Oakland, California, and was cofounder of the Graduate Program in Transpersonal Counseling Psychology at John F. Kennedy University, Orinda, California.

◻

Permissions

The editors would like to thank the following publishers for permission to reprint:

Chapter 1 consists of excerpts from Daniel Goleman, "Perspectives on psychology, reality, and the study of consciousness," 1974, *J. Transpersonal Psychology* 6, 73–85.

Chapter 2 consists of excerpts from Ken Wilber, "Psychologia perennis: The spectrum of consciousness," 1975, *J. Transpersonal Psychology* 7, 105–32.

Chapter 3 consists of excerpts from Charles Tart, 1983, *States of Consciousness*, Psychological Processes, El Cerrito, Calif. Reprinted by permission of the author.

Chapter 4 contains a chart reprinted from *The Spirit of Shamanism*, by Roger Walsh, M.D., Ph.D. (Tarcher, 1990). Reprinted by permission of the publisher.

Introduction, Roger Walsh and Frances Vaughan, "Royal Road to the Transpersonal," includes an excerpt from William Blake, *Complete Writings*, G. Keynes, ed., 1966, Oxford University Press, Oxford, U.K.

Chapter 5 consists of excerpts from Jack Kornfield, 1978, *J. Transpersonal Psychology* 10, 113–33.

Chapter 7 consists of excerpts from Jack Kornfield, "Even the best meditators have old wounds to heal: Combining meditation and psychotherapy," 1989, *Yoga Journal*, September/October, 1989, pp. 46–102. Reprinted with permission of *Yoga Journal*. All rights reserved. Copyright © 1989 by *Yoga Journal*.

Chapter 8 consists of excerpts from Judith Malamud, "Becoming lucid in dreams and waking life," 1986, in B. Wolman and M. Ullman, eds., *Handbook of States of Consciousness*, Van Nostrand Reinhold, New York.

Chapter 9 consists of excerpts from Stephen LaBerge, 1985, *Lucid Dreaming*, J. P. Tarcher, Inc., Los Angeles.

Chapter 10 consists of excerpts from Jayne Gackenbach and Jane Bosveld, 1989, *Control Your Dreams*. Copyright © 1989 by Jayne Gackenback and Jane Bosveld. Reprinted by permission of HarperCollins Publishers, New York.

Chapter 11 consists of excerpts from Sri Aurobindo, 1970, *The Life Divine*, 5th ed., 1970. Reprinted by permission of Sri Aurobindo Ashram Trust, Pondicherry, India.

Chapter 12 consists of excerpts from Stephen LaBerge, 1985, *Lucid Dreaming*, J. P. Tarcher, Inc., Los Angeles.

Chapter 29 consists of excerpts from Ken Wilber, "Eye to eye: Science and transpersonal psychology," 1979, *ReVision* 2, 3–25. Reprinted by permission from Rudi Foundation, Cambridge, Mass.

Chapter 30 consists of excerpts from Fritjof Capra, "Science and mysticism," 1976, *J. Transpersonal Psychology* 8, 20–40.

Chapter 31 consists of excerpts from Charles Laughlin, John McManus, and Jon Shearer, "Transpersonal anthropology," 1983, *Phoenix Journal of Transpersonal Anthropology*, vol. VII nos. 1, 2, pp. 141–59. Reprinted by permission of Charles Laughlin.

Chapter 32 consists of excerpts from Ken Ring, "The near-death experience," 1986, *ReVision*, winter/spring, 75–84. Reprinted with permission of the Helen Dwight Reed Educational Foundation. Published by Heldref Publications, Washington, D.C. Copyright © 1986.

Chapter 34 consists of excerpts from Aldous Huxley, "The perennial philosophy," taken from Introduction, 1972, in Prabhavananda and Isherwood (Trans.) *The Song of God: Bhagavad-Gita*, Vedanta Press, Hollywood, Calif.

Chapter 35 consists of excerpts from Ken Wilber, 1993, "The Great Chain of Being," *Journal of Humanistic Psychology*. Reprinted by permission of Sage Publications, Inc., Newbury Park, Calif.

Chapter 37 consists of excerpts from The Dalai Lama, "The Nobel peace prize lecture," 1989. Reprinted by permission of the Office of Tibet, New York.

Chapter 38 consists of excerpts from Ram Dass, "Compassion: The delicate balance." Reprinted by permission from the author.

Chapter 39 consists of excerpts from John Welwood, 1990, *Journey of the Heart*. Copyright © 1990 by John Welwood. Reprinted by permission of HarperCollins Publishers, New York.

Chapter 40 consists of excerpts from an article, "Transpersonal Ecology," printed by permission of the author, Warwick Fox, that is based in part on portions of a previous article by Fox, "Introduction: From Anthropocentrism to Deep Ecology," that appeared in *ReVision* 13 (3), 107–108, (1991). Permission to reprint portions of this article (Introduction) in "Transpersonal Ecology" was granted to Fox by the Helen Dwight Reid Educational Foundation, published by Heldref Publications, 1319 18th St., NW, Washington, D.C. 20036-1802, Copyright © 1991.

Chapter 41 consists of excerpts from Bill Devall and George Sessions, *Deep ecology: Living as if nature mattered* 1985, 65–69. Reprinted by permission of Gibbs Smith, Publisher, Layton, Utah.

Chapter 42 consists of excerpts from Duane Elgin, "The Tao of personal and social transformation." Reprinted by permission of the author.

Chapter 43 consists of excerpts from Stanislav Grof and Christina Grof, eds., 1989. *Spiritual Emergency*. Reprinted by permission of the publisher, J. P. Tarcher, Los Angeles.

Chapter 44 consists of excerpts by Peter Russell. Reprinted by permission of the author.

Chapter 45 consists of a paper by Ken Wilber. Printed by permission of the author.

About the Editors

ROGER WALSH, M.B., Ph.D., is professor of psychiatry, philosophy, and anthropology at the University of California at Irvine. He has published over a hundred articles and seventeen books on science, philosophy, medicine, religion, and ecological issues, and his work has received over a dozen national and international awards.

FRANCES VAUGHAN, Ph.D., is a psychologist in private practice in Mill Valley, California, and was formerly president of the Association for Transpersonal Psychology. She is author and coeditor of several books on psychotherapy and spirituality.

Other Books by the Editors

BY FRANCES VAUGHAN AND ROGER WALSH

Gifts From A Course In Miracles

BY ROGER WALSH

The Spirit of Shamanism

Meditation: Classic and Contemporary Perspectives (with Deane Shapiro)

Essential Spirituality: The Seven Practices Common to World Religions

BY FRANCES VAUGHAN

Awakening Intuition

The Inward Arc: Healing in Psychotherapy and Spirituality

Shadows of the Sacred: Seeing Through Spiritual Illusions